CW01024239

Tank Combat in Spain

TANK COMBAT
IN SPAIN

Armored Warfare during the
Spanish Civil War 1936–1939

Anthony J. Candil

CASEMATE
Philadelphia & Oxford

Published in the United States of America and Great Britain in 2021 by
CASEMATE PUBLISHERS
1950 Lawrence Road, Havertown, PA 19083, USA
and
The Old Music Hall, 106–108 Cowley Road, Oxford OX4 1JE, UK

Hardcover Edition: ISBN 978-1-61200-970-4
Digital Edition: ISBN 978-1-61200-971-1

A CIP record for this book is available from the British Library

Printed and bound in the United States of America by Sheridan

Typeset by Versatile PreMedia Services (P) Ltd

For a complete list of Casemate titles, please contact:

CASEMATE PUBLISHERS (US)
Telephone (610) 853-9131
Fax (610) 853-9146
Email: casemate@casematepublishers.com
www.casematepublishers.com

CASEMATE PUBLISHERS (UK)
Telephone (01865) 241249
Email: casemate-uk@casematepublishers.co.uk
www.casematepublishers.co.uk

With appreciation for the work of the storytellers who record the history,
the archivists who preserve it,
and the historians who help interpret it for the new generations to come.
If you ain't Cav, you ain't!

To my children and grandchildren, even if they do not share my passion for tanks.

To my close friend Walter G. Radencic, a gentleman and of course, a cavalry officer.

To my friend Stanley G. Payne, who deserves to be a cavalry officer.

To my father, who instilled a passion for tanks in me.

To the U.S. Army Armor School, where I learnt so much.

To the men and women of the 37th Armor Regiment, with whom I spent some memorable days at their Regimental Recall, in September 2018, at Nashville, Tennessee.

To Major Ronnie Nall and Captain Dwight McLemore, both my instructors at the U.S. Army Armor School, who were so patient with me.

To Lieutenant Colonel David A. H. Sievwright, British Army, 13/18 Queen Mary's Own/ Royal Hussars, a "red coat" who shared with me unlimited time at the Spanish Staff College.

To U.S. Army Lieutenant Colonel Charles J. Piraneo, my friend and comrade at the Spanish Staff College.

To Major General Peter Nagel, Bundeswehr, whose father fought in the Spanish Civil War.

To Major General Itzhak Rabin, Israeli Defense Forces, an outstanding armor officer and close friend, and a classmate at the U.S. Army Armor School.

And to the best team I ever had as director for the Leopard 2 Project in the Spanish Army.

Thank you all for making my life so thrilling!

Contents

Acknowledgments

Firstly, I need to state that I feel fully indebted to Professor Stanley G. Payne, who encouraged me to write and set an example for me, and who has only ever had words of appreciation and support for me.

I also wish to thank professors Shannon Fleming and Jose Alvarez for their efforts and time spent with my manuscript, and for urging me to do a presentation of the subject at the 59th Annual Missouri Valley History Conference at Omaha, Nebraska, in 2016.

Above all, I would like to thank my classmate and good friend, U.S. Army Major Walter G. Radencic, who has stood by me since those times back in 1977, when, at Fort Knox, we were once "young and soldiers." My friend Walter has found time enough to read both my draft and my final manuscript and to make the appropriate suggestions.

I must also thank my friend and classmate, U.S. Army Major Michael Masterson—today known as the Reverend Mike Masterson of the Evangelical Lutheran Church—who found time among his community work, worship and family to read my manuscript draft and encourage me to publish it. Thank you, Mike, for your suggestions and your time.

I would also like to express my gratitude to Brigadier General Fernando Cano, of the Spanish Army, for reading the manuscript and making appropriate suggestions. Brigadier General Cano is an old friend and a graduate from the U.S. Army Armor School.

Last, but not least, I would like to thank the Spanish Institute of Military History, in Madrid, for allowing me to access their archives during my research quite some time ago, as well as the library of the Italian Military Academy in Modena, Italy.

Anthony J. Candil,
2021

Foreword

It was at the U.S. Army's Armor Advanced Course in 1977 that I first encountered young Captain Anthony Candil, relatively fresh from his assignments in Spanish Western Sahara. Tony, as he was known to his peers and to me, was intense, formidably intelligent, and well-versed in history and military science, particularly with regards to tank design and development as well as the tactics of mechanized maneuver.

I was most impressed by his affable nature, ready wit, and apparent affection for the Confederate and United States of America, and at once seized the opportunity to become the course sponsor for Tony and his family. During the months of our classroom and field training we became friendly with other young officers from France, Israel, and pre-revolutionary Iran, and although we sincerely mourn the disappearance of the latter and their lovely wives, our French and Israeli classmates rose to deserved ranks of the highest import to their nations and peoples. Tony himself rose to become Spanish military attaché to Her Majesty Queen Elizabeth II, and in that capacity and in his dress uniform, during my first wife's visit to London with her aunt, he not only broke but thoroughly shattered the heart of that elderly East Texas lady over the course of an introduction and a brief tea, a circumstance from which she never recovered.

Forty-plus years on from Armor School has found each of us awaiting that complete rebuild at Fiddlers' Green, for our torsion bars are sprung, our telescopes foggy, and our gun tubes long past their last recoil exercise. Nevertheless, our onboard computers remain vital, if occasionally the hard drives are overworked. Since that time, despite intermittent periods of radio silence, we have remained closer than many brothers: Tony became a U.S. citizen, our families have often visited one another's homes in Georgia and Texas, and in 2018 we had the good fortune to attend the recall of my old regiment, the 37th Armor, where Tony first disclosed to me his plans for this history of armored warfare in Spain.

Despite my many years' experience with armor in both field and classroom, the history of the tactical and operational levels of armored warfare in the Spanish Civil War never appeared on our official curricula. This is perhaps as it should be, for during our time in the Cold War the technical and maneuver aspects of warfare were changing so dramatically that little opportunity was available to examine the increasingly remote dawn of the age of tanks. Today, with the advantages of age, familiarity with armor operations, and insatiable professional interest, we have the luxury of discovering the details of those post-World War I decades in which the newer weapons of industrialized Europe were brought to bear by and against the superpowers of their time. A study of *Tank Combat in Spain* will go far toward answering the "Whys" of armor development and design, will firmly establish the bases for the subsequent doctrinal failures and successes of each of the combatants, and will disclose a vital part of the story of armor development and employment from 1918 to the beginning of World War II.

It is possible to appreciate *Tank Combat in Spain* without recourse to other works on the Spanish Civil War, a circumstance made almost inevitable by the remarkable dearth of publications in English which treat the war in detail, especially from the perspective of military history. Volumes have been written on the war's clash of ideologies, the politics of the contestants, and the personal experiences of international volunteers, journalists, and even units, but at this time there is very little in the way of a meticulous, lucidly written, and comprehensive military history of the war. An understanding of that war and its complex political issues is nevertheless necessary in order to fully grasp the effects upon the governments and military organizations which participated, and which in their turn so greatly influenced—or failed to influence—international relations and armor development specifically. Readers are encouraged to assess for themselves the variety and validity of available publications, for among these are *just* enough to offer a sufficiently robust historical background to Spain's Civil War.

What might one expect to learn from *Tank Combat in Spain*? Here is a taste:

> Does the oft-repeated assertion that the Spanish Civil War was a proving ground for World War II have a factual basis?
>
> What effect did the less-than-modest achievements of Spanish armor during the Alhucemas campaign have upon the Spanish General Staff?
>
> In what ways did the Spanish Civil War affect subsequent Soviet tank design and doctrine?

Why was the Soviet Union the principal provider of armor to the Nationalist army?

What were the differences between German and Soviet involvements, specifically with regards to maintenance, training, and logistics?

Why did Italy, whose armored forces performed very creditably in the Spanish Civil War, come away from Spain unprepared for World War II?

How did the civil war affect the development of anti-tank weaponry?

Tank Combat in Spain reveals answers to these questions that are far from straightforward, often ironic, occasionally paradoxical, and always thought-provoking. A unique and invaluable contribution to military history, the informed understanding offered by this volume should forever prevent the profound and costly lessons arising from the employment of armor in the Spanish Civil War.

Walter G. Radencic,
Lieutenant Colonel, U.S. Army (Retired),
Atlanta, GA, July 2020

Preface

As a senior Armor officer in the Spanish Army, I had direct experience of the struggle of the tank concept in Spain, not only to replace the horse, but to establish it as the primary combat arm in mobile warfare and to create an armored branch within the Spanish land forces, as in most Western armies; however, it was to no avail.

Nevertheless, I was fortunate in being intimately involved in armored warfare and the improvement of Spanish armor since I joined the Spanish Army, almost from the beginning and my early days at the military academy. Since then I have been both directly and indirectly concerned with all kind of developments in tanks and armored warfare, until I voluntarily ended my military career in Spain and relocated to the United States in 2007.

As a theoretical practician of the art of warfare—or business, whatever we may call it—I have always been interested in theory, and in the relation between theory and practice. My classical education with the Jesuits, combined with a naturally argumentative personality, had always led me to question generally accepted, established responses, methods, or systems. Certainly, without war experience it has been difficult to support my rationale, but my learning and experience gained alongside the U.S. Army—as a graduate of the U.S. Armor Officers Advanced Course—and the British, French, Israeli, Italian, and German armies, led me to question a great deal of what I had been taught or told in Spain. Indeed, one of the most important lessons I learnt was to distrust almost everything I was told and to test its validity by relentless probing.

At the end of my military career I spent several frustrating years linked to armor procurement, concerned with the design and development of the Spanish version of the Leopard 2, the main battle tank for the Spanish Army, and other related vehicles. This led me to initiate a thorough re-examination of all the factors which affected their design, during the course of which I came to the conclusion that many views, decisions, or opinions were based on very flimsy evidence indeed, and as proven later, had come to be reviewed—certainly not in Spain, but in Germany and even the United States—as a consequence of the asymmetric fighting taking place in new theaters of operations.

When I began to study and write about the history of tank employment in the Spanish Civil War, having access to new accounts written by various authors, I was struck by the differences between what I learned and the generally accepted view that developed immediately following the conflict and soon crystallized into a myth which, until now, has been hard to dislodge from people's minds.

I have long been interested in clarifying how much success, or failure, can be related to the official history or the unofficial influence that came from it. Clarity of thought, allied to imagination and the willingness, if not the propensity, to discard unfruitful traditional methods—aided by an always ready pen or outspoken attitude—combined with my knowledge of the history of warfare, have been useful tools in achieving results in my work.

The army that developed in Spain following the Civil War failed to understand what tanks could do, if properly used, and as a consequence no armor branch of any sort was created, with tanks merely subordinated to support the infantry. Luckily for Spain, the need to demonstrate how wrong this policy was never came to light.

For a long time, the Spanish Civil War has been portrayed as a romantic episode of the 20th century where defenders of freedom and democracy were confronted by the evil forces of totalitarianism and dictatorship, appearing as such in some of Ernest Hemingway's books and in various Hollywood movies. The reality was quite different, with neither side being quite as they were portrayed. The truth was that behind the flag of democracy and freedom rallied a mixture of romantic and idealistic people, who were mostly ignorant of the covert Communist attempt to seize power in Spain; while on the Nationalist side, most of the conservative forces of the nation were prey to Fascist and Nazi ideologies. In the end, the Spanish Civil War came to be a clash between Soviet Communism and Nazi/Fascist-inspired ideologies, resulting in over half a million deaths and the complete destruction of a country.

Historians of armored warfare have often misinterpreted the role of armor in the Spanish Civil War. Some have stated that the conflict was merely a laboratory to test modern armored tactics, while others concluded that there were few if any lessons to be learned. The confusion of historians is understandable, as the conflict was not a demonstration of brilliant tactics and great battles, but rather a series of battles of attrition.

At no point during the conflict did either side possess enough armor to execute the tactically independent operations envisioned by some of the interwar armor theorists. Nevertheless, tank forces proved useful once effective tactics were developed. Moreover, lessons were learnt by all the warring parties and both sides quickly found that the type of tanks employed were not always ideally suited for the missions they performed, which probably led their leaders to make the wrong assessments.

The Spanish Civil War has been described frequently—but inaccurately—as a contest between democracy and fascism. While it is true that Italian Fascism supported the Nationalist side, there was no real democracy on the Republican side. The uprising was designed, at first, as an exclusive military affair to remove the radical left from power and convert the existing regime into a conservative republic, in which democracy—as we understand it today—would have been severely curtailed. The military was divided, as was Spanish society. However, instead of a successful coup d'état, the so-called Nationalists ended up in control of only half the country's army, less than a third of the air corps and the navy, and about a third of the country's resources. Without the full weight of the military or the country behind the Nationalists, a civil war broke out in which the military rebellion would have soon been defeated had its leaders not been able to lobby Italy and Germany for military aid.

To understand the role that tanks were to play in the conflict, one must first develop a basis for understanding what the war was truly about. The Spanish Civil War was not only a clash between two systems, two societies, and multiple ideologies, but a host of other systems as well. On the battlefield, different doctrines, training, and military intelligence affected the outcome of battles as much as weapons and manpower. The Nationalists managed to maintain the all-important systems of national mobilization, logistics, finance, and—to a certain extent—research and development. Ultimately, the Republican side was engulfed in chaos, both from a societal and military perspective.

In the end, the war was a clear-cut revolutionary/counterrevolutionary contest between left and right, with the fascist totalitarian powers supporting the right and the Soviet totalitarian power backing the left. It was not, as many historians have perpetuated, a precursor to World War II, which began only when a pan-totalitarian coalition was formed through the Nazi-Soviet Pact, with the aim of allowing the Soviet Union to conquer a sizable swath of Eastern Europe while Germany was left free to conquer much of the rest of the continent. Spain, on the other hand, led then by General Franco—who was the unquestionable victor of the Spanish war—never officially entered World War II.[1]

The Republicans, also called "Reds," were fighting against conservative society, the power of the Church, the landlords, the military, and anybody who was considered as being wealthy and privileged. The Rebels, nicknamed "Nationalists," under General Francisco Franco, targeted their revolution against Marxism, anarchism, disorder, dictatorial trade unions, atheism, and in general against anybody not respecting the ideas of God, Motherland, and King; but ultimately, they became easy prey for totalitarianism.

For both sides, the struggle was a kind of holy war. The Nationalists even managed to convince Pope Pius XI to declare the war as a "crusade against Bolshevism," but the cruel truth was that it gave way to Nazism and Fascism, the concentration camps, and World War II. During the Spanish Civil War, new tactics were tested, including terrifying Stuka air attacks, bombing of defenseless cities, and an almost total war against civilians. Stalin, Hitler, and Mussolini were the main actors behind the scenes; however, Spaniards were just trying to establish their identity and future. Even if, at the beginning, most intellectuals and artists supported the Republic, later most withdrew their support due to the rising influence of the Communist Party and the terror campaigns conducted in Republican Spain against Catholics, monarchists, and even ordinary conservative people.

When the war started in 1936, the so-called Nationalists and their supporters represented authority, the interest of free-economy, and centralized government, as opposed to a regional decentralized autonomy. On the other hand, the Republicans formed an incompatible alliance between authoritarian communists and libertarian anarchists. Spain, at that time, had little industry and an agricultural system with more than four million workers, kept at the limits of human endurance and sacrifice. Corruption, financial scandals, and speculations in public office often made the headlines, together with a tax system that was little more than a farce.

Just as the revolutionary Spanish Republic was *"sui generis"* politically speaking, the war was uniquely military, as Professor Stanley Payne very cleverly points out. It was typical neither of World War I nor of World War II, but rather represented a kind of transition war halfway between the two and displayed certain traits of each. Most of the weaponry used was more typical of World War I, though occasionally the employment of armor and aircraft was more characteristic of World War II.

The Spanish Civil War was an event of interest to the Military Intelligence Division (MID) of the U.S. War Department.[2] Through the Army attachés stationed in the major embassies in Europe, the MID received technical and tactical information concerning weapons used in Spain by the Germans, Soviets, and Italians. Although the information gathered by the attachés was often random and incomplete, they—and their sources—saw trends in the development and use of modern weapons, especially the tank and antitank guns. The efforts of the attachés provided the MID with information that could be analyzed, and from which it could draw conclusions about the nature of a future European war. That the United States Army could not or would not make use of the "lessons" of the war in Spain was not due to a lack of information.

To many, the Spanish Civil War proved inconclusive regarding mechanized warfare. Despite attempts by Soviet, German, and Italian advisers to use newly devised mechanized theories, the lack of quality of both crews and the tanks employed, as well as the insufficient number of tanks used in operations, provided wrong impressions on the usefulness of armored forces.

As for lessons from the war, even if they were amply attested, it was not of much value to draw too detailed deductions of general application from individual episodes. Nevertheless, many tended to support the view that the ultimate effect of mechanization could be to enhance the power of defense rather than revive that of the offensive, while the Germans proved the opposite to be the case in the earlier stages of World War II.

CHAPTER I

Overview of Military Operations

July 18, 1936–April 1, 1939

It is difficult to understand tank combat in the Spanish Civil War without an overall military grasp of the conflict. For almost three years, Spain was tainted in blood. Conflict in a country that was neither a major player in European politics nor a cornerstone in the struggle for supremacy in Europe, ultimately led, even if unwillingly, to the major global disaster that was World War II.

To start with, we must bear in mind that the military rebellion was not initially a success, which was why the war began, as not all the armed forces joined the military uprising against the Republican government. Indeed, from a total of more than 80 generals on active duty in July 1936, fewer than 30 joined the uprising. A great number of those who joined were summarily executed at the outbreak of the war by both sides.

For the purposes of this study and a quick understanding of the conflict, we can establish four main stages in the development of the war:

- Stage one: from July 1936 until November 1936, when the Nationalist forces, outnumbered but superior in combat procedures, managed to consolidate their capacities and reached Madrid, circling the city from the west and the south, but failed to take over the capital.
- Stage two: from mid-November 1936 until late October 1937, when supplies and aid received by both sides managed to establish some balance of power, although the conquest of the Basque Country by the Nationalists gave them a substantial superiority.
- Stage three: from late October 1937 to mid-November 1938, when the Republican side was clearly on the defensive and conducted mainly delaying operations. Among them, the battle of attrition at "el Ebro" —the longest battle of the war—is the main example.
- Stage four: from mid-November 1938 until the end of March 1939, when the Republican side collapsed completely and stopped all resistance, with General Franco announcing the end of the war on April 1, 1939.

Stage one

In the beginning, the Nationalist side faced numerous unknown situations as their local commanders actively tried to consolidate their positions all over the area they seized control of, fighting off the Republican forces. There was little coordination, which ultimately led to the establishing of a unified command on October 1, 1936, which was entrusted to General Franco.

In spite of the Nationalist numerical inferiority, following orders from General Emilio Mola—the military commandant at Pamplona, and the effective head of the uprising in the north—a mobile column[1] began moving from Pamplona towards Madrid, threatening the capital and the government, forcing the Republican leaders onto the defensive. From Pamplona, the Nationalists also managed to take Irun and San Sebastian at the same time, cutting all links between the Basque Country and France by mid-September 1936.

However, it became obvious that these forces would be incapable of achieving any important objectives, and much less obtain any decisive victory. Reinforcements were key for the uprising, and these could only come from the Army of Africa, which comprised the best troops Spain then had, deployed in the Spanish Protectorate of Morocco.

By the end of July 1936, the Nationalist forces were in dire straits. The Republic held two-thirds of the country, including the capital and major urban centers, along with the gold reserves and most of the industry. The Republic also controlled most of the Spanish Navy,[2] and from July 19, Republican warships started patrolling the waters between Morocco and the Spanish mainland.

Even though Franco managed to land two battalions of colonial troops in southern Spain and some minor units were airlifted to Seville, it was clear that without substantial air and naval transportation, along with air support capability, not much would be achieved. Therefore, General Franco sent emissaries to Berlin and Rome, requesting transport aircraft in order to carry on the airlift of his troops. Germany sent 20 Junkers Ju-52 transport aircraft, and Italy 12 Savoia SM-81 transport/bombers, plus some fighter aircraft. As a result of their help, between July 29 and August 5, the Nationalists managed to fly 1,500 men of the Army of Africa across the Straits of Gibraltar, thereby establishing the first military airlift[3] in history.

On August 5, Franco challenged the Republican naval blockade with a convoy of merchant ships, carrying some 3,000 soldiers, equipment, and heavy weapons, then about 15,000 more men were moved between August 5 and August 15. This achievement, a clear military success, was a major psychological blow for the Republican government, for even though the

Republican Navy continued to deploy around the Straits, it was no longer a threat to the Nationalists.

From August 6, cargo ships regularly crossed the Straits of Gibraltar, under the cover of Italian bombers. By the end of September, the Republicans had completely lost control of the Straits of Gibraltar, with the Nationalists enjoying free passage between Spanish Morocco and the mainland until the end of the war. This was a major success for the Nationalist rebels and a huge setback for the Republic.

After landing in Spain, the forces of the Army of Africa advanced north, capturing Badajoz near the border with southern Portugal and linking with other Nationalist forces at Cáceres. Making remarkably rapid gains—and closing all land communications of the Republic with Portugal—they then turned north-eastwards towards Madrid and liberated Toledo, where the Infantry School (the *Alcazar*) had been under siege by Republican militias since the early days of the uprising. Another small force spread throughout Andalusia, took control of key locations, and reinforced the cities of Granada and Cordoba.

Due to the Army of Africa's advance, almost all western Spain was in Nationalist hands by the end of September 1936, and Franco reached the outskirts of Madrid late in October, forcing the government to flee to Valencia, on the eastern coast. That was a considerable psychological blow to the Republic, badly hitting the morale of its supporters.

Without doubt, the most important military development of this first stage of the war was the effective campaign of the Army of Africa, with its surprise airlift and impeccable crossing of the Straits of Gibraltar, and immediate advance towards Madrid, breaking all effective links between the Republic and Portugal, as well as isolating the Basque Country in the north once the Nationalists closed the border with France. Overall, it was a great leap forward for the Nationalist forces. To paraphrase a later quote from Churchill, it could be said that "perhaps it wasn't the beginning of the end, but it was the end of the beginning." However, there was still a long and arduous journey ahead. It was only at the end of this stage of the conflict that serious employment of tanks began.

A key fact at the time was the Republican government's inability to crush the military rebellion, failing not only to anticipate the rebels' intentions, but to react with initiative and bold determination. Allowing the Nationalists to cross, practically unopposed, the Straits of Gibraltar was a grave mistake, that in the end they would pay for dearly. Failing to confront Franco's columns on their advance to Madrid until they almost reached the southern suburbs of the capital, while trying to block the wrong avenue of approach from Cordoba, was also a monumental error. The government's inability to mobilize its troops and establish an effective military force to confront the rebels until it was too late had already sealed the fate of the Republic.

Stage two

From mid-November 1936 onwards, the war began to rage, becoming more complex and even reaching an almost international dimension. There were several great battles throughout 1937, a year when both sides consolidated their positions and the Spanish Civil War became not only a Spanish affair. It was also the year when, within the Republican government, some leaders[4] realized that they could not win the war, mainly due to the fact that the entire northern part of country—the Basque provinces and Asturias—fell into Nationalist hands, thus depriving the Republic of its main industrial base and logistical support, apart from considerable materiel losses in armament, equipment, and personnel.

Quoting once more Stanley Payne,[5] the Spanish Civil War was without a doubt a low-intensity conflict, but full of high-intensity battles. In the Central front, around Madrid, the main clashes during this period were the battle of Jarama in February 1937, the battle of Guadalajara in March 1937 and the battle of Brunete in July 1937. None of these battles were decisive and none allowed the Nationalists to capture Madrid, but all severely weakened the Republican forces and drained their manpower. Tanks were also widely employed in all these battles.

During the first of these battles—fought between February 6 and February 27—Franco tried to cross the Jarama River to cut off the road between Madrid and Valencia, where the Republicans had relocated their government. The battle's results were inconclusive: Franco's troops managed to get onto the east bank of the Jarama River, but failed to sever communications between Madrid and Valencia. However, the Nationalists did put parts of the main road between the two cities under machine-gun and rifle fire. By the end of February, the front lines had stabilized, with both sides consolidating and fortifying their positions to the point where no useful assault could be undertaken. Nationalists and Republicans alike had suffered very heavy casualties, and their troops were exhausted and low on ammunition and food. The battle was well described by Hemingway, and perpetuated in many songs of the time, including some performed later by folk singers such as Woody Guthrie and Pete Seeger in the United States.

Although the Nationalists succeeded in crossing the Jarama River and resisted all efforts to dislodge them from their footholds, the Madrid–Valencia road remained out of reach and firmly in Republican hands.

Consequently, the area lost much of its strategic importance and merged into the wider front.

The battle of Guadalajara was an operation that, even if well conceived and planned, was executed only after some misplaced Italian optimism due to the relatively easy walkover of the Italian volunteers in the capture of Malaga early in February 1937. Following the battle of Jarama, the Nationalists were incapable of any major efforts in the Central front, and Guadalajara became an almost exclusive Italian affair. The goal of the Italian High Command was to take the cities of Guadalajara and Alcala, the latter only 20 miles from Madrid. They hoped the Republican forces would crumble, Madrid would be occupied, and a quick surrender would follow, thus bringing an end to the war. However, matters did not turn out that way.

The most important strategic consequence of the Italians losing the battle was the abandonment of the Nationalist goal of conquering Madrid, the capital thus remaining in Republican hands until the end of the war on April 1, 1939. Italian morale was devastated and Mussolini was furious, as the battle became the most publicized Republican victory of the entire war. The battle soon became a propaganda trophy, but it was not a turning point. On the contrary, it helped the Nationalists adopt a long-term indirect strategy, firstly by reducing any vulnerable Republican positions they could find.

The summer of 1937 witnessed one of the bloodiest clashes of the Spanish Civil War, the battle of Brunete, from July 6 until July 25. It proved an unsuccessful attempt by the Republicans to alleviate the pressure exerted by the Nationalists in the north, especially against Santander and on the Madrid front. Although initially successful, the Republicans were forced to retreat from Brunete and in the end suffered devastating casualties. From a political standpoint, the offensive at Brunete was chosen to satisfy Communist demands, to prove to the Russians that the Spanish leadership possessed military initiative. Russian advisors had been pressing for an attack on Brunete since the early spring of 1937, but in the end the Communists suffered a major loss of prestige as the offensive failed to prevent Nationalist troops from completing the encirclement of Madrid from the north.

After Brunete, with the occupation of the north by Franco's forces almost completed, the war effort focused on northeastern of Spain, largely due to a Republican decision driven once more by political considerations rather than military procedures. Following the failure of their offensive at Brunete, the Republicans admitted that nothing of importance could be achieved by major operations in the Central front. The Republican government soon moved again, this time from Valencia to Barcelona, and thus the war's operational goals changed once more.

Elsewhere, the Nationalists had secured clear victories. Early in the year—from mid-January to mid-February 1937—the capture of the coastal city of Málaga, on the southern Mediterranean coast, contributed to further complicating the logistics of the Republicans, confining the Republican Navy to operating only in the eastern littoral, and even then, under permanent threat of attack from aircraft operating from Nationalist bases in the Balearic Islands. Only a handful of Italian tanks were employed in these actions by the Nationalists.

In the north, starting in April 1937, the Nationalist forces under the leadership of General Mola[6] initiated an all-out offensive against the province of Biscay, finally entering Bilbao on June 19 and kicking out the Republicans beyond the province of Santander. The intended offensive against Santander was delayed by the Republican offensive in Brunete, but it finally commenced on August 14, and by September 1, Santander had been captured. Immediately after, the Nationalist forces entered Asturias, liberating Oviedo—which had been under siege since the early days of the uprising in 1936—and the harbor of Gijon, ending the whole campaign on October 24. The entire northern region of Spain, from Galicia to the French border, was then under Nationalist control.

The only overland channel of communication left between the Republic and France was through Catalonia. The Republic had lost a key region, along with about 200,000 troops plus a huge amount of military equipment. It was a disaster with serious strategic consequences: without doubt, this was the beginning of the end.

By this time, both sides had received considerable aid from abroad, so their armies bore little resemblance to those when the war began in July 1936. Italy was the country that diverted the most resources in helping the Nationalists, contributing not only equipment and armament, but a large number of troops. Italian submarines began to attack all Spanish, Soviet and other nations' merchant ships that were transporting materiel and supplies for the Republic through the Mediterranean,[7] making it very difficult for supplies from the Soviet Union to reach the Republic. There was also German involvement, including contributions from the Kriegsmarine, besides the technical and military aid that had been sent to General Franco since the beginning of the war.

The Nationalists' attempt to capture Madrid had some serious tactical drawbacks. First and foremost, General Franco's troops were outnumbered by more than two to one by the defenders, and although the Nationalists were far better trained and equipped, another disadvantage was their inability to surround Madrid and cut if off completely from outside help as the road to Valencia always remained open.

Following the first battle for Madrid, the Republican government tried to reorganize its armed forces from a collection of people's militias into a regular army, the so called "*Ejército Popular*" or Popular Army mirrored on the Soviet Red Army. This was achieved by integrating the militias into the structure of elements of the pre-war army which had sided with the Republic. While in theory reducing the power of political parties in relation to the government, in practical terms it increased the influence of the Communist Party, which was the main source of Soviet arms and foreign volunteers and advisors.

A new limited offensive commenced on August 24, aiming to break into the Nationalist rearguard and disrupt their final battles in the north. The Republican objective was the town of Zaragoza, on the banks of the Ebro River, but they failed and only managed to capture the ruins of Belchite, a small town in the middle of Aragon of no tactical or strategic value. For the Republicans, Zaragoza was more than a symbolic target; it was the communications hub of the entire front in Aragon. The whole operation lasted just 13 days, and once again the Republicans suffered a considerable loss of badly needed armament, equipment, and personnel.

Stage three

By early September 1937, the Aragon front was stabilized at an average of 20 miles from Zaragoza, and the Republicans and Nationalists both took a brief break. The Nationalists intended to take advantage of their occupation of the northern zone, while the Republicans were hoping that, given time, the international situation would help their situation. By the end of the year, both sides had completed their reorganization and mobilization reached its highest, each having about 700,000 personnel in their field armies.[8] However, the quality, discipline, and morale of troops was clearly superior on the Nationalist side.[9]

The Nationalist High Command thus decided to mount an offensive on the Madrid front by the end of the year, again in the Guadalajara sector, but slow preparations and accumulation of troops and supplies, combined with good Republican intelligence, gave away the operation. The Republicans therefore decided to launch an "offensive-defensive" battle to disrupt the Nationalist plan, aiming for limited destruction of forces and obtaining some advantage for further exploitation. The area chosen was the weakest point of the whole Nationalist front, near the town of Teruel in southern Aragon. The Republicans deployed some 40,000 men, with the armored force, inefficiently, split up among the attacking units. The Nationalist forces consisted mainly of the 52nd Infantry Division, with less than 10,000 men; consequently, the Republicans initially managed to obtain some local success.

The Republican attack began on December 15, just three days before the intended Nationalist offensive in the Guadalajara sector; by December 19, the Republicans had reached the outskirts of Teruel, and on December 25, they proclaimed victory. However, the city didn't surrender until January 7, 1938. Franco's headquarters were taken aback upon hearing of the offensive, and against all advice, and at the cost of canceling the prepared offensive against Madrid via Guadalajara, Franco decided to re-establish the front and recapture Teruel. Uppermost in Franco's mind was to never lose ground.

Following the battle of Teruel, the Nationalists, rather than reorganizing, regardless of the great losses suffered, decided to continue the action and take advantage of the momentum; after only a two-week break, they launched the battle of Aragon, nicknamed the "March to the Sea," on March 9, aiming this time to split apart the Republican-held area and isolate the central and western regions from Catalonia in the northeast. The Nationalist offensive opened with massive artillery and aviation support, and by April 15 they had captured the seaside town of Vinaroz on the Mediterranean coast, thus establishing a corridor that effectively separated Catalonia from the rest of the Republican area and cut the Republic in two. It was here where tanks were employed at their best by the Nationalists and where the principles of mobile warfare were validated, even if in a limited way.

For the Republic, it was once more a complete disaster, of similar consequences to the loss of the northern area in 1937. The severe blow inflicted on the most experienced formations of the Popular Army, while at the same time separating Catalonia from the rest of Republican-held Spain, yet the only remaining source of Republican manpower and industry, was of fatal consequences. Without Catalonian industry and supplies from abroad, the central region was vulnerable to falling in short order. The Republic had already lost the war; the end was just a matter of time.

Some small tactical successes were obtained by the Republicans at sea when they managed to sink the Nationalist heavy cruiser *Baleares* on March 6, 1938, although this failed to make any difference to the outcome of the war. The international situation was becoming very difficult and challenging, and was perhaps the main reason why, after reaching the sea, rather than turning northwards, the Nationalists initiated operations throughout Castellon towards Valencia rather than closing on the French border, to avoid any risk of France joining the fight.

On April 25, the offensive towards Valencia began, but bad weather forced the Nationalists to call off the operation. On May 4, the offensive recommenced and the Nationalists launched one attack after another, but they could not break the Republican front. Progress was slow and painful. At the beginning of July, Franco ordered the Italian Corps (CTV) and four newly formed infantry divisions to reinforce the front and continue the offensive on July 13. The Nationalists tried in vain to crush the Republican defenses for 10 days. The Republican slogan "to resist is to win" was finally beginning to have some meaning. Then something unexpected happened: the battle of the Ebro, which was about to start, changed the whole picture.

The battle of the Ebro was the most decisive clash of the entire war. It was the battle that definitively sealed the fate of the Republic and proclaimed the Nationalists as the victors. But it was not easy. On the Republican side, the Popular Army had managed to create 12 new divisions, calling to arms almost 200,000 men, and establishing a new Army Group nicknamed "*Ejército del Ebro*," under the command of "General"—in reality just a lieutenant colonel—Modesto, a communist leader and a former construction worker. Taking advantage of a huge delivery of armaments, equipment, and supplies recently arrived from the Soviet Union through the French border, a total of 80,000 men, with nearly all the armor, artillery, and aircraft then available to the Republic, were committed to battle.

The Nationalists facing the Republicans were mainly General Yagüe's Moroccan Corps (three divisions) that, even if they were in high alert readiness, considered it unthinkable that the Popular Army would be ready to undertake so soon any sort of offensive operations, especially after having been so severely mauled in Aragon and now having to cross one of the biggest rivers in Spain if they were thinking of attacking.

General Franco, upon hearing of the Republican offensive, halted all operations in the Valencia region, and fresh forces were turned around to march against the Republican bridgehead. All available air forces were also tasked immediately for operations on the Ebro, and by the early afternoon of July, 25, Spanish Nationalist aircraft—together with German and Italian expeditionary air forces—began attacking the crossing points on the Ebro, giving the highest priority to the pontoon bridges.

Just less than a week later, on August 1, "General" Modesto ordered the Army of the Ebro to go on the defensive. The Republicans had lost more than 12,000 men to once more gain minimum terrain of no strategic value whatsoever. To continue the battle in such circumstances had no military justification, especially when there was no hope of achieving the original purpose of the offensive. Furthermore, the Republic was so vulnerable that saving its troops to fight another battle was the most sensible course of action.

Yet political considerations—and a desire for propaganda—ultimately lead to another disaster. The Nationalists didn't react as expected, and once more committed themselves to destroying the forces which had taken Nationalist territory. The Republican plan was deeply flawed from the start, and once the initial surprise was achieved, the commanders had no idea of how to handle the situation or what to do next. Choosing to fight with a large river behind them, when the Nationalists had full air superiority, led to the useless sacrifice of an army they could never replace.

Committed to a battle of attrition, the Nationalists launched six counter-offensive operations in a row against the Republican-held positions. The first began on August 6, with the last commencing on September 3, but fighting continued until November 14. The last Republican soldiers crossed back over the Ebro on November 16. Thus ended the battle of the Ebro. It had been a hundred-day battle in a thousand-day war, and practically marked the end of the Republic. The Republican Army of the Ebro had ceased to exist, the eponymous battle being its swansong.

Stage four

Barely two weeks after the fighting on the Ebro had died down, the Nationalist forces were ready to attack again and redeployed all along the Segre and Ebro rivers that bordered Republican territory in the Catalonian region. Franco and his general staff, not wishing to give the Republicans time to recover, were making final preparations to continue their offensive to reach the French border as soon as possible. It was merely a matter of exploitating their success and pursuing an enemy that had already been defeated.

The situation was dire on the Republican side, with the Popular Army already looking beaten before the last battle even began, and with little equipment remaining. Its estimated strength of *circa* 250,000 men had no more than 100 artillery guns, 40 tanks, and less than 100 aircraft. On October 28, while the battle of the Ebro was still raging, the International Brigades were withdrawn from the front and disbanded under the auspices of an agreement following the proceedings of the International Committee for Non-Intervention.

The final offensive was finally launched on December 23. Even if surprise wasn't achieved, it was no longer necessary as there wasn't much for the Republicans to do. However, to alleviate the Nationalist pressure, several diversionary attacks were mounted by Republican forces, both on the Central front and at Extremadura, but to no avail.

On January 22, 1939, the President of the Republic, and almost the entire government, made their way to Gerona, Figueras,[10] and ultimately into exile by crossing into France. However, the Prime Minister, Juan Negrín, later arranged to return to Madrid.

In the early evening of January 26, Barcelona fell, and the Nationalists troops entered the city without any real opposition. On February 9, the remnants of the Republican forces crossed into France, while the Nationalist troops reached the border and all fighting came to an end. The whole of Catalonia had been captured by Franco's forces.

There was still some minor resistance on the Central front, with several dramatic episodes taking place, but military operations had almost come to a halt. A military coup in Madrid orchestrated by Republican forces resulted in the removal of Prime Minister Negrin and his colleagues. They fled to France, this time by air, while a new National Defense Council was organized in Madrid, with Republican general José Miajaon as chairman. The new Madrid regime was committed to a policy of "peace with honor," but this at once led to conflict with the Communists in the capital, even before the war was over. After the Communists were defeated, General Miaja tried to reach a compromise with Franco. Failing to secure assurances of leniency, the National Defense Council was finally obliged to accept unconditional surrender, and Miaja fled to Algiers, where he received the protection of the French authorities.

Nationalist troops finally entered Madrid on the morning of March 28, and on April 1, 1939, the war was over and the Republic defeated. A chapter of Spanish contemporary history had been closed, and something very different was coming for all Spaniards.

On the ground, the Spanish Civil War had largely been an infantry war, waged between untrained or partially trained conscripts and volunteers, often led by inexperienced officers and noncommissioned officers. It was a war of trenches and street fighting, with each side largely depending upon light or hand weapons. Yet both sides also introduced technical elements to the fighting that changed the nature of the war. Tanks, antitank weapons and antiaircraft guns—supplied by the Germans, Italians, and Soviets—were used with varying degrees of success. And although neither side employed these weapons in great numbers, their use provided information that reflected the technical and tactical improvements and changes made since the end of the Great War, while also demonstrating the growing complexity of modern weapons and warfare.

CHAPTER 2

Foreign Intervention

In 1936, most countries of the world sided with either one or the other Spanish warring parties. The Republic, however, received material aid and could purchase arms almost only from the Soviet Union, due to a Franco-British arms embargo.

Using foreign Communist parties to recruit volunteers for Spain was first proposed in Moscow in September 1936, at a Comintern meeting, very likely following a suggestion by Stalin, after Italy and Germany had already begun sending aid to General Franco. As a security measure, non-Communist volunteers would first be interviewed by an NKVD agent. The main recruitment center was in Paris, where entry to Spain was arranged, providing all needed assistance, money, and passports for volunteers from Eastern Europe. They were then sent by train or boat from France to Spain, and thereafter to a training base near Albacete, between Madrid and Valencia.

Albacete soon became the International Brigades' headquarters and its main depot, while the French Communist Party provided uniforms and other support. Discipline was extreme, and for several weeks the brigadists were locked in their base while they underwent strict military training. Their first engagement was during the siege of Madrid in November 1936, when the role of the International Brigades in stopping the advance of Franco's forces was generally recognized.

Though the government of France did not send direct support to the Republican side, the left-wing government of Prime Minister Leon Blum was sympathetic to the Republicans, and therefore in the early days of the civil war provided some combat aircraft to them through covert means. Even though France initially supported the Spanish Republic with some military equipment, this was soon vetoed by the British and by its own conservative parties, with an agreed shipment of French military aid being canceled. The actual French policy, however, continued, with extensive assistance to the

Republic; while short of the direct sale of military equipment, this support did provide financial and commercial facilities, serving as a conduit for the International Brigades and of large-scale shipments of Soviet military supplies. On at least two occasions, the French government actively considered the possibility of direct military intervention, prompting General Franco to react cautiously, but the French finally decided against such action.

The British government,[1] under Conservative leadership, quickly adopted a hands-off policy, which was maintained throughout the conflict. Yet although the United Kingdom proclaimed itself neutral, its government was strongly anti-communist and tended to prefer a Nationalist victory. The UK ambassador to Spain, Sir Henry Chilton, believed that a victory for Franco was in the establishment's best interests and worked to covertly support the Nationalists. British financiers, with interests in Spain, were not enthusiastic for the Republic. British Foreign Secretary Anthony Eden publicly maintained the official policy of non-intervention, but also privately expressed a preference for a Nationalist success, testifying that his government "preferred a Rebel victory to a Republican victory." Admiral Lord Chatfield, the British First Sea Lord at the time of the conflict, was an admirer of Franco and, with the government's support, the Royal Navy favored the Nationalists during the conflict. However, the British government claimed to be acting solely in the interests of general peace.

Nevertheless, the British government discouraged activity supporting either side by its citizens. There was wide popular support for the non-intervention plan, but the Labour Party was strongly in favor of the Republic. Part of the reasoning for the official British position was based on an exaggerated belief in Germany's and Italy's preparedness for war. Sir Winston Churchill, initially an enthusiastic supporter of non-intervention, was later to describe the workings of the arms embargo as "an elaborate system of official humbug." On August 15, 1936, the United Kingdom banned exports of war materiel to Spain, while the League of Nations condemned intervention, urged its council's members to support non-intervention, and commended mediation. The great issue of the struggle between democracy and fascism seemed to be at stake in Spain. However, this appearance was misleading. The Spanish Republic had never been "securely democratic" and, as the war went on, increasingly fell under the direction of the Communists, who ultimately controlled the supply of arms from the Soviet Union.

When the Spanish Civil War erupted, U.S. Secretary of State Cordell Hull followed American neutrality laws and moved quickly to ban arms sales to either side. However, from the outset, the Nationalists received important support from some elements of American business. Claude Bowers, the American ambassador to Spain, was one of the few ambassadors friendly to the Republic. He later condemned the Non-Intervention Committee, saying that each of their moves had been made to serve the cause of the rebellion, and that "This committee was the most cynical and lamentably dishonest group that history has known."

On August 5, 1936, the United States had made it known that it would follow a policy of non-intervention, but did not announce it officially. This isolationism regarding the Spanish war would later be identified as disastrous by Undersecretary of State Sumner Welles. President Roosevelt had ruled out U.S. interference with the words "[there should be] no expectation that the United States would ever again send troops or warships or floods of munitions and money to Europe." Then on January 6, 1937, at the first opportunity after the winter break, both houses of Congress passed a resolution banning the export of arms to Spain.

In the American private sector, allegiances were unsurprisingly tilted in favor of the military uprising. Texas Oil canceled unilaterally a contract to supply oil to the Republic, and instead began supplying Nationalist forces. Historian Pierpaolo Barbieri[2] mentions an unconfirmed story that states that Henry Ford told Texas Oil chairman Torkild Rieber, "With my trucks and your oil, we will prevent Communism in Spain." It is estimated that during the war, more than 1.5 million tons of fuel were provided to the Nationalist forces, almost all on credit and without any collateral. Nevertheless, the United States also decided that partisan involvement was far too dangerous and that isolating Spain was the only practical way to contain the conflict. Speaking to his cabinet on January 27, 1939, Roosevelt called a Franco victory a defeat for American national interests. He called the embargo "a grave mistake," suggesting that Spain could well be the first round in another general world war. After the war was over, Spanish diplomat José Maria Doussinague, who was at the time Undersecretary of State at the new Spanish Foreign Affairs Ministry, said, "Without American petroleum and American trucks, and American credit, we could never have won the Civil War."[3]

Mussolini's response to appeals from the Spanish insurgents for armed assistance, following their military coup on July 18, 1936, was initially very cautious. Only when he had guarantees, on the grounds of reports received from Italian diplomats, that neither France, Britain, nor Soviet Russia intended to intervene, did the Italian dictator give the green light on July 27 for the dispatch of aircraft to assist General Franco with the airlift of Spanish Moroccan forces to the mainland, as well as arms and ammunition to those fighting already in Spain. Mussolini's decision to intervene was made on the expectation that just a small amount of Italian war materiel would be decisive for the rebellion. This was based, partly at least, on Franco's personal assurances to the Italian authorities that victory for the rebels would be certain and quick, provided some assistance was received, and that once this was achieved he would establish "a republican government in the Fascist style."[4]

Nevertheless, the request for aid that finally provoked Italy's intervention in Spain came from the mastermind of the military uprising, General Emilio Mola, and not from General Franco. General Mola had met with Italian Foreign Minister Count Ciano in Rome on July 24 and requested urgent assistance, advising the Italians about the danger of possible French support for the Republic. Mussolini then assured the former Spanish King Alfonso XIII that "Italy would not permit the establishment of a Soviet regime in Spain."[5]

Following the victory of the "Popular Front" coalition of left-wing parties at the general election in Spain in February, 1936, Mussolini was worried that success for the left in Spain might encourage revolutionaries in France and Western Europe, including Italy. He told his wife, Rachele, that: "Bolshevism in Spain would mean Bolshevism in France, Bolshevism at Italy's back and the danger of [the] Bolshevization of Europe."[6] The Duce and Count Ciano continued regarding their intervention in Spain throughout the civil war as safeguarding Fascism in Italy, and as Count Ciano reflected later, in October 1937: "At Malaga, at Guadalajara, at Santander, we were fighting in defense of our civilization and revolution."[7] Mussolini also became fully committed to the Spanish conflict for geostrategic reasons. The vision of a leftist revolutionary Spanish Republic, oriented towards France and the Soviet Union, would constitute an intolerable challenge to the Fascist concept of "*Mare Nostrum*"[8] ("Our Sea").

All along, Mussolini acknowledged and understood that Italy provided more aid to Franco than Germany. Supporting Franco with troops, Italy far outdid its German friends. While sharing common ideological concerns with Italy, the Germans invested less in terms of military support for Franco, both in personnel and armaments. It has been estimated that the total cost of Italian war materiel supplied to Nationalist Spain amounted to between 6 billion and 8.5 billion Lire (about U.S. $120–$180 million) while in the case of Germany the figure was between 412 million and 540 million *Reichmarks* (close to U.S. $70–$90 million).[9]

Throughout the civil war, more than 16,000 Germans helped the Nationalist forces, although the maximum number in Spain at any one time was no more than 10,000. These forces included the "Condor Legion" dispatched in

December 1936, which consisted of 5,000 men for both the ground and air detachments. At the maximum, Italian forces in Spain numbered between 40,000 and 70,000 troops, including air service personnel, though more than 80,000 went to Spain throughout the war. Italy sent men from the Italian Air Force, the Army, and the Fascist militia, and supplied artillery guns, mortars, machine guns, motor vehicles, light tanks, and bomber, assault, and fighter planes, in greater numbers than Germany. German casualties in the war were light, amounting to no more than 300 dead. Italian losses were far heavier, with almost 4,000 dead and 11,000–12,000 wounded.[10]

In regard to the conduct and progress of the war, both the Italians and Germans experienced increasing exasperation with the slow attritional strategy of Franco and his military command.[11] After the debacle of Guadalajara in March 1937, contemptuously referred to as a "Spanish Caporetto" (a major Italian defeat in World War I) by critics of the Fascist regime, Mussolini was highly critical of Franco's failure, as he saw it, in bringing the Red forces to a decisive confrontation. Yet in October, the Duce complained to the German ambassador that while the Spaniards were very good soldiers, they had no idea of modern warfare and were making "exceedingly slow progress" at the front. Count Ciano was equally critical of Franco's military leadership, accusing him in December 1937—while the Republican offensive to capture the city of Teruel was underway—of "missing the most opportune moments to attack and giving the Reds the opportunity to rally again."[12]

In the case of Germany, the proposal to assist the military rebellion in Spain seemed to come as a surprise to Hitler, who, until then, had paid little attention to whatever was happening in Southern Europe. The request for military assistance came directly to him from General Franco, with the help of Nazi representatives based in Spanish Morocco, and ultimately from Rudolf Hess, the deputy Führer. It has been wrongly believed, and still is, that the military uprising was just one stage in a deliberate Fascist strategy of conquest, and that the Spanish rebels were merely puppets of Italy and Germany. However, anyone with knowledge of Spanish history and the Spanish character should know better and recognize this view as wrong. Spaniards are too proudly independent to be anyone's puppets, and the revolt had been prepared without consulting either Rome or Berlin. That is why General Franco requested help immediately following the uprising and not before it.

The Mediterranean theater was an area in which Hitler had shown little interest, and had preferred to leave it to Mussolini. However, on July 22, 1936, Franco and Lieutenant Colonel Beigbeder[13] approached the German consul at Tetouan, in Spanish Morocco, informing him of the "new Spanish Nationalist

Government" and requesting him to "send ten troop-transport planes with maximum seating capacity through private German firms."[14]

It has also been said that none of the German intelligence organizations had direct prior knowledge of the Spanish military uprising, even though Spanish rebel agents had made some low-level contacts with Nazi Party officials. However, it has been generally agreed that none of these contacts were reported to higher levels of the German government. Nevertheless, there is ample evidence that the outbreak of the Spanish Civil War came as no surprise to Admiral Wilhelm Canaris, the chief of the German military intelligence, or *Abwehr*. Therefore, there is some doubt whether he had reported his views to Hitler. Whatever the case, the Führer knew no more than anyone else beforehand of the rebellion.

Apart from Hitler himself, probably no one in Germany played a greater part in aiding the Nationalist war effort than Admiral Canaris. The *Abwehr* outstations in France and around the Mediterranean had been picking up all kinds of warnings for weeks in advance. One member of General Franco's close personal staff, Lieutenant Colonel Juan Beigbeder, was in contact with Canaris. From him and other Spanish sources, Canaris got hints of what was about to happen in Spain and was even asked if Germany would support the military uprising. Initially, Canaris was probably evasive and didn't bring the issue to Hitler's attention; however, he soon realized that he could not turn his back on the call for aid from his Spanish friends.[15]

Canaris's name was not unknown to Franco, who had met him in the summer of 1935 while attending arms procurement negotiations between Spain and Germany. It appears that it was Franco who instructed Beigbeder to mobilize Canaris and his other German friends. Admiral Canaris must have been involved in organizing aid for Franco no earlier than July 26, and representatives of the *Abwehr* took part in *Sonderstab W*, which was charged with immediately setting up an airlift to Spanish Morocco. Although Canaris was not completely familiar with all the details of the situation in Spain, he was undoubtedly better prepared than anybody else to deal with both Spanish generals, Mola and Franco. It was no mere coincidence that General Mola had been chief of Spanish State Security and had cooperated with Canaris during the Weimar Republic. Canaris was the only high-ranking German official who appeared wholeheartedly committed to support the Spanish revolt from the beginning. It was Canaris who created a durable alliance between Nazi Germany and Franco's Nationalist Spain.

Hitler's decision to intervene was taken on July 26, apparently against the advice of his foreign and war ministries. In response to the personal appeal from Franco, delivered while the Führer was attending the Wagner festival at Bayreuth, he ordered the dispatch of transport and fighter aircraft, along with armaments, to the rebel forces in Spain.[16] Under the Wagnerian codename *Unternehmen Feuerzauber* (Operation *Magic Fire*), the organization of a support operation, *Sonderstab W*, was immediately set in motion within the German General Staff.[17] German aid to the Nationalists increased during August, and on August 28, 1936, Hitler authorized a small number of German soldiers and airmen to be sent to Spain, if necessary to engage directly in combat operations.

Maybe Hitler and the Nazis were initially ignorant of Spain and Spanish affairs, but that was not the case with everybody in Germany. Some Germans had a definite and military plan for the Mediterranean based on geographical facts, relating to the interests and trade routes of Great Britain and France. The main exponent of this plan was Karl Haushofer, a professor at Munich University. In Haushofer's view, Spain was Germany's natural ally against France and it was in Germany's interest to make Spain strong again. The summer of 1940, following France's defeat, witnessed illusions for Francoist expansionism, with war considered as a chance to redress a half-century of injustices against Spain's legitimate demands in Northern Africa. Admiral Canaris was always harping on the issue of Spain and Italy, which he regarded as natural allies of Germany, and along with his friends he was very close to Professor Haushofer.

The German plans for Spain were laid down in many documents, but the most significant appeared in Professor Ewald Banse's 1933 book *Germany, prepare for War!*[18] Professor Banse, in a chapter on Spain, explained how Spain was now again "Germany's natural ally against France, as it was during the 16th and 17th centuries." Banse outlined (more than three years before the military uprising in Spain and General Franco's emergence) that having a strong Spain ruled by a dictator would make it possible for the Spanish nation to play a part worthy of its past, and it was in Germany's interest to make this happen. Was the Nazi leadership aware of such thoughts? There is no evidence pointing at Hitler being familiar with these studies, but such a possibility cannot be ruled out. Undoubtedly, Admiral Canaris knew about them all. Nevertheless, there is no solid evidence that Germany was involved in any way in the Spanish military uprising.[19]

However, from the outset, both Hitler and Mussolini concentrated their support on Franco rather than any other Spanish general,[20] a decision that undoubtedly reinforced Franco's political status. Intervention in the civil war in Spain motivated both the Italians and Germans due to ideological, strategic, and economic considerations, but it was the first of these that initially drove their involvement and sustained it thereafter. The common struggle against

Bolshevism, above all preventing the rising of a communist republic in Spain—with its consequences for international communism and against the advance of Fascism and National Socialism in Europe—produced "a sudden increase in the warmth of German-Italian cooperation,"[21] in the words of Ulrich von Hassell, the then German ambassador to Italy.

While sharing common ideological concerns with Italy over the Spanish conflict, the Germans were content to support a greater Italian commitment while deliberately limiting their own contribution, rather than—as has been claimed by some historians[22]—wishing to prolong the conflict and thereby keep alive the tensions engendered by it, using them as a distraction from Nazi political and military expansion in Central and Eastern Europe. However, Hitler apparently told his military leaders at the Hossbach Conference[23] that Germany was more interested in a continuation of the war in Spain and of the tensions arising between Italy and France in the Mediterranean.[24] At the time, he was convinced that dispatching a large number of German combat troops to Spain would risk a general conflagration, for which Germany was not yet ready.

Although less critical towards Franco during the first part of the civil war, the German military authorities eventually came to sympathize more with the Italian view of Franco's military leadership, agreeing that the Nationalist war effort could be conducted more energetically and effectively, particularly during 1938, as the war seemed to drag on endlessly. In February 1938, prior to the big Aragón offensive, in concert with Italian demands, the German embassy in Nationalist Spain was instructed to ascertain Franco's further military plans. It was to impress on him the need for a "speedy decisive military blow," well as to warn him not to take German material assistance for granted nor "be misled by confidence in our continued armed assistance, into regarding the heretofore rather one-sided performance in the relations between Germany and Nationalist Spain as a permanent condition."[25]

Franco's failure to break the stubborn resistance of the Republicans at the Ebro during the summer of 1938 was a source of increasing concern to the Axis powers, particularly to Italy. According to Count Ciano, Mussolini used violent language about Franco for "his flabby conduct of the war," letting victory slip away when he already had it in his grasp. He accused the Spanish leader of "serene optimism" in the way he conducted the war, advising him that serene optimists "find themselves under a tram as soon as they leave home."[26] At one point Mussolini was considering the withdrawal of all his ground forces, but with Franco's agreement, arrangements were begun to pull out only 10,000 Italian soldiers from Spain, a decision that was made politically easier by the withdrawal of the International Brigades from the Republican side during September and October 1938.[27]

At that time, Germany's attention was too engaged with the developing crisis over Czechoslovakia to be unduly concerned about events in Spain. But, following the settlement of the crisis at Munich in September 1938, the German and Italian authorities agreed that the Rome–Berlin Axis should aim at a speedy and victorious conclusion to the civil war in Spain as soon as possible and to approve no further shipments to Franco until agreement had been reached with him as to the means of achieving such a victory. On November 18, 1936, Germany officially acknowledged the Spanish Nationalist government, claiming that General Franco's administration had now "taken over the greater part of the Spanish national territory" and that "no government authority in charge could be said to exist any longer in the rest of Spain." The German government certainly intended to do everything it could to draw Franco's regime into a Rome–Berlin–Madrid axis, and the first substantial test of this relationship took place in September 1938 during the Czech crisis.

The substantial arms deliveries provided by Germany late in 1938, along with further Italian reinforcements during the winter of 1938–39, contributed to Franco's victory in Catalonia and the capture of Barcelona in January 1939, and finally, the fall of Madrid at the end of March 1939.[28] The intervention of Germany and Italy[29] without a doubt had prevented Franco's defeat, even if initially Soviet military aid gave to the Republic the means to beat back the military uprising.

Regarding the Soviet Union intervention, it is now evident that Stalin didn't decide to aid the Spanish Republic until late in September 1936. Following recent revelations, it has come to light that the blueprint for the support operation to the Republic was presented to him by the NKVD on September 14 and was approved by the Politburo on September 29. The Soviet Union then sent more than 3,000 personnel, mainly tank crewmen and pilots, who actively participated in combat on the Republican side.

Stalin had signed the Non-Intervention Agreement, but nonetheless decided to break the pact. However, unlike Hitler and Mussolini, who openly breached the pact, Stalin initially tried to do so secretly. He created a special section of the Soviet Union's military general staff to head the operation, coined "Operation X." The scope of the Soviet military contingent's intended operations in Spain was ambitious indeed, for these extended across the entirety of the Republican war effort. But the work of Soviet advisors and direct combatants in Spain did not proceed smoothly; on the contrary, "Operation X" was to some extent a failure.

Often, the Soviets' assignment in Spain was a struggle against numerous major obstacles that rendered their work ineffective or counterproductive. The factors contributing to these difficulties were numerous, and included the corrosive attitude of Soviet advisors and diplomats towards the Republic's political leaders and their decisions; personal conflicts between the Soviets themselves and with the Spanish officers; the kind of recruits they were intended to advise or train; the unbridgeable cultural and social differences between the Russians and Spaniards; the personal shortcomings of some advisors; and last but not least, the inability of the Soviet Defense Commissariat and Kremlin to provide full support to their men on the battlefield and issue timely and constructive orders.

Under "Operation X," a high-level committee was intended to work out feasible terms, amounts, and logistics for direct Soviet military assistance to the Republic. The planning committee created a special section within the NKVD, called "Section X," under Semyon Uritsky, head of the military intelligence, or GRU. The ultimate commander of "Operation X" was Marshal Kliment Voroshilov, the Soviet Defense Minister.

The first cargo ship carrying Soviet arms, the *Komsomol*, arrived in Cartagena on October 12, 1936, which ironically is now Spain's national day. By November 5, the NKVD had already overseen a massive mobilization of Soviet weaponry for sale to the Republic. This materiel initially included aircraft, tanks and armored vehicles, artillery, machine guns, rifles, and ammunition. Sizable amounts of Soviet equipment, including the latest-model tanks, were accompanied by numerous Soviet advisers and specialized personnel, who helped to turn the tide in the civil war by November 1936; at least for a while.

One problem was caused by the Soviet Union exacting a harsh price from the Spanish Republic for the delivery of military aid. British historian Gerald Howson has furnished overwhelming evidence showing the full extent to which Stalin shortchanged and double-crossed the Spanish Republic. It is now clear that the Soviet Union pursued a dual goal, with any intervention having to take place within the framework of the overall Soviet policy of the intended alliance with France and Britain. Consequently, Stalin would provide enough military aid to allow the Republic to defend itself, but not enough to frighten or outrage the Western democracies. It is unclear just why the Soviets determined to help the Spanish Republic, and the available documents are so far unhelpful in this regard. It could have been a desire to aid ideological comrades; fears about encouraging further aggression in Europe if the Nationalists were not stopped; or a willingness to support France's strategic position. All these issues may have played a part in the decision. But initially it was not Western inaction that forced the Spanish government into the Soviet sphere, as many biased historians have suggested; the Republicans had already decided to request Soviet aid, not realizing how dependent they would become on the Russian bear. As for the Soviet response to this request, the general view among scholars has been that Stalin[30] resolved to intervene in Spain only in late September.

Military dispatches from the front lines suggested that the Republicans would collapse if they did not receive immediate and massive aid. There were also reports from the first Soviet advisers on the scene, which emphasized the lack of modern technology in Spain and the dangers that the situation represented. These considerations, added to the blatant disregard that Hitler and Mussolini showed for the embargo agreement, may have convinced Stalin[31] to overcome the idea of just sending small arms and begin sending tanks, airplanes, and greater numbers of men early in October 1936.

As Stanley Payne clearly explains, at least by the summer of 1937, the Soviet intention changed to enable the Republic to win a military victory, even though major intervention was delayed so long that the main concern eventually came to be simply avoiding defeat. Stalin, however, made "haste slowly, as he always did."[32] In the end, Stalin wanted only to be sure that there would be no quick and easy Franco victory.[33]

There is some indication that at the initial concept of the operation, Marshal Voroshilov proposed to Stalin the sending of regular Soviet Army combat units,[34] but leading military commanders, including Marshal Tukhachevsky, argued that this would be too difficult and too risky. However, in August and September, the first Russian fighting men arrived in Spain to help organize the war effort against the Nationalists. By late November 1936, there were more than 700 Soviet military advisers (most of which doubled as GRU informers), NKVD agents, diplomatic representatives, and economic experts in Spain.

The military advisers were under the leadership of Yan Berzin (real name, Pavel Ivanovich Kiuzis Peteris), the head of the GRU until he left for Spain, and also under the name of Vladimir Gorev, the acting military attaché in Madrid. He was aided, among others, by Colonel Semyon Krivoshein, the first commander of Soviet tank units in Spain. The advisers usually complained about the incompetence of the Spanish military but expected them to follow Soviet advice entirely and ultimately, they forced out those who stood in their way.

The NKVD initially guaranteed the secrecy and security of the shipment of arms to the Republic as organized by "Section X." The largest shipments arrived in Spain during October and November 1936. Supplies then diminished, increasing slightly in volume by the spring and summer of 1937. After that, shipments were fewer and intermittent, though they continued at varying intervals almost to the end of the war.

One advantage that Soviet arms gave to the Republican forces lay in their initial timing. No matter the speed with which Italian light tanks, and even German tanks, were sent to Spain, the large shipments that arrived in Spain from the Soviet Union during October and November 1936, combined with the arrival of the International Brigades, gave the Republicans temporary superiority and strength on the Madrid front, though this advantage was soon superseded in 1937. In general, Soviet supplies were enough to provide the Republicans with at least equality, or superiority, of arms for a brief time. However, the Republicans were unable to make good use of it.

There has been much debate concerning the quality of Soviet arms. While Soviet sources stress their quality, there have been a great number of allegations from Republican sources that some of the equipment was outdated. Indeed, there is truth to both sides, depending on which set of arms they speak about. Aircraft provided by Moscow were equal to those sent by Germany and Italy, at least initially, while in tanks the superiority of Soviet equipment was undisputed until the end of the war. Artillery and antitank guns sent by the Soviet Union were also generally good, being the same as those in service with the Soviet Army early in World War II. Nevertheless, the main priorities for the Soviet advisers were to help organize the defense of Madrid in October and November 1936 and to help plan the organization of the new Spanish People's Army.

The issue of Soviet involvement in Spain is still a controversial issue to this day. Soviet support increased the influence of the Spanish Communist Party (PCE) within the Republic, and Soviet officials worked with and influenced the Republican leadership to suppress dissidents. A Republican victory would have turned Spain into a kind of "people's democracy," very close to a Soviet satellite state. For how long that would have been the case, on the eve of World War II, is unknown.

The Spanish Civil War was important not only to Spain, but also to the whole of Europe and even the world. Germany's involvement in the war was crucial to helping Franco's Nationalists claim control of Spain. Despite some historians' views as to a functional foreign policy, evidence suggests that involvement in Spain was perfectly consistent with Hitler's goal of distracting Britain and France and driving a rift between them, Italy, and the Soviet Union, while Hitler was making plans for eastern expansion. Indeed, the result of Germany's involvement in the Spanish Civil War was that Britain and France, although drawing closer together, moved further away from Italy and alienated the Soviet Union. Both Italy and, to a lesser extent, the USSR were subsequently drawn toward Germany. Furthermore, Britain and France's non-intervention policy in the Spanish Civil War led Hitler to believe that he could manipulate the weak democracies to achieve his foreign policy aims. Ultimately, this led to an acceleration of his plans for eastern expansion, which in turn helped to accelerate Europe's movement toward World War II.

The major Western powers, including the United States, stayed out of the conflict. Rather than stand up with a fellow democracy and come to its aid, they ignored it. In Spain, the debate over the civil war has its own unique views.

CHAPTER 3

The Beginning: The Early Days of Tanks in the Spanish Army

The Spanish Army's interest in tanks began near the end of World War I, in light of the Allies' experiences on the Western Front. A formal request for the purchase of a single Renault FT-17 light tank was made to the French government in October 1918. This purchase, however, was not processed by the French administration until January 1919, once the war was over.

The Spanish War Ministry's Commission for Experiences, Projects and Confirmation then issued a formal order for one FT-17, armed with a 37mm gun, and days later extended the order to include another request for three cannon-armed tanks and one FT-17 armed only with machine guns. In May 1919, the French acceded to the sale of a single FT-17 light tank to the Spanish Army, which was delivered the next month. Upon inspection by the Spanish government, it was decided to procure another 10 tanks, including eight armed with machine guns and two with cannons. The French government declared that there weren't any vehicles available for sale, and consequently denied the purchase. As a result, Spain began to approach other governments, including the UK and the United States, but to no avail.

Following Spain's colonial defeat at the battle of Annual[1] during the Rif rebellion in northern Morocco on July 22, 1921, another petition was sent to France for new tanks. This time, the French government consented and agreed to the sale of 10 machine-gun armed FT-17s and a single command tank. The command tank was an FT-17 chassis, with the turret replaced by a superstructure, carrying a single communications radio. These were presented to the *Escuela Central de Tiro* (Central Gunnery School) in January 1922, and subsequently organized into a company of 12 light tanks. In September 1921, the Spanish government procured six Schneider CA1 assault armored vehicles and deployed them to Spanish Morocco in February 1922. In March 1922, another six new FT-17s were unloaded at the enclave of Melilla in northern Morocco.

On March 18, 1922, the first company of 12 Renault FT-17 light tanks, integrated into the infantry, had a baptism of fire in its first combat operation, fighting alongside units of the newly created Spanish Foreign Legion. The force was ordered to capture a small rebel town in northern Morocco.[2]

Surprising the defenders, the armored company and the legionnaires captured the town, but later, after advancing further, the tanks began to come under heavy fire. As they had separated themselves from the legionnaires due to their speed, they were forced to fall back and search for the infantry's protection. Two FT-17s were abandoned by their crew due to mechanical problems and were later destroyed by the Moroccan insurgents with dynamite.

A post-action analysis determined that the poor performance of the tank company was due to poor cooperation with the infantry, lack of reliability of the tanks' machine guns, and lack of prior training before being rushed to the front. The Spanish Army's General Staff examined the lackluster performance of the tanks and also concluded that the determining factor in the fiasco was the lack of cooperation between the infantry and tanks. The gap which developed in the field between the two elements, as well as the failure of the machine guns, were found to be important contributing factors. It was also noted that the tanks had been sent to the front without the opportunity for coordinated training exercises with the infantry.

For the remainder of the campaign in Morocco, tanks were used on a smaller scale to provide support during retreats, in punitive operations, in wheeled-vehicle recovery, and in reconnaissance operations with cavalry and infantry units. Thereafter, Spain's only armored company was used almost continuously in small-scale operations between late 1922 and September 1925, but always as a fire support team. On September 9, 1925, Spain's available armor took part in the first amphibious military landing with tanks in history: the landing at Alhucemas.[3]

After being refitted with brand-new FT-17s to replace losses incurred during the three years of operations in Morocco, the tank company was transferred to Ceuta, the most western Spanish enclave in Morocco, to prepare for the amphibious operations planned to take place at Alhucemas Bay, today's Al-Hoceima. Upon landing, the armored company's vehicles were used to support the left flank of the Spanish forces and aided in the capture of the heights surrounding the beaches, and in controlling the exit points leading inland. The war came to an end in May 1926, and the armored company was relocated back to the Spanish mainland.

Despite some tactical improvement, the colonial experience of Spanish armor does not seem to have been an outstanding success. It certainly didn't impress the Spanish War Ministry. Some officers shrewdly enumerated the mistakes made in this early period as being "using the tanks in isolation as mobile pillboxes, for too long periods in action (exceeding the nine hours' autonomy of the Renault FT), lacking adequate reconnaissance, and losing contact with the infantry during the advance." Lack of experience undoubtedly contributed to these mistakes, and it is not surprising that it was concluded that the Moroccan experience proved the need for a greater subordination of tanks to infantry, using them as fire support and under the cover of the infantrymen.

Spain's first use of armor during the Rif rebellion in Morocco had resulted in a minor setback. There were lessons to be learnt, but the Spanish Army largely failed to act on them. Nevertheless, some farsighted officers realized that the use of tanks in a colonial setting, where difficult terrain would be encountered, was a reality. In this type of campaign, it was of the utmost importance that armor and infantry should provide mutual support; otherwise, either could be easily cut off and destroyed. This not only happened to Spanish tanks at Ambar, but to Italian armor during the Italo-Ethiopian war of 1935–36. A manuscript written by a Spanish military officer noted the following causes for the failure of the tanks at the battle of Ambar, and what needed to be done to rectify the situation:

> It was necessary to install at least two machine guns instead of the single one provided, it was needed to improve the quality of the ammunition to avoid interruptions, and personnel better trained with combat experience was also significant. Tanks, in this type of campaign, should be employed with mutual support from infantry. The threat to tanks will come from artillery, antitank rifles and machine guns.

Greater mechanical reliability, along with improved ammunition, would have enhanced the fighting abilities of the Spanish tanks during the rebellion, and even though they did not play a major role during the Alhucemas Bay landings, they were available to provide fire support if called upon to do so. Nevertheless, within the Spanish Army, there was no going back: armor was there to stay. In spite of the experiences in Morocco, the Spanish Army decided to fund a development program to build a new genuinely Spanish light tank. The vehicle was to be based on the French Renault FT-17, which was the most numerous armored vehicle in service with the Spanish Army at the time and one widely used by many foreign armies. It was felt that the tank would become an extremely important asset in future conflicts, and thus the Spanish Army would require a Spanish-built model.

The design that was at first chosen was called the Trubia A-4.[4] Although the prototype performed well during testing, the tank was never put into mass production. Spain also experimented with the Italian Fiat 3000, acquiring one tank in 1925, and with another indigenous tank program called the "Landesa." However, none of these evolved into a major program, so the FT-17 remained the only tank in the Spanish Army until the beginning of the civil war.

These early ideas about armored warfare made little difference to the overall military thinking, and the Spanish Army continued to consider the tank as a simple fire-support platform. The cavalry continued relying on horses, and rejected tanks and motor vehicles, considering them unreliable. Consequently, armor on the eve of the civil war was almost irrelevant in Spain.

In general, the Spanish Army was not sympathetic to the modern ideas current in Europe between the two world wars. Its military technology was backward, and, in any case, resources were lacking to motorize or mechanize the army. The tank was considered as just one more available weapon system, and as such it was just provided to the infantry; however, some armored vehicles, such as the Schneider armored assault guns, were given to the artillery. The cavalry was entirely horse-mounted and only limited mechanization took place with the introduction of some armored cars, but not until the mid-1930s.

At the outset of the Spanish Civil War, most of the troops were just young men completing their term of compulsory draft service who had very little training in military skills. Despite the reforms of the Second Republic, military equipment and training were deficient. After the final pacification of the Spanish protectorate of Morocco in 1927, and given the lack of funds for realistic and extensive maneuvers, the Spanish Army had no further war experience and lacked modern equipment.

Organization and Structure of Armor in the Spanish Army on the Eve of the Civil War

The reorganization of the Spanish Army after the coming of the Second Republic in April 1931 affected the possibility of creating an armored force. According to Stanley Payne, War Minister Manuel Azaña "had scant interest in tanks." Nevertheless, the new government created two infantry tank regiments and a squadron-sized cavalry armored car group in June 1931.

The tank regiments were based in Madrid (the 1st) and Zaragoza (2nd), while the armored car group was an organic unit of the one cavalry division, located in Aranjuez near Madrid. However, the tank units were regiments on paper only (in practice, each regiment had just five of the surviving Renault tanks), and the cavalry squadron did not receive its first armored cars until 1935. Consequently, at the outbreak of the civil war, Spain had only two small tank units equipped with outmoded machines. Spanish military intellectuals described and commented on tank experiments carried out abroad, but reactions were mainly hostile. Neither J. F. C. Fuller nor fellow mechanized warfare advocate Sir Basil Liddell Hart were well known in Spain at the time.

Therefore, to speak of "Spanish armored forces" is simply a utopia. On July 18, 1936, neither side had any tank force of real military value. Therefore, during the civil war, armor operations in Spain on both sides would be mainly led by officers with little or no tactical training on tanks, and on missions conceived by senior commanders who had no grasp of the tactical capabilities, or shortcomings, of armored units in combat.

Republican armor's performance was poor, and as had happened in the army before the war, interest in tanks quickly faded and did not turn into a policy of mechanization. This was a consequence of sheer neglect and negative attitudes, but was also due to Spain lacking the means to implement a policy of mechanization in the 1920s and 1930s, along with the limited manufacturing capacity of Spanish industry and very low army budgets, which in the end had ruled out the creation of an armored force.

The tank was set to become one of the glamour weapons of 20th-century warfare, combining mobility, armor, and firepower into one deadly package, as advocated by German general Heinz Guderian. Tanks maneuvered where other units could not, survived in environments where no others could, and spearheaded mobile operations. From soldiers to historians, everybody loved the tank in the 1930s. Intertwined with the technology and tactics of the period, the tank dominated first the imagination and then the actual doctrine of the era's war makers. Wielded by commanders of vision, men who understood its strengths, weaknesses, and possibilities, the tank became the arbiter of victory and defeat; but not in Spain.

Spanish officers on both sides were influenced by the experience in the Moroccan war, where tanks did not prove to be a war-winning weapon; a fact that strengthened the skeptics' view against creating an armored force at the expenses of horse-mounted cavalry or conventional infantry. During the Spanish Civil War, there was some evolution in Republican military thinking as a result of the battlefield experience obtained so far and the advice provided by Soviet officers, but neither side had enough tanks to attempt large-scale operations.

The Spanish military resigned itself to the passive role of following foreign experts' guidance. Spain was behind the main European armies in 1936, not only in terms of tank strength, but in innovative thinking too, the blame for which can be placed at the door of various governments of the already-gone monarchy, but also of the Republic as well as the army's leading generals, including General Franco, who had even been Chief of the Army General Staff for a short time.

The knowledge of writings of contemporary foreign military thinkers, as well as experience of mechanization, were very limited among Spanish officers. Due to reasons of geographical and cultural closeness, the Spanish Army was more exposed to French military influence than to that from any other country, and the experience of the French was used to endorse conservative views on armor within the Spanish Army during the early years of the period. A widespread view among the Spanish General Staff in the 1920s was that the tank was a very limited weapon, whose usefulness for the army was almost none. Moreover, they believed that the improvement and increased employment of specially designed antitank weapons nullified any achievements made by the tank, which they deemed to be a very expensive tool.

Furthermore, the Spanish infantry was looking at the use of motor vehicles as a way to prevent the cavalry from being turned into mounted infantry, since mobile infantry forces could be created only through motorization, with the additional advantage of the better cost-effectiveness of mechanical transportation. Therefore, the policy in an army dominated by the infantry was to keep the cavalry horse-mounted and out of modernization for a while, even at the cost of jeopardizing the efficiency of the entire army.

Knowledge of British mechanization experiences was very limited in Spain. In general, it was considered too radical. The Spanish General Staff was particularly skeptical about General Fuller's theories of armored forces, no matter how little they actually knew about them, as they modified too radically the traditional features of the land battle validated during World War I. According to their views, Fuller neglected the value of land. They also warned against a too radical mechanization due to the danger of being overconfident in machines, saying it would harm morale by making the armed forces too dependent on the quality and quantity of the weapons systems available.

Given the Spanish Army's background of corporate rivalries, it is not surprising that tanks became an area of professional responsibility to fight for. The initial idea was to assign armor to different branches, depending on the characteristics and tactical missions of the tank. The light tank, armed only with machine guns or a small-caliber gun, was thought best assigned to the infantry, whereas the heavier tank, cannon-armed, should be under the artillery branch, whose personnel were considered the most proficient for operating its armament. However, nothing was specified over the differences between the missions for both types of tanks. The cavalry was not even mentioned.[1]

Nevertheless, it seems that General Fuller's ideas raised the interest of Vicente Rojo[2] when he was just a young captain with the Infantry School at Toledo, who would later become the Republican Army's Chief of the General Staff during the Spanish Civil War. However, Vicente Rojo was at this time only a junior officer and had no influence over Spanish military thinking. Fuller recognized a peculiar factor related to the Spanish situation, saying that if he had written his ideas for the Spanish Army, he would have done it in a different way, "because Spain is a unique country, divided, as it is, by a series of almost parallel mountain ridges, from west to east. In my view, such a country is ideal for combining the methods of muscular and mechanized warfare; for the older weapons can occupy the mountains, while the newer ones can go over the plains." This was an assessment that was not necessarily true, as German armored units would prove later when bursting through the forests of the Ardennes or the Greek mountains.

Key personalities in the Nationalist Army, such as Colonel Juan Beigbeder, who became secretary of state after the civil war and witnessed maneuvers of the German Army with cavalry in the early 1930s when he was military attaché in Berlin, concluded that "the future indeed lay in the combination of motor and horse, since both assets complemented each other."

The first reference to tanks in the Spanish Army's official doctrine appeared in the field manual "Doctrine for Tactical Employment of Arms and Services," published in 1924. Tanks were defined as weapons which were essentially offensive, while it also pointed out that armor should be used massively. The 1924 army doctrine also dealt with the tactical roles of infantry and artillery tanks, explaining that artillery tanks were those which would first break into the enemy lines, followed by the infantry tanks, but then it asserted that the employment of tanks should only be occasional. Armor, according to the field manual, should be organized into separate units that would support the infantry according to each mission, but just as fire-support platforms.

The first official specific doctrine on armor was finally issued in 1928 as a supplement to the 1926 "Infantry Tactical Regulations." This doctrine established the tank's role as an exclusive infantry support weapon, dispelling categorically any doubt over the tank's mission by banning their use in any other task. The stubbornness of Spanish official military thinkers reached a climax when it was established that the tank, as a new weapon, was accepted into service to be used occasionally within the existing doctrine, on the condition that it posed no serious threat to roles already assigned to the traditional Army branches.

However, the organization established by the 1928 Army regulations was not applied to the tank regiments set up in 1931. These were formed according to tables of organization and equipment established on June 5, 1931. Two first-echelon and one second-echelon platoons (five tanks each) formed a first-echelon company; two first-echelon companies formed a battalion; and each regiment included two battalions. The regiment's total tank strength, after adding one signals and command tank for every company, battalion, and regimental headquarters, was 67 tanks. But this was only wishful thinking, as no tank regiments as such were ever organized.

This proposal seems to contradict the Republic's executive order of May 25, 1931, on the reorganization of the army, which stated that the organization of the basic tactical units should be in perfect agreement with the regulations. There is no explanation of the new organization in sources consulted, though this matter becomes purely academic when talking about units that were armored regiments on paper only, as in reality there were only five Renault tanks available for each regiment. Perhaps the answer is related to Minister of War Azaña's personnel policy. Since the War Department wanted to reduce the size of the officer corps, and there were no prospects in the near future to procure more new tanks, he was probably satisfied with a reduced organization that saved a number of useless appointments.

There was no intention whatsoever of creating a large tank force under the operational control of a single commander, as proposed by the leading British and German theorists of armored warfare. The regulations did not consider a tank regiment or a tank battalion operating as an independent whole unit under its commanding officer. Regiments were only administrative units, with battalion commanders reduced to an advisory and liaison role close to the brigade or divisional headquarters. Spanish Army regulations provided even for minor tank support to infantry battalions, such as one tank platoon per infantry battalion as the standard ratio, though the armored component could be increased to tank-company size if the enemy defense was very strong, a procedure regularly implemented at most battles in the Spanish Civil War on both sides. After 1930, the Spanish Army seemed to develop a greater interest in the increasing of motorized transport, but with no real consequence in practice. The lack of efforts to pursue a clear-cut policy of motorization—even on a small scale—led to an appalling situation. In 1933, the Spanish Army had a motor fleet of 2,655 vehicles of 92 different models. Moreover, the civil motor fleet would not be a great help in wartime, as just 20–30 percent of requisitionable vehicles would be of any use due to the diversity of models and spare parts.

Under the right-wing cabinets of the 1933–35 period, there were two attempts to increase the level of motorization within the Spanish Army, but these did not become anything more than mere projects before the outbreak of the civil war. Late in 1934, Prime Minister Lerroux thought of organizing a new motorized division as a purely volunteer formation and a general reserve unit for the army, ready to operate in the home territory or in northern Africa. The second attempt was planned in June 1935, when it was decided to motorize one of the existing divisions as a first step towards a gradual motorization of the army.

There was some evolution from the pre-war doctrine in the Republican Army during the conflict, and in the end, both sides launched offensive operations that tried to exploit the principles of mechanized warfare. Both the plan of the Republican summer offensive against Zaragoza in 1937 and the Nationalist offensive in Aragon in March 1938 showed that Spanish commanders could manage to understand, and even grasp at random, the possibilities of mechanized forces and mobile warfare. Notwithstanding the efforts of the officers who tried to open up the Spanish military's mind to innovations such as the tank and mechanized warfare, this eventually proved to have little success.

Another issue affecting armored warfare prior to the Spanish Civil War was antitank defense. This matter was also neglected in the Spanish Army, with neither regulations on the subject nor specialized weapons. The Spanish Army was supposed to be equipped with an antitank gun designed in 1926: the Ramirez Arellano gun (named after its designer, an Army officer), which was theoretically able to pierce the Renault tank's armor at more than 2,000 yards. About a dozen guns were manufactured at the artillery factory of Trubia in Asturias, but remained untested by 1931. These weapons were still stored in the factory when, during the radical socialist uprising in Asturias before the war in October 1934, the insurgents used them against military forces, amongst them—ironically—the gun's designer himself.

The making of a Spanish armored force in the 1920s and 1930s faced serious obstacles that contemporary professional literature did not fail to highlight. One such impediment was the underdevelopment of Spanish industry: in the early 1920s, Spain's lack of an industrial base solid enough to produce and maintain these types of mechanical systems was insurmountable, especially regarding engines, suspensions, tracks, optics, and even ordnance. By 1928, any attempt to implement mechanization would end in failure as Spain was not an industrial country capable of producing such systems, not to mention the problems of getting an adequate supply of fuel.

Foreign aid and limited intervention during the Spanish Civil War constituted, in some ways, the most extensive military action since World War I for the countries involved, especially the Soviet Union, Germany, and Italy, regardless of the latter's experiences in north-eastern Africa. Unlike other equipment used in the civil war, armor was provided only by the Soviet Union, Germany, and Italy. Neither American, French, nor British armored vehicles were employed by either side. This made mechanized warfare limited both in terms of scope and lessons to be learned from it. Nevertheless, the tank combat that did take place was fierce enough for those involved.

Each nation, specifically Russia and Germany, unquestionably welcomed the opportunity to acclimatize soldiers to combat, especially their airmen and pilots, but when it came to actual practice, neither was able to employ the most sophisticated tank theories, which were still untested, and for a variety of reasons they tended to make a confusing post-operational analysis. Although in the case of the Soviet Union, the Spanish Civil War experience did have some consequences in later tank technology, many tactical lessons were ignored, distorted, or misunderstood.

Nevertheless, the Spanish Civil War was the first conflict in which the opposing sides possessed armored vehicles in similar numbers. The war also witnessed the first tank-versus-tank battle in history early in October 1936 on the Madrid front. Throughout the war, however, tank units were generally employed in an infantry support role and were never used alone in independent operations. Indeed, the limited number of tanks available—a few battalions at the most—largely dictated their employment and tactical size unit. Furthermore, by the time foreign tanks did arrive, the overall strategic situation was at a stalemate, a state of affairs that their appearance did little to change.

CHAPTER 5

Soviet Participation

The two opposing armies of the Spanish Civil War were essentially Spanish in nature, though the Nationalists included significant Italian ground forces, while the Republicans integrated several brigades of international volunteers. However, both armies were based on the traditional Spanish model and were nothing more than offshoots of the pre-war Spanish Army, even if the Republican People's Army (with its official insignia of the red star and the institution of political commissars) had become formally a Spanish variant of the Soviet Red Army.

The Soviet Union's efforts in tank design and production must be understood in the context of the experience of the Russian Civil War and the growth of Soviet industry. During the Russian Civil War, the use of armored trains was common. This tended to lead to a greater interest in tanks and armored cars compared to some Western nations. The rapid growth of heavy industry in the USSR under the Five-Year Plans made a large tank fleet possible. Following the Great War, Britain continued its technical dominance of tank design, and British designs, particularly those from Vickers-Armstrong, formed the basis for many Russian tanks of the 1930s, including the T-26 and BT series.

The Soviets also spent tens of millions of dollars on U.S. equipment and technology to modernize dozens of automotive and tractor factories, which would later produce tanks and armored vehicles. Stalin's enthusiasm for industrialization and mechanization drove an aggressive military development program, resulting in by far the largest and broadest tank inventory of all nations by the late 1930s.

Based on a mixed force of foreign tanks and imported prototypes, the Soviets developed a large domestic design and production capability. The T-26 light tank was based on the British Vickers E (as were many other tanks of the period), chosen after it beat a Soviet FT derivative in trials. In the spring of 1930, a Soviet buying committee arrived in Great Britain to select tanks, tractors, and cars to be used by the Red Army. The Vickers 6-ton was among four models of tanks selected by the Soviet representatives during their visit to the Vickers-Armstrong Company.

The Vickers-built 6-ton tanks had the designation V-26 in the USSR. Three British tanks were successfully tested for cross-country ability at the small proving ground near Moscow in January 1931. On February 13, 1931, the Vickers 6-ton light infantry tank, under the designator T-26,[1] officially entered service in the Red Army as the "main tank for close support of combined arms units and tank units of High Command reserve."[2]

By 1936, when the Spanish Civil War started, the Soviet Army had a total of four mechanized corps, six independent mechanized brigades, and six independent tank regiments. This approach to the use of armor was much more advanced than that of most Western countries, where conversion to mobile warfare was slower. The Soviet tank formations, bigger than the entire tank forces of the world put together, made a less impressive showing, however, in terms of reliability.

It is generally agreed that Soviet progress in this direction was brought to a halt partially by Stalin's incorrect evaluation of the Soviet experience using armor during the Spanish Civil War. The result was that the mechanized corps were disbanded, and tanks returned to the simplest job of providing support to the infantry. As events would later prove, the Soviet Army would pay dearly for this fateful decision.

Among the Soviet military personnel fighting for the Republican side were a number of officers who later rose to prominence during World War II and were still active in the 1950s and 1960s, among them Malinovsky,[3] Konev,[4] Voronov,[5] Batov,[6] and Meretskov,[7] all of whom reached four-star general rank or even higher and contributed much to the shaping, role, and employment of the armored forces of the Warsaw Pact. As a result of their studies of the war, the Soviet leadership at the time acknowledged that their own military doctrine, strategy, and tactics were seriously deficient. Major changes were made in the Soviet Armed Forces, based on their Spanish experience, changes that during the Russo-Finnish War and War World II often proved to have been ill-advised. However, it was the Soviet military attaché in Madrid, Colonel Vladimir Gorev,[8] nicknamed "Sancho," who apparently first ordered, even though he was not an expert in armored warfare, the sending of tanks into combat on the Madrid front, early in October 1936.

The first modern and new Soviet tanks had arrived at the Spanish naval base of Cartagena, on the Spanish southeastern coast, on October 12, 1936, on board the Soviet cargo vessel *Komsomol*. This first shipment of Soviet military aid to the Republican forces contained 50 T-26B tanks and about 40 BA-6 armored cars. Soviet equipment always came to Spain with full crews and auxiliary personnel, even if Spanish troops were going to be trained to use the equipment as they were supposed to handle them.

At this early stage of the war, Germany was still a neutral country, at least officially, with effective diplomatic relations with the Spanish Republic. However, the unloading of the tanks was observed from a German Navy fast boat anchored in Cartagena harbor, and the news was quickly reported to Berlin, and henceforth to General Franco. Thus, the Nationalist forces knew that they could encounter Soviet tanks at any time. By the end of November 1936, four cargo vessels from Leningrad had also arrived at Bilbao's harbor, bringing at least 20 wheeled BA-6 armored cars equipped with the same turret and armament as the T-26 tank.

In total, during the last quarter of 1936, 106 T-26B tanks were delivered to the Spanish Republic by the Soviet Union, and during the first quarter of 1937, another batch of 100 Soviet T-26 tanks were unloaded in various major harbors in the Mediterranean, all of them from ships sailing from Odessa. In May 1937, another 50 tanks arrived, taking the total of T-26 tanks so far delivered up to 256. Fifty of the newest, and fastest, BT-5 tanks arrived from Odessa on board the Spanish vessel *Cabo San Agustin* on August 18, 1937, along with a great deal of supplies and spare parts. The BT-5 tanks were organized into a tank regiment under full Soviet command, and crewed entirely by Soviets.[9] These BT-5 tanks were possibly sent to Spain with the idea of proving and comparing them, while the T-26s were sent as they were the standard armor in the Red Army. More tanks and wheeled armored cars were subsequently delivered to replace loses. The last tanks supplied to the Republic by the Soviet Union were 25 T-26Bs, which arrived on March 13, 1938. By mid-May 1938, before the battle of the Ebro, the Spanish Popular Army was considering acquiring at least 300 more new tanks from the Soviet Union, but this project never came to fruition, likely due to the lack of financial resources available to the Republic. It was too late anyway.

Nevertheless, in July 1938, the Republic still had in active service more than 100 T-26s, plus at least 28 BT-5s and over 50 wheeled armored vehicles of different kinds. The Republicans managed to reorganize their available armored forces once more, splitting and deploying them with the Army Group East (*Grupo de Ejercitos de la Region Oriental*—GERO), located in Catalonia, and Army Group Center (*Grupo de Ejercitos de la Region Central*—GERC), still fighting around Madrid. After the summer of 1938, there are no records of more tanks being delivered to the Spanish Popular Army; their number began to decline quickly after combat loses, with many tanks being captured by Nationalist forces.

The total number of tanks delivered to Spain by the Soviet Union between 1936 and 1938 was 331,[10] of which about 178 were recovered and repaired by General Franco's forces[11] by the end of the war. It has been estimated than no less than 80 T-26s remained in service within the new Spanish Army after the war until the early 1950s, when they were finally replaced finally by brand-new modern tanks supplied by the United States.[12] Soviet tanks, if employed correctly and supported by air power, would have made a real difference in the outcome of the war, but that is just wishful thinking. The truth is that the Republic proved incapable of developing successful military operations, no matter how superior they were in terms of equipment.

Nevertheless, the contribution of Soviet tanks to the Spanish Civil War could be considered as decisive in Soviet armored design for World War II. Soviet tanks dominated their foreign rivals in Spain due to their firepower, but their thin armor—which was common in most tanks of the period—made them vulnerable to the new towed antitank guns supplied to infantry units. This weakness eventually led directly to a new generation of Soviet tanks. However, in 1939, the most numerous Soviet tank models were still the T-26 light tank and the BT series of fast tanks.

On the eve of World War II, the Red Army had around 8,500 T-26s of all variants. The T-26 was a slow-moving infantry tank, originally designed to keep pace with soldiers on the ground, while the BT cavalry tanks were very fast-moving light tanks, designed to fight other tanks. Both were, however, thinly armored, protected against small-arms fire but not against antitank guns such as the German 37mm antitank cannon, and their gasoline-fueled engines—commonly used in tank designs throughout the world in those days—were liable to burst into flames when hit by gunfire.

Soviet T-26 tank shipments during the Spanish Civil War[13]

Date	Ship	Number of vehicles	Additional information
October 15, 1936	*Komsomol*	50	Led by Lieutenant Colonel Semyon Krivoshein
November 30, 1936	*Cabo Palos*	37	Led by General D. G. Pavlov
November 30, 1936	*Mar Caribe*	19	
March 6, 1937	*Cabo Santo Tomé*	60	
March 8, 1937	*Darro*	40	
May 7, 1937	*Cabo Palos*	50	
March 13, 1938	*Gravelines*	25	Last shipment received
Total		281	

CHAPTER 6

Italian Aid and the Volunteer Corps

Patriotic and chauvinist Italians may claim that Italy was the first country to use armored vehicles in battle back in 1912,[1] when primitive armored cars were deployed against the Turks during the battle of Zanzur in Libya, but there was little similar from those almost mythical beginnings to the highly mobile troops that the Italians employed in Abyssinia and later in Spain.

Like Spain later did, Italy first imported the French Renault FT-17 and produced a slightly improved clone, the Fiat 3000, launching its own designs. While the Fiat 3000 was being developed, France sent 100 FT-17 tanks to Italy in 1918 so that Italian troops could get acquainted with tracked combat vehicles. In Italy in 1918, Fiat of Turin and Ansaldo of Genoa were the only industrial companies capable and large enough to deal with tank production. In 1933, a new design was built jointly by Fiat and Ansaldo. This vehicle was introduced as the Fiat-Ansaldo CV-33 light tank,[2] which, armed only with two machine guns, was widely used at the beginning of the war in eastern Africa.

In 1935, a slightly improved model of the CV-33 was introduced and designated the CV-35. The primary differences were that the armor was bolted rather than riveted and the single 6.5mm machine gun was replaced with twin 8mm machine guns. Many older CV-33s were retrofitted to meet the specifications of the CV-35. In 1938, the vehicles were renamed as L3/33 ("L" stands for *Leggero*, or light, in Italian) and L3/35.

On the night of August 6, 1936, the first Italian armored vehicles—a platoon of five Fiat-Ansaldo CV L3/35 tanks—accompanied by an officer and 10 crewmen, left the Italian port of La Spezia bound for Melilla, a Spanish enclave in northern Morocco. Unable to get to Melilla due to Republican Navy activity, they were redirected to the Galician port of Vigo in northern Spain and then made available to the Spanish Military District Commandant at Valladolid. The Italian armor arrived at the port of Vigo on August 26 on the vessel *Aniene*, Italy thus becoming the first country supplying armored vehicles to one of the warring parties. The whole Galicia region, in northwestern Spain, was already in the hands of the military rebellion, and this aid was therefore addressed to General Emilio Mola, who was in command of the whole area. This first tank platoon was extremely well organized, with a services support section, including maintenance and field repairs.

The Italian crews and specialists that came with them had orders to act as instructors and not become involved in combat operations, so the Spanish Nationalist Army Command immediately decided to assign the tanks for operations under control of the Northern Army, which had no armor at all and was already engaged in combat against the Republican militias.

On September 29, 1936, the second shipment of Italian armor[3] arrived, again at the harbor of Vigo, on board the Italian ship *Città di Bengasi*, with 10 more L3 light tanks, seven regular combat tanks, and three flamethrower tanks, with three officers and 25 Italian soldiers, under the command of Captain Oreste Fortuna of the Italian Army, who, in Spain, adopted the nickname of Major Oswald Ferrini. Early in October 1936, these tanks were joined by the initial five-tank platoon, therefore integrating a full tank company (known as the Fiat Tank Company), with a total of 12 combat tanks, structured into three platoons of four tanks each, plus a flamethrower tank platoon with three tanks.

In the meantime, Franco requested additional Italian aid in the form of arms, materiel, and personnel to be used in the formation of mixed Spanish–Italian units. The man behind all the Italian aid between August 28, 1936, and December 1937 was Lieutenant Colonel Emilio Faldella,[4] a peculiar officer who had been Italian Consul at Barcelona from 1930–35, and therefore spoke fluent Spanish and knew about Spain.

A special department, *Ufficio Spagna*,[5] was set up in Rome, led by the Italian diplomat Count Luca Pietromarchi, under Count Ciano's direct authority. Its role was to centralize all requests from the Italian Military Mission in Spain and to coordinate responses to them. The *Ufficio Spagna* was beyond the control of the Italian military and functioned as a situation room, for exclusive communications between Italian forces in Spain and civilian authorities in Rome. Special radio facilities were established, and the Italian military were kept out of direct contact with events in Spain and the decision making process.

At the same time, on December 7, 1936, Mussolini placed all Italian forces in Spain under General Mario Roatta's command, who was until then chief of Italy's military intelligence, and instructed him to make contact with General Franco and with the Germans. On December 8, a third batch of 20 L3 33/35s arrived in Spain, and on December 13, the Italian government agreed to send organic units to Spain, although it was already clear that the

Nationalists would not be able to take Madrid before the end of the year. Later that month, a company of eight Lancia 1Z y 1ZM wheeled armored cars landed at Cadiz in southern Spain.

Italian L3 CV-33/35 tank shipments during the Spanish Civil War	
Date	Number of vehicles
August 26, 1936	5
October 7, 1936	10
December 8, 1936	20
January & February 1937	24
March 1937	24
April 1937	12
September 1937	16
April 1938	12
November & December 1938	32
Total	155

The combat history of the L3 tank was not good. In Spain, L3 tanks were totally outclassed by the T-26 and BT-5 tanks provided to the Republican forces. Italian armor, consisting for the most part of L3/CV-35 light tanks, proved to be no match for that sent by the Soviets. Italian armor was never employed en masse, and therefore it never displayed its full efficiency. Tank companies were employed mainly just as infantry support, distributed among the main infantry divisions of the Italian Volunteer Corps (CTV).

In the final analysis, the Italians failed to absorb the key military lessons of the Spanish Civil War—despite their more extensive intervention—such as the superiority of the more heavily armored Russian tanks, even though they were less maneuverable than lighter Italian models, and the coordination of air and ground forces. Both of these lessons, however, were taken on board by the Germans.[6] Unlike the Germans, who supported the integration of captured Russian armor within Nationalist units, the Italians failed to do so, and they only occasionally requested the use of any captured Soviet armored vehicles.

CHAPTER 7

Germany Enters the Arena

The Treaty of Versailles had prohibited the design, manufacture, and deployment of tanks within the German Army (*Reichswehr*). Paragraph 24 of the treaty specified a 100,000 Marks fine and imprisonment of up to six months for anybody who "manufactured armored vehicles, tanks or similar machines, whose purpose could be for military use."

Despite the manpower and technical limitations imposed by the Treaty of Versailles, several *Reichswehr* officers established a clandestine kind of general staff to study the Great War and develop future strategies and tactics. One such *Reichswehr* officer was General Hans von Seeckt, who as Commander-in-Chief of the Army took to heart the lessons learned in the war and set about rewriting the foundations of the new German Army. The infantry remained the heart and soul of any planned offensive, but tanks would become the spearhead of actions that could shatter enemy defenses through their speed, force, and firepower. Tactics involved the splitting up of enemy formations and counteractions involving pincer movements to surround and ultimately decimate the enemy entirely. By 1926, German Army doctrine had been fully rewritten to fulfill this vision. Although at first the concept of the tank as a mobile weapon of war was met with apathy, German industry was secretly encouraged to develop a tank design.

German tank theory was pioneered by two figures: General Oswald Lutz and his chief of staff, Lieutenant Colonel Heinz Guderian. In the end, Guderian became the more influential of the two, and his ideas were widely publicized. Like his British contemporary, General Sir Percy Hobart, Guderian initially envisioned an armored corps (*panzerkorps*) composed of several types of tanks. During the early 1930s, the German Army studied how other nations were approaching mechanization, the employment of tanks, and the theoretical promises of mobile warfare.

During the early 1930s, as it became clear that the tank could play a significant role on the battlefield, the German Army called upon various German firms to create prototype light and medium tanks, but only a small number were completed. At this time, the German Army did not have a formal plan of action in terms of what it realistically needed. Light tanks could be made available in large quantities for a relatively low price, while medium tanks afforded firepower but came at a higher price. Germany's industrial infrastructure, taking into account both postwar limitations and the economic hit caused by the crash of 1929, made the call easy for the German Army, so the initial target was for the development of only light tanks. Thus, the *Panzer I* was intended not just to train Germany's *panzer* troops, but to prepare Germany's industry for the future mass production of tanks; a difficult engineering feat for the time being.

In July 1932, the Krupp corporation unveiled a prototype heavily influenced by the British Carden Lloyd tankette. The Krupp tank was armed with two 7.92mm MG-13 Dreyse machine guns. Machine guns were already known to be largely useless against even the lightest tank armor of the time, thus restricting the *Panzer I* to a training and anti-infantry role by its design.

Its baptism of fire took place during the Spanish Civil War, and lessons learned from the *Panzer I* provided the German designers and manufacturers with valuable experience for the design and production of the next generation of German tanks that would soon follow. Although the *Panzer I* was not a superb combat tank, it proved to be an excellent training tank, and most of the *panzer* crews were trained on it almost until the end of the Spanish conflict. Many even operated it in combat as their first armored vehicle.

The Germans also built the *SdKfz 265 Panzerbefehlswagen*, which was the German Army's first purpose-designed command and control tank, converted from the *Panzer I Ausf B*, which was the primary German command tank in service not only in Spain, but during the early days of World War II. The creation of the German armored force was an amazing accomplishment, but the truth is that by 1939 the German Army did not field better tanks, or better-armed ones, than those in service with the French, British, or Soviet armies. The German armored force was by this time superior only in terms of procedures, organization, methods of employment, and cooperation with other arms, especially with the air force. Most of this was learnt while in Spain.

Between August and November 1936, following the outbreak of the war in Spain, Lieutenant Colonel Walter Warlimont[1] served as the Reich War Minister (OKH General Staff)'s *Wehrmacht* plenipotentiary delegate to General Franco. Reich War Minister General Werner von Blomberg[2] directed

Warlimont to coordinate German aid in support of Franco's battle against the Spanish government forces. Warlimont replaced Major Alexander von Scheele, a *Luftwaffe* officer who had lived in Argentina and was fluent in the Spanish language.

Before flying to Spain to meet with Franco, Warlimont[3] met various Italian intelligence officials to discuss the Spanish Civil War. When Warlimont learnt that the Nationalists had no tanks, antitank guns, or heavy artillery, he suggested supplying these items to them.[4] Warlimont advocated in November 1936 that German troops provided for Spain be combined into the so-called Condor Legion. Military aid from the USSR had by this time also begun for the Republican government, and as the conflict began to snowball, it became obvious that the Condor Legion, even with Italian help, would prove unable to tip the balance, but only to maintain parity. Hitler nevertheless gave his agreement for the formation of the Condor Legion. Meanwhile, in Berlin, a special section at the Air Ministry called *Sonderstab W*, led by *Luftwaffe* Lieutenant General Helmuth Wilberg,[5] was set up for planning and implementing the aid program to the Nationalists.

Nonetheless, General Franco had to agree to several conditions: first, that all German forces and their attendant services would be grouped in a special autonomous corps, under German command; second, that Nationalist forces would guarantee the security of their bases; and finally, that the Nationalist command would conduct the war in an "active and rational manner," with priority given to the neutralizing, destruction, or seizure of the Mediterranean ports through which Soviet assistance to the Republic was provided.

The Condor Legion was a unit composed of volunteers from the German *Luftwaffe* and *Heeres* (Army), which served during the war in Spain between July 1936 and March 1939. The Condor Legion, upon establishment, consisted of a transport-bomber unit—*Kampfgruppe 88*—with three squadrons of Ju-52 aircraft and *Jagdgruppe 88* with three squadrons of Heinkel He-51 fighters, a reconnaissance group, an air defense group—*Flakbteilung 88/Fk 88*—and a signals group. Overall command of the Condor Legion[6] was given initially to *Luftwaffe* General Hugo Sperrle.[7] There were also two armored units under the command of Colonel Wilhelm Ritter von Thoma, equipped with *Panzer I* tanks.

On December 20, 1936, Warlimont and Major General Wilhelm Faupel, the then German Ambassador to Nationalist Spain, met in Berlin with Hitler, Goering, Colonel General Ludwig Beck, and Von Blomberg to discuss the situation in Spain. Colonel Warlimont's report of his meeting with Hitler is revealing. He wrote:

Faupel wanted three infantry divisions to be sent to Spain immediately. I objected on the grounds that although the Spanish soldier was quite a good fighter, it would not add to the German troops' morale to fight beside Spaniards. Goering and von Blomberg agreed with me, and Hitler expressed fear that it would be impossible to camouflage the identity of 60,000 German troops and that such an action on Germany's part would also force France to intervene on the Republican side, with fatal results for the Fascists. Moreover, Hitler added that if they could focus the world's attention on Spain, it would help Germany. He was not anxious to finish the war quickly. Therefore, Hitler decided not to send three divisions but only to increase the scope of German training for the Spanish troops and send additional war materiel.

A key person in the fulfillment of the German help to Nationalist Spain was Lieutenant Colonel Baron Hans von Funck,[8] who became the German Army's representative at the headquarters of General Franco for the duration of the war, first in Salamanca and later in Burgos. He took over most of the responsibilities of Lieutenant Colonel Warlimont once the latter returned to Germany, and became leader of all German ground forces in Spain except the armored contingent.

Germany delivered to General Franco's Nationalist Army a total of 132 *Panzer I* light tanks between 1936 and 1939. Seventy-two tanks were assigned to the armored branch of the ground forces of the German Condor Legion, and 50 additional tanks were acquired later, when the Nationalists requested more from Germany.

German *Panzer I A/B* tank deliveries to Spain (1936–39)

Date	Number of vehicles
October 1936	41
December 1936	21
August 1937	30
End of 1937	10
January 1939	30
Total	122

As mentioned, only 72 tanks—68 *Ausf A* and *Ausf B* and four *Panzer Befehlswagen I* command tanks—saw service with the Condor Legion under Colonel Ritter von Thoma's *Panzer Abteilung 88*, also known in German as *Abteilung Imker/Drohne*. Group *Imker/Drohne* maintained initially two, then three *panzer* training companies equipped with *Panzer I* light tanks. The other 50 tanks supplied later were under direct command of the Nationalist forces.

The first shipment of German tanks took place on October 8, 1936, with 41 *Panzer I Ausf A* tanks in two batches of 16, plus nine additional tanks and 24 37mm *Pak 35/36* antitank guns, which arrived at the port of Seville in southern Spain on the boats *Pareachssages* and *Girgenti*. Soon after arriving, the whole group went to Caceres by rail, reaching there between October 8 and 10. Almost immediately they were inspected by General Franco at the Castle of Arguijuelas, which was their provisional and main base for the duration of the war. The first 41 *Panzer Is* came along with three *Panzer Befehlswagen I* command tanks. Soon after, on November 25, another batch of 21 *Panzer Is* —in this case *Panzer I Ausf Bs*—arrived on the *Urania*, forming the 3rd Tank Company of the group; meaning a total of 62 tanks were supplied in the second half of 1936, about half of the total number provided by Germany during the entire war.

Contrary to the standard procedure implemented by both the Soviets and Italians—who rotated their troops, especially at battalion level and above—the Germans usually kept their personnel in Spain for the duration of the war.

CHAPTER 8

The Cost of Foreign Aid

Both warring parties—the Republican government and General Franco's civil administration—followed similar financial strategies. Money creation, rather than new taxes or the issue of debt, was the main mechanism used to cover the expenses of the war. Contrary to what is commonly thought, both sides consumed a similar amount of domestic and foreign resources. Inflation was higher for the Republican side, not only because money grew faster, but due to a greater fall in production and because expectations turned against the Republican currency as the so-called People's Army failed to contain the advance of Franco's troops. Given the equality of resources employed by the two sides, we must conclude that the Spanish Republic did not lose the war due to a lack of means.

Furthermore, the Spanish conflict suggests that the outcome of wars—civil or otherwise—is somehow irrespective of the point of departure. It shows that the economic and financial position of the combatants undoubtedly influences the development of wars, but also that the evolution of the economy is affected by the changing military fortunes of each side.

When the civil war began in July 1936, the Spanish economy was divided in two, with most of the industrial base and financial wealth concentrated in the area controlled by the Republican government. Nevertheless, the Republicans lost the war three years later, when in March 1939, General Franco's Army secured total victory over a demoralized Republican Army. The American scholar John R. Hubbard was the first author to approach the issue in 1953, showing that Franco financed the war essentially with German and Italian long-term credits. The Spaniard Angel Viñas has tried to clarify the central issues about the financial requirements of the war. He examined how the Republicans financed their civil and military purchases abroad by depleting the gold reserves of the Bank of Spain, and how Franco, besides receiving most of his resources from Germany and Italy, also obtained help from financiers in Portugal and Switzerland.

Both sides were eventually forced to resort to all possible means to meet the huge expenditure requirements of the three years of conflict. Taxes, requisition, confiscation, payment moratoria, sale of assets, borrowing, and money creation were all used to finance the war effort, the two parties spending roughly similar amounts.

On the eve of the war, Spanish industry, the armed forces, and Spanish diplomacy were entirely unprepared for any kind of conflict, whether civil or international, short or long. In 1935, the level of public expenditure stood at around 13 percent of the nation's GDP. Reported military spending was low, at around 16 percent of the total budget expenditure. The quantity and quality of the military equipment and supplies was clearly insufficient to wage a long war. The rebel forces planned a coup d'état and expected to seize power within a few days, but as the Republic did not immediately crumble, the military coup turned into a drawn-out and devastating war.

Two central banks—one in Madrid and another in Burgos—and two different *pesetas* (the former Spanish currency) coexisted during the war. Financial institutions on both sides were closely supervised. Republican authorities suspended the operations of the stock exchange, took measures to defer the redemption and payment of interest on public debt, and declared a moratorium on bank mortgages. They also introduced rigorous foreign exchange controls and enforced strict measures to regulate the financial system. Franco's administration adopted similar measures: price and exchange controls were introduced and the financial system was subjected to strict regulations.

The Non-Intervention Agreement promoted by Paris and London, signed in September 1936 by 34 nations, drastically reduced the initial economic superiority of the Republic. The agreement prevented the sale of arms to either side, but in fact penalized the Republic, as Franco's army was well supplied by its allies—Germany and Italy—from the beginning of the war, blatantly disregarding the agreement. However, the Soviet Union also ignored the arms embargo and supplied materiel massively to the Republic.

Foreign resources to pay for the war were especially relevant as Spain did not have the capacity to produce military goods. Hence, imports were essential to maintain the war effort. Franco was able to purchase his military equipment with German and Italian aid, along with loans from private banks in Portugal, Switzerland, and the United Kingdom. The most important source, due to its magnitude and strategic significance, was the aid received from Germany and Italy, which included troops, military experts, and military supplies on credit.

The terms for this financial assistance varied over time and from country to country. The mechanism, timing, and control of the funds were always in the hands of nations providing the goods, in the case of the Nationalist side. Nonetheless, in all cases it was agreed that the advances and credits were to be settled at the end of the conflict. As it turned out, the total amount to be paid by Spanish Nationalist authorities was established in bilateral diplomatic negotiations once the war was over.

In the case of Italy, the total aid has been calculated at between 7 and 8.6 billion lire ($377–$467 million), including both military supplies and the expenses of voluntary troops, plus the interests of a revolving credit (300 million lire in all). It is not easy to establish precise figures, particularly because after the war and following long negotiations, the Italian government acceded to a substantial decrease of the Spanish debt that was finally established at 5 billion lire; an amount that was accepted by the Spanish government in 1940. Spain was to reimburse the Italian government up to 1961, even if the Fascist government had already fallen.

German assistance to Franco included supplies to the three services channeled directly through the administration and indirectly through private agents; the cost of the personal expenses of the German military forces; obligations with HISMA (the German company responsible for bilateral trade); and finally various credits granted by the Department of Economy and by private agents. In addition, the Nationalist government bought and paid in cash part of the supplies that came from Germany and hence these payments also had to be included in the total of the German aid. The total amount of German aid was 629 million Reichmarks ($253 million), a considerable amount at the time.

Taking into consideration loans from all sources, it is estimated that the Nationalist administration borrowed as much as $729 million. Italian aid accounted for about 60 percent and German aid roughly 35 percent of the grand total.

The Republic did not receive any significant foreign financial assistance, except two Soviet credit loans in 1938 (a little over $170 million for both). The Republican government did not float debt in London, Paris, or New York, despite having a large amount of gold to be used as guarantee. But it was not short of international means of payment, as it controlled most of the gold and silver reserves of the Bank of Spain. At the outbreak of the civil war, the reserves in the Bank of Spain that could be mobilized to finance the war amounted to 635 tons of fine gold, equivalent to $715 million. These reserves ranked fourth in the world, behind those held by the U.S. Federal Reserve System, the Bank of France, and the Bank of England. By the end of the war, the Republican government had used up these reserves completely to purchase military equipment, ammunition, food, and raw materials abroad.

The transfer to Moscow's Gosbank[1] of almost all the gold amassed over the centuries by the Spanish crown was one of the most sensational episodes not only of the Spanish Civil War, but indeed of all 20th-century international history;[2] however, that is another story beyond the scope of this book. The initial decision to use the Bank of Spain's gold reserves as a means of financing the Republic's war effort came just days after the Nationalist uprising. On July 24, 1936, Prime Minister Giral authorized the first dispatch of gold to Paris, where Blum's government accepted it in exchange for weapons. Sales of gold to France continued until March 1937, when 26.5 percent of all Spanish gold reserves had been transferred to the Bank of France.

The Republicans paid the Soviets for the military aid they received; it was not a magnanimous gesture from one benevolent state towards the besieged folk of another, even if Republican and pro-Soviet propagandists went to extreme lengths to suggest this. The Republic paid dearly for Soviet help, and it did so with their gold stock, amounting to 73.5 percent of what was left after the initial delivery to France.

The Republican government never expected, of course, to receive military assistance at anything less than the market price. Indeed, throughout the war, Soviet aid to Spain remained squarely within the parameters of normal commercial exchange. Some 7,800 crates were shipped to Moscow. The gold was received in the Russian capital by representatives of the Spanish government, the Bank of Spain, and senior Soviet officials.[3] The amount sent to Moscow was just over 510 tons, with a value in 1936 prices of U.S. $518 million. This monetary figure, however, ignored the numismatic value of the gold coins shipped. Had this value been factored into the assessed amount, the Republic no doubt would have established a larger credit line with the Soviets.

The transfer of the world's fourth-largest gold stock to the world's most demonized state unquestionably demands a full investigation.[4] Stalin did not, of course, steal the gold; on the contrary, shipping the gold to Moscow may have been the Republic's only hope of survival. First, the gold would be required to pay for the Soviet weaponry that, by late September, Spanish officials were assured of receiving. Second, the gold could be converted into hard currency through Moscow's financial front organization in Paris, the *Banque Commerciale pour l'Europe du Nord* (Eurobank). The Republic's account at Eurobank would permit the Republicans to finance the war effort, including not only the purchase of arms but also foodstuffs and raw materials, especially oil. That the gold was sent to Moscow simply for safekeeping—a claim maintained for years by some Republican leaders—makes little sense. The besieged Republic had no need for a large, safeguarded gold deposit; it required the rapid mobilization and conversion of all possible resources. The gold was sent to Moscow because, given the international climate, only from Russia could it be best used to the Republic's advantage.

Once in Moscow, the gold's conversion to hard currency proceeded apace. Through additional conversions, the Spaniards depleted their resources by early 1938. Even before the gold was used up, Prime Minister Negrín had instructed the Spanish ambassador to prepare for this contingency by establishing a credit line with the Soviets. In March 1938, the Soviets agreed to grant the Republic a credit line of $70 million. The Republicans sought a second credit in December of the same year, when General Hidalgo de Cisneros traveled to Moscow to plead the Republic's case for more arms.

Various writers have frequently drawn unfavorable contrasts between the credit extended by Hitler and Mussolini to Franco and that which Stalin offered the Republic. According to this line of reasoning, the fascist dictators are often portrayed as extremely generous when compared to Stalin, who allegedly would not sell weapons to the Republic but was interested only in obtaining most of the Spanish gold stocks. However, a large cache of Soviet weapons was sold to Spain on credit, though it appears clear that Stalin's principal motivation for issuing the credit was the promise of an eventual transfer of the Republic's gold. Stalin's decision to aid the Republic seems almost certainly to have depended on the promise of Republican officials to immediately begin transporting the gold out of Madrid.

The total cost of the arms sold by the Soviets to the Republic, much like the issue of the total amount of weapons sold, remains somewhat elusive. Determining the value of the weapons is made difficult by the various indirect expenses related to the complicated transfer of arms, costs which included loading and unloading at port, shipping, rail passage, and pay for the officers and crew of each participating vessel. The Soviets added such costs to the initial price of the weapons. These expenses, ultimately added to the Spaniards' bill, were clearly not insignificant. Multiplied by dozens of voyages, they constituted a sizable drain on the Republic's limited resources.

Another expense added to the Republic's bill was the cost of training Spanish crewmen in the Soviet Union. Here again, a comprehensive tally of total expenses incurred would be difficult to estimate. Charges included hours of instruction, use of equipment, the cost of room and board in the Soviet Union, and transportation within the USSR. In the light of these added expenses to material costs, it is not surprising that no satisfactory total cost spreadsheet exists. From different sources, we can arrive at a figure of approximately $307 million. However, certain Soviet Defense Commissariat documents complicate the matter, though only slightly. It may be reasonable to assume that the numbers, such as those from the Defense Commissariat, do not reflect the indirect expenses, while the separate calculation of $307 million does. Nevertheless, a total "just weapons bill" cautiously estimated at $250–300 million does not look unreasonable.

The total weapons bill is quite important in assessing whether (or not) the Spaniards received fair exchange for their gold. The value of the gold sent to Moscow was approximately $518 million. As we have seen, the gold was converted into hard currency and applied toward the purchase of weapons in Russia and other wartime financing in Paris. But the issue cannot be dismissed so easily. The Kremlin could not have profited from the war if the prices the Soviets charged the Republic were fair ones, prices that reflected market values. The late British historian Gerald Howson's research[5] reveals in incontrovertible fashion that, throughout the entire period of Soviet military assistance, Moscow was overcharging the Spanish Republic for nearly all the weapons sold. The Soviet authorities succeeded in gouging the Spaniards by manipulating exchange rates between rubles to dollars and dollars to pesetas. The Spaniards never saw the original ruble price and were thus never aware that the prices they were being charged were, on average (per Howson's estimate), over 25 percent higher than they should have been. Howson believes that this price-jiggering resulted in overcharges of not less than $51 million. Howson's research and conclusions on this question cannot reasonably be doubted, and he is not exaggerating at any point.

On the other hand, recently declassified documents from Russian military archives indicate that, on at least one occasion, Moscow used hardware earmarked for Spain to pursue military objectives elsewhere. In April 1938, the Soviet Air Force purchased 10 American-made DC-3 cargo aircraft directly from the Douglas Corporation. The purchase, evidently the sole occasion during which the Soviets bought American aircraft for delivery to Spain, was requested by Republican officials and approved by Stalin. All these planes were not, however, immediately deployed to Spain. Three of the DC-3s were expropriated for use in Moscow's other ongoing activities in support of the Chinese communists. So Moscow was charging the Spaniards for planes that they would never receive and that the Soviets would in fact use in another military venture on the other side of the world.

How do all these unveiled new discoveries alter the final tally? Even if we subtract Howson's overcharges, acknowledge possible unpaid loans, and subtract the cost of the DC-3s, the total value of the Soviet assistance provided to the Republic comes to approximately the equivalent amount their gold should have bought. Of course, the matter of the gold's numismatic value effectively throws into doubt the estimated value of $518 million agreed initially. But that does not allow for unfair prices and indirect expenses. Whatever the case, the debate over the financing of the Republican war effort is likely to rage on for years to come.

Things were not too different on the Nationalist side. Under orders from leading members of Hitler's regime, representatives of the Nazi Party deliberately steered Germany's economic relationship with Nationalist Spain in a new direction. A unique trading system was established to deal with the special conditions created by the civil war in Spain. The available evidence leaves no doubt that the Nazi leadership actively pursued policies to ensure that the balance of the new economic relationship would tilt irreversibly in favor of Germany. Indeed, a large-scale exploitation of Spain's economic resources—and specifically its raw material wealth—was planned early on during the civil war and rapidly initiated. By early 1939, at the end of the civil war, the Nazis had established a foothold in Spain's mining industry and further expansion seemed to face no major restraints.

Germany's direct involvement with the military uprising in Spain started with Hitler's decision on July 25, 1936. There currently seems to be general agreement that economic considerations did not account for Hitler's initial decision. Undoubtedly, Hitler's foremost motive was ideological. Hitler emphasized that Germany could not accept a Communist Spain under any circumstances. Hitler had important reasons for initiating Germany's intervention in favor of Franco, and while economic considerations did not contribute to Hitler's initial decision, they soon achieved greater significance.

For the supplies that Hitler had promised, an organized system had to be introduced. In the event, the problem was solved by founding a private company which, being officially Spanish, would handle all the operational details. It became better known under the name of HISMA,[6] an abbreviation of its commercial name *Sociedad Hispano-Marroquí de Transportes, Sociedad Limitada*. HISMA's rise to its ultimate position of virtual monopolistic representation of Germany's economic interests in Spain was officially initiated when the company was registered at Tetuan, in Spanish Morocco, on July 31, 1936. As its first main task, HISMA was simply supposed to act as an administrative organization and payments office for German help given to the Nationalist movement of Spain. In practice, this included the organization of the transportation of Franco's troops and their equipment to the mainland, the camouflaging of these transports, and the arranging of the acquisition of additional war materiel from private companies. Hitler finally decided on August 24 that General Franco should be supported with supplies and militarily as much as possible. Goering, whom Hitler had finally put in charge of the Spanish operation, was already talking about the payment for German deliveries of war materiel with iron ore. It is easy to see why Goring would have considered such a form of payment. According to American historian Roger Whealey, in July 1936, at the start of German aid to Franco, Hitler expressly ordered Goering to secure economic rewards.

Franco amassed huge debts with Italy and Germany. During the war, Italy remained largely lenient in its demands for the payment of the ever-mounting debt, but the Third Reich acted in an aggressive way to secure payments and, increasingly, Germany demanded raw materials in exchange, though an interest in payment in foreign currency was also added. According to British historian Hugh Thomas, German aid to the Nationalists amounted to approximately $215 million in 1939 prices. That was broken down in expenditure to 15.5 percent for salaries and expenses, 21.9 percent for direct delivery of supplies to Spain, and 62.6 percent for the Condor Legion. However, no detailed list of German supplies furnished to Spain has so far been found.

While Italian military aid to the Spanish Nationalists was more extensive in quantity, Germany contributed military and technical aid far superior in quality. German military aid included not only large quantities of heavy equipment, but the technical services necessary to wage modern war as well. At least as important was the swiftness of organization and dispatch of the German aid to the Nationalist forces. Compensation from the Spanish Nationalist government for German war materiel was not as extensive as Germany expected. Thereafter cited as "conversations," there were various German–Spanish agreements, protocols, and treaties outlining in general terms future German participation in the Spanish economy, but no definite agreements existed between the two countries by which the Nationalists acknowledged a definite area of the Spanish economy available for German exploitation. As late as September 1940, Franco still proved to be obstinate over the matter of repayment of the civil war debt. He refused to mix what he considered idealistic matters—the Nationalist cause—with crass economic matters such as the Nationalist debt to Germany.

By the time Franco's troops had finally secured complete victory over the Republic at the end of March 1939, Franco Spain's debt to Nazi Germany had reached the preliminary figure of nearly 430 million Reichmarks. According to the final German government calculation of December 1940, Spain's debt turned out to be even higher. Regardless of how much the bill was, at least an additional $20 million must be added that Spain had to pay to Texaco for all the oil supplied, without taking into account all the trucks and motor vehicles provided by Ford.

Germany's intervention in the civil war had been an extremely costly affair. Undoubtedly, some economic gains had come out of the intervention: HISMA had been successful in challenging the traditional trading pattern between Germany and Spain by securing substantial amounts of raw materials for Germany. However, this did not change the fact that—purely from an orthodox financial Nazi point of view—Germany's costly intervention had few tangible economic returns. It could even be argued that the vast amounts of German war materiel which found their way to Spain should instead have been sold to other countries.

Undoubtedly, the supply of raw materials continued to be at the heart of Nazi intentions to maintain Germany's special economic relationship with Franco. In view of the financial strength of Germany's economic competitors, the Nazis desired to secure Germany an important role in the reconstruction of Spain. Following the acknowledgment of Franco's regime by France and Britain, this became an even more pressing goal as businessmen from both countries as well as the USA immediately offered Franco's Spain goods on credit.

A report of the Spanish *Comisión de Investigación de las Transacciones de Oro Procedentes del III Reich durante la II Guerra Mundial* (Commission for Investigation of Transactions of Gold coming from the Third Reich during World War II), in 1998, stressed the devastation of the Spanish economy after the three years of the Spanish Civil War. By the end of hostilities, Spain was in debt to Germany for more than $212 million for supplies of war materiel and other items to the forces of General Franco. The report maintains that settlement of this debt was the fundamental financial issue between Germany and Franco's Spain during the wartime period. In its conclusions, the report states that the Third Reich did not make payments to Spanish authorities for Spanish goods during the war, except to pay back earlier debts; the debt was gradually settled by payments in goods as well as by other means, such as the Blue Division and Spanish workers sent to work in German factories. In fact, Spain ended World War II with a favorable trade balance with Germany, but kept paying because Spain had been asked in October 1944 to state its adherence to Bretton Woods Resolution VI (following a conference of the same name to regulate international monetary and financial order after the conclusion of World War II), and did not do so until May 5, 1945, days before the end of the war in Europe. In early May 1945, in response to an

Allied request, Spain issued a decree freezing all assets with Axis interests and arranged for a census of Third Reich assets. In October 1946, Spain agreed to turn over to the Allies—to the Inter-Allied Reparations Agency—an estimated $25 million in official and semi-official German assets.

The Allies estimated German external assets in Spain at the end of the war at about $95 million. However, American officials conservatively estimated in 1946 that between February 1942 and May 1945, Spain acquired about 123 tons of gold worth nearly $140 million: 11 tons directly from Germany and German-occupied territories, 74 tons from the German account at the Swiss National Bank, and about 38 tons directly from the Swiss National Bank, which the Allies believed included some looted gold. United States estimates indicated that 72 percent of the gold, worth approximately $100,000 million, acquired by Spain had been looted by Germany from the nations it occupied; all a consequence of German aid during the civil war. War is an expensive business, and if we conclude that the Republic, by expending the gold reserves, had used up the savings of Spaniards from centuries past, then Franco had mortgaged the Spaniards for many years to come.

As an approximate example of the manufacturers' sales price, it is possible to establish the following costs for each armored vehicle supplied to Spain's warring parties in 1936:

BT-5 tank	$29,600
T-26 tank	$21,500
Panzer I Ausf B	$15,000
Fiat L3 CV-33	$3,600

The cost of a *Pak 36* 37mm antitank gun has also been established at $2,280, while a *Flak 18* 88mm antiaircraft gun was $13,000.

Taking into account such figures, we can conclude that the total amount the Republic spent on tanks was about $7.5 million, while the Nationalists spent approximately $2.5 million. This means that at 2021 exchange rates, both sides in the Spanish Civil War spent some $190 million on battle tanks, which does not look like much nowadays.

CHAPTER 9

Organization and Structure of the Nationalist Armored Forces

The Nationalist forces coming to mainland Spain from Morocco—then a Spanish protectorate—had no armor at all. Tank Regiment 2[1] at Zaragoza in northeastern Spain was loyal to the Nationalists, but the city was surrounded by Republican forces, so its few tanks available—just five Renault FT-17s—were employed in defensive operations only; however, until late in 1937 they could not be employed in their intended offensive role anyway. Similarly to the Republicans, the Nationalist Army had almost no available armored forces until the Italian and German aid materialized.

The Nationalist armored strength was almost negligible during the early weeks of the war. Nevertheless, the Nationalists realized that even a small number of tanks could mean a significant advantage. A month after the outbreak of the conflict, Lieutenant Colonel Yagüe, commander of the Nationalist task force named Column Madrid, advancing towards Madrid from the south, wrote to Lieutenant Colonel Franco Salgado-Araujo (then General Franco's aide de camp) that "half a dozen tanks would be very useful for my troops. They would save casualties in the occupation of villages and small towns and provide more speed in the envelopment of enemy positions."[2]

The first modern Nationalist armored unit was the platoon of Italian Fiat L3 light tanks which came late in August 1936 and had curiously been assigned to an artillery regiment.[3] This first platoon was under the command of 2nd Lieutenant Giovanni Battista Barbaglio of the Italian Army (*Regio Esercito*), and he became the first Italian tanker to set afoot in Spain.

The Italian crewmen and accompanying specialists had orders to act as instructors only and not get themselves involved in combat operations, so the Spanish Nationalist Army Command immediately decided to assign the tanks for operations under control of the Northern Army that was already engaged in combat against the Republican militias. This first tank platoon then came under command of Spanish Army First Lieutenant Julio Tamarit, an artillery officer who entered the war not within his original branch but with the armor. Initially, the first modern tanks received were thus under administrative control of an artillery battalion at Valladolid—Field Artillery Information Battalion 2—a decision that revealed clearly that tanks were considered as fire-support platforms rather than for maneuvering on the battlefield.

The second shipment of Italian armor arrived on September 29, 1936, with 10 more L3 light tanks, seven ordinary combat tanks, and three specially converted flamethrower tanks, accompanied by three officers and 25 Italian soldiers. All these tanks were immediately assigned administratively to the Spanish Foreign Legion in order to disguise the presence of Italian soldiers on Spanish soil, even if the decision fooled no one. The unit set out by rail for the Torrijos–Talavera zone—heading to the Madrid front—where it was joined by several Italian artillery batteries.

On October 6, the unit was based at the castle of Las Arguijuelas in the province of Caceres, in northern Extremadura, where it was joined a few days later by the first platoon, and the whole component was organized immediately as the Fiat Tank Company, at the time the first and only modern tank unit of the Nationalist Army. The formation received more Spanish personnel from the same artillery unit as the first platoon and was put under the command of Spanish artillery Captain Guillermo Vidal-Quadras. It was also joined by the Italian artillery unit which had come with the second shipment of Italian equipment, some 38 65/17mm field guns that would double as antitank weapons.

Even if, in the beginning, the tanks so far provided were under Spanish orders, all Italian-equipped mechanized troops would later be under direct command of the Italian Volunteer Corps (CTV), as was the case with the Germans. The Fiat Tank Company—also known as the Tank Company *Navalcarnero*[4] (*Compagnia Carri Navalcarnero*)—would become the Assault Tank Battalion (*Battaglione Carri d'Assalto per l'OMS/Oltre Mare Spagna*) once a third shipment from Italy with 20 new tanks arrived in early December, led by Italian Captain Paolo Paladini. The whole unit later changed its name again to the Special Units Task Force (*Raggruppamento Reparti Specializzati/RRS*), and finally to the Tank Task Force of the Italian Volunteer Corps(*Raggruppamento Carri/CTV*).

Between January and February 1937, 24 further L3s arrived, which allowed for the formation of two more tank companies, together with several thousand Italian volunteer troops, and by March 1937, the Nationalist Army had received another 24 L3 tanks. Consequently, it was possible to create an armored battalion with four companies of 10 tanks each. This, together with a second battalion and the armored car unit, formed the bulk of the armored force for the Italian CTV.[5] On April 12, 12 more L3s arrived, then 16 more in September. With 12 new L3 tanks in April 1938 and a final delivery of 32 more L3s between November and December that year, a third battalion, manned completely by Spanish crews, was added. By the end of the war, a total of 155 Fiat-Ansaldo L3 CV-33/35 tanks had been delivered to the Spanish Nationalist Army.

To give some idea of the overall Italian contribution, by the fall of 1938, the Italians had organized within the framework of the Italian Volunteer Corps a kind of Armored Task Force (*Raggruppamento Carri*) comprising:

- one HQ company, with a platoon of L3 flamethrower tanks;
- one tank regiment, with three tank battalions (one was manned by Spanish soldiers), each with three tank companies;
- one mixed mechanized battalion, with one motorized infantry company (*Bersaglieri*) on trucks, one company of machine gunners on motorbikes, and an armored wheeled car company.; one engineer battalion reinforced with a machine-gun company;
- and one fire support battalion, which included one motorized 65mm assault battery, one antitank company (with German 37mm *Pak* guns), one mixed antitank battery (with Italian 47mm guns and Russian 45mm guns), and one air defense company (with 20mm Breda-35 guns).

By the end of the war, all Italian equipment had been officially delivered to the Spanish Nationalist Army. A total of 60–70 Fiat L3 tanks remained in active service within the new Spanish Army, in cavalry units, until the early 1950s. The rate of attrition, slightly over 50 percent, was the highest suffered by any armored force during the Spanish Civil War and should have taught a lesson to the Italian High Command with a wider war looming in Europe.

Between September 23, 1936, and June 8, 1939, Lieutenant Colonel Wilhelm Ritter von Thoma was sent to Spain by the German General Staff as provisional commander of the Group *Imker/Drohne* (beekeeper), the ground contingent of the German Condor Legion. Arriving in Spain early in October 1936, the personnel of Group *Imker/Drohne* were originally volunteers from a *panzer* division and were tasked with training Franco's Spanish Nationalist officers and men in tank and infantry tactics, but also on artillery and signals employment. Group *Imker* went under the direct authority of Lieutenant Colonel von Funck, but the armored component of Group *Imker/Drohne* was exclusively under the direct orders of Colonel von Thoma.

Von Thoma, a frequent visitor to combat zones, personally led an armored assault on Madrid during the battle of Madrid in November 1936. He later claimed to have taken part in no less than 192 tank actions in Spain,[6] which may have been slightly exaggerated.

Among the subordinates of von Thoma were Major Eberhard von Ostman[7] as second in command, chief instructor Heinrich Becker,[8] instructor Rudolf Demme.[9] Other officers included Major Joachim Ziegler,[10] the first tank company commander, Captain Gerhard Willing,[11] and Lieutenant Karl Pfannkuche, who commanded a *panzer* battalion in Normandy in 1944 and was a recipient of the Knight's Cross; after the war, he joined the new German *Bundeswehr* as full colonel.

After the Spanish Civil War ended on June 8, 1939, von Thoma was assigned back to Berlin as a staff officer. From August–September 1939, he was transferred to the 2nd *Panzer* Division, and was then assigned to command a tank regiment. In November 1942, von Thoma was captured by the British at El Alamein in Egypt. For the remainder of World War II, von Thoma was a prisoner-of-war in British captivity.[12] Churchill's high regard for Thoma is evident from his many later quotations of Thoma's opinions on strategic matters in his writings about the war. After Montgomery invited Thoma to dine with him in his private trailer, Churchill remarked: "I sympathize with General von Thoma: defeated, in captivity and having dinner with Montgomery."[13] Only a few months after his repatriation following the end of the war, Thoma died of a heart attack in 1948 in his hometown of Dachau, near Munich.

The group's command post moved to Cubas de la Sagra near Toledo, near the front at Madrid, where a training school and logistics base were set up. The armored unit of the Condor Legion, *Panzer Abteilung 88*, was then organized with three tank companies, and was also based at Cubas de la Sagra, where German instructors trained future Spanish crews. The unit was thus used for both training duties and combat missions.

Thirty new *Panzer I* tanks for the Nationalist Army[14] arrived in August 1937,[15] with another shipment of 10—this time for the Condor Legion—following by the end of the year, making a total of 40 *Panzer I Ausf A* tanks delivered during 1937. There were no new shipments from Germany in 1938, and a final delivery of 30 *Panzer Is* arrived in January 1939 when the war was almost over. Of the latter group, 20 *Panzer I Ausf A* tanks were for the Nationalist Army and the remaining 10 for the Condor Legion detachment to cover losses.

After completing their training, Spanish troops took custody of the first tanks when a new shipment of *Panzer Is* arrived from Germany. As had happened before with the Italians, the new tank units provided by Germany came under the administrative umbrella of the Spanish Infantry Regiment *Argel 27* (*Regimiento de Infanteria Argel 27*), organized as a tank battalion,[16] commanded by Spanish Major Jose Pujales Carrasco, a former instructor at the Infantry Central Gunnery School, soon to be promoted to lieutenant colonel. While ostensibly in Spain in a training capacity only, the German Army instructors also rotated to the front to provide further technical advice to the Spanish, engaging briefly in direct combat operations.

Group *Drohne* later made use of large numbers of the superior Russian tanks captured from Republican forces (the T-26 tank was particularly prized). Thus, on February 13, 1937, the battalion was reinforced with an experimental platoon of four T-26B Russian tanks captured in combat around Madrid. On March 5, 1937, the battalion received a new tank company equipped entirely with 16 new *Panzer I B "Maybach"* tanks, and it was then organized with four tank companies plus the Russian platoon.

On October 1, 1937, the battalion was transferred administratively to the original Spanish Army Tank Regiment 2, from Zaragoza, continuing under the command of Lieutenant Colonel Pujales. The battalion was then restructured and organized into two armored task force groups; Group One was formed with two tank companies with *Panzer I B*s, while Group Two was made of three companies with *Panzer I A*s. A month later, on November 1, another tank company with Renault FT-17 tanks, captured on the Northern front, was added to Group One. The Nationalist Tank Battalion then had a total strength of six tank companies. An important innovation was that from that moment, one Russian T-26B tank was integrated into each *Panzer I* platoon. Therefore, each tank platoon had four German tanks and one Russian tank. Although this represented an increase in the platoon's firepower, it brought many logistical issues (spare parts, ammunition, etc.).

On February 12, 1938, a new reorganization of the battalion under Spanish control began again, which resulted in the battalion becoming part of the Foreign Legion (*La Legion*) and being renamed as *Bandera de Carros de Combate de la Legion*.[17] From an administrative point of view, the battalion was then under the control of the Foreign Legion *Tercio Duque de Alba*, still with headquarters at Ceuta in Spanish Morocco.[18] Moreover, once the tank battalion became a unit to be manned by the Spanish Legion, the pool of trainees decreased in terms of numbers and quality: personnel unsuitable for the Legion infantry battalions were often sent compulsorily from depots to the tank battalion, disregarding their educational qualifications. Assignment to tank units seemed like a punishment. This must have been shocking for the Germans, as in Germany the tank crews were hand-picked from the best manpower available.

Von Thoma thought that the standard of officers, regarding training and combat skills, was no better than that of private ranks, either on technical or tactical issues. Moreover, since trained officers were transferred from time to time from the armored forces to new appointments, the basic courses for officers had to be repeated over and again, with almost no opportunity for advanced training.

From March 1938, the *Bandera* consisted of two battalions (renamed as *Agrupaciones de Carros 1* and *2*), with a total force of six companies, equipped with *Panzer I* tanks as previously, but with the third platoon in each company equipped only with captured T-26 Soviet tanks,[19] and the sixth tank company equipped entirely with Russian tanks. All the Renault FT-17 tanks were withdrawn and taken back to the rear for training purposes, forming a seventh tank company. With German advisors at the battalion and company level, the *Bandera* organization was as follows:

- Command, and HQ Company, under Lieutenant Colonel Jose Pujales Carrasco. (German advisor: Colonel Wilhelm von Thoma.)
- Group 1, under Captain Gonzalo Diez de la Lastra (with three tank companies). (German advisors: Major Joachim Ziegler, Hauptmann Ferdinand von Planitz, Oberleutnant Erwin Strauchmann, Major Heinz Wolf.)
- Group 2, under Major Modesto Saez de Cabezon (with three tank companies). (German advisors: Major Karl-Ernst Bothe, Hauptmann Gerhard Willing, Oberleutnant Karl Pfannkuche, Oberleutnant Ottfried Sanfft von Pilsa.)
- Antitank Company, under Major Jose del Toro. (German advisor: Major Peter Jansa.)
- Transport Company, under Captain Jose Alfaro Paramo. (German advisor: Hauptmann Hans Schruefer.)
- Maintenance and Workshop Company, under Captain Felix Verdeja Bardales.[20] (German advisor: Hauptmann Albert Schneider, who was awarded a Knight's Cross while serving with the German 78th Infantry Division on the Russian Front in 1942.)

At its height in March 1938, the armored detachment of the Condor Legion amounted to 6,200 men, organized into two tank battalions, under whatever name the Nationalist Army wanted to use, with a total of four tank companies of *Panzer I A/B*s (16 tanks per company), plus two reinforced tank companies of captured Soviet T-26Bs (22 tanks each), and 10 antitank companies of *Pak* 37mm guns (10 guns each).

Finally, on September 28, 1938, another bureaucratic reshaping took place and the *Bandera* was renamed again as the Tank Task Force of the Foreign

Legion (*Agrupacion de Carros de la Legion*), returning once more to the administrative umbrella of Tank Regiment 2 at Zaragoza, while the former Tank Groups became Tank Battalions 1 and 2. Thus, at the end of October 1938, the Nationalists had two tank battalions available, each with three companies, one company of each battalion equipped with captured Russian T-26B tanks. It also had a tank transport column, which consisted of a medium cross-country Wanderer car, two BMW motorcycles with sidecars, 14 Vomag diesel trucks, 10 Büssing diesel trucks, 19 low bow trailers, and four mobile loading ramps, plus the 10 antitank companies.

On April 4, 1939, with the war already over, General Franco's Army still fielded a total of 84 *Panzer I A/B* light tanks, having lost in combat 38 tanks from the 122 supplied. About one-third of the force had been destroyed, a high rate of attrition that should have taught something to those involved in the fighting. However, the losses were not as high as those the Italians had suffered, because the *Panzer I* was a better tank than the Fiat L3 and the German tanks were better employed in combat.

Approximately 40 percent of T-26s supplied to the Republic had fallen into Nationalist hands by the end of the war. The Nationalists used captured T-26 tanks in almost all their battles: Brunete, Bilbao, Teruel, the Ebro, and the final Catalonia campaign. They employed a total of 123 Russian tanks,[21] making the equipment captured from the enemy far more numerous than all the surviving equipment that was supplied by both Italy and Germany.

The end of the war also marked the end of the "love affair" between tanks and the Spanish Foreign Legion. A new organization was set up and the Foreign Legion remained without tanks and armored vehicles for many years until some American- and French-made tanks were sent to the Spanish Western Sahara. There was neither much innovation nor imagination on the Nationalist side regarding armor organization during the war. Battalion-level organization and employment were never exceeded, and at platoon level either the Italian or German pattern of organization was adopted, lasting even to modern times. Administrative organization, nevertheless, did not contribute to a more effective employment of tanks. But as Nationalist General Solchaga once said, the Republicans did far worse, as will be shown below.

CHAPTER 10

Organization and Structure of the Republican Armored Forces

At the outbreak of the war, the Republicans had control of Tank Regiment 1 at Madrid,[1] besides various armored cars and artillery assault armored vehicles, plus the Gunnery School and all existing depots. Yet almost without exception, all this equipment was destroyed or severely damaged in combat between July and October 1936.

On the Republican side, indigenous effort was initiated early on to provide the militias and the Popular Army with armored vehicles to replace their combat losses, but although some armored cars were locally produced, generally with results were disastrous. Nevertheless, more effective armored forces soon materialized under foreign aid programs, mainly from the Soviet Union but also some from France, which was then under a Popular Front government too. However, no armored force of any value was organized until Russian aid arrived.

The Republican armored force was really born in mid-October 1936 following the arrival of Soviet tanks and armored cars. The shortage of time and the Soviet tankmen's eagerness to obtain combat experience meant that only one company could be manned with Spanish crews when the Republican tank force, grouped into two battalions, went into action before the end of October 1936 on the Madrid front. Though the number of Spanish tankmen increased in the following months, the tactical command of the armor was often held by Soviet officers well into 1937. This makes assessment of the pre-war Spanish armored doctrine's effectiveness difficult, since Soviet thinking and procedures weighed heavy at this time. It suffices to say, for this book's purposes, that the Soviet-led Republican tanks did not achieve any offensive success during the early months of the war, but proved effective in delaying and defensive actions during the Nationalist offensive on Madrid between November 1936 and March 1937.

The restructuring of the Spanish Republican Army—the People's Army—showed the Communist influence imposed by the Popular Front authorities. The new Republican People's Army instituted, among other things, the political commissars who were tasked theoretically with lifting the morale of the troops and ensuring cooperation with their high-ranking officers in all units. The political commissars had to overcome the mistrust of the troops towards the officers in order to achieve the necessary discipline for proper coordination. The militias that had been hurriedly armed in the wake of General Franco's coup had been loosely coordinated by the Popular Front coalition. The new structure was seeking to impose a more effective coordination of loyalist forces, as the Republican government had lost all effective control of the armed units.

Nobody has better explained the parlous state of Republican armored forces at this time, than Colonel Segismundo Casado,[2] who said: "[D]uring the entire war the Tank Corps was not controlled by the Ministry of National Defense, nor in consequence by the Central General Staff. The minister and his staff were not even aware of the quantity and types of machines and only knew the situation of those that were used in actual operations." The Soviets, rather than Republican military officers, organized the government's armored forces. Therefore, we must assume that not only the tactical employment, but also the organization and even administration of the armored units were under the control of Soviet advisors.

The key Soviet combat participants in the war were the tank crewmen, who entered battle late in October 1936 on the Madrid' front, conducting a mobile assault against advancing Nationalist troops. As Spanish crewmen were included in tank units from the very beginning, the number of Soviet tank crews that remained in combat declined well into 1938. Soviet crewmen nonetheless continued to serve in diminishing numbers until at least the spring of 1938, fought with courage and skill, and had some local successes, though they never won any major victory.

The Spanish Republican Army often lacked proper equipment. The situation improved somewhat by spring 1937, but certain units remained short of equipment and ammunition throughout the war. The shortage of proper clothing, boots, weapons, and ammunition was especially acute during the first months of the war, immediately after the reorganization.

By mid-October 1936, two months after the Nationalists had been supplied with German and Italian weapons, the first Soviet war supplies arrived to alleviate the lack of materiel on the loyalist side. Taking advantage of its arms shipments, the USSR used this opportunity to implement its control over the Republic. In April 1938, the Socialist Secretary of Defense, Indalecio Prieto, resigned in protest against Soviet influence over the Spanish Republican Army.[3] The People's Republican Army would reach its highest level of organization at the battle of the Ebro during the second half of 1938, but this was also the place where its back would be broken and its last battle.

The first 50 T-26 tanks that arrived in Spain, under the command of Colonel Semyon Krivoshein, were manned by Soviet personnel. Krivoshein had apparently led the training department of the Soviet Tank School at Ulyanovsk.[4] Immediately after disembarking with all his armored forces, Colonel Krivoshein was given, by the Spanish Republican Army, the facilities at the famous thermal baths station of Archena, not far from Cartagena, to instal the main base and training center of the Republican armored forces. Before the end of the month, a reinforced tank company entered combat against Nationalist forces south of Madrid, entirely with Soviet crews and under exclusive Soviet command.

By the end of November 1936, the training center in Archena was initially under the command of Soviet Captain Pavel Arman, nicknamed "Major Greisser," Krivoshein's deputy. At the Archena tank school, Soviet instructors attempted without success to teach with hand signals alone, a practice that contributed in no small measure to the poor preparation of the Republican armor specialists and led to a minor disaster when the cadres saw their first action at Seseña, in the vicinity of Madrid. Colonel Krivoshein then went to the city of Alcala de Henares—seat of the first Spanish university, some 20 miles northwest of Madrid—where he began organizing a second training center for the Republican Army.

Poor preparation led to bad orientation for tank drivers, who did not know where they were, while lack of fuel many times forced them to return to their starting points as advanced refueling checkpoints were not set up. While it took about a year to train a Soviet tank driver in the Soviet Union, the Republican Army pushed to get its tank drivers ready in a month. This led to instances such as one tank commander who broke contact with the enemy because he had not learned how to fire his main gun. Furthermore, the Soviet instructors did not initially have language interpreters to communicate with their Spanish students. Krivoshein felt very frustrated in the face of such Spanish bureaucracy and poor administration.

Really desperate for Spanish volunteers, Krivoshein was also constrained in matters of recruiting. However, only Communist soldiers were allowed to be assigned to the new Soviet tanks. As a result of this policy, the pool of soldiers to recruit from was very narrow, and less adept drivers were often picked over better ones due to their political ideologies. Because the T-26 was a "clear manifestation of proletarian revolutionary might," only devout Communists were to operate it. Accounts from the ranks indicate that non-Communists with mechanical backgrounds were often rejected in favour of more politically acceptable but technically unqualified inductees. It is noteworthy that at this stage of the war, the Republican Army had officially changed its name to the Popular Army and adopted the Red Star to be worn on its uniform.

With training still underway, the tanks were nonetheless sent into combat. The first 50 were organized into the Popular Army's first tank battalion. The battalion was equipped with three tank companies (each company containing 10 tanks) and a headquarters company; each company had three platoons, with three tanks each, plus a command tank. By mid-November 1936, two tank battalions were operational, and they were deployed for the defense of Madrid, which was already threatened by the advance formations of General Franco.

In December, these two tank battalions defending Madrid, then under attack from Nationalist forces, were withdrawn from the front line to start a major reorganization with more equipment that had arrived from the Soviet Union. Both Colonel Krivoshein and Captain Pavel Arman were called back to Russia.[5] Krivoshein[6] reappeared as commanding officer of a Soviet armored brigade that linked with then-ally Guderian's armored forces after the invasion of Poland in September 1939.

Krivoshein was replaced by General Dimitry Pavlov, who in December 1936 organized new Soviet armored vehicles into an armored brigade, made up of four tank battalions and a reconnaissance company. This brigade, known as the *Brigada de Carros de Combate* (Tank Brigade),[7] was comprised of 56 tanks and 68 other armored vehicles, and immediately saw combat around Madrid, including in the battles of Jarama and Guadalajara in early 1937. However, being mainly constrained to defensive duties, it never achieved as much success as had been hoped.

This 1st Armored Brigade, the first major armored unit ever formed in Spain—thus the merit of first creating and employing a mobile force should after all be credited to the Republicans—was made up of four tank battalions and a reconnaissance company with wheeled armored cars, a Spanish motorcycle company, and a transport battalion. The Soviet volunteer tank commanders and drivers sent to Spain were from the best tank units of the Red Army: the *Volodarsky* Mechanized Brigade, the 4th Separate Mechanized Brigade from Babruysk—whose previous commander had been General Pavlov himself—and the *Kalinovskiy* V Mechanized Corps. The tank gunners were usually Spanish communist soldiers.

There were around 70 T-26s in the Republican Army at the beginning of 1937. At the time that Pavlov's brigade went into operation in January 1937, it had received only 56 new tanks since the original October shipment, bringing its total to date to 106. However, during the first quarter of 1937, with the new Soviet tanks received, it was possible to reorganize the armored force into two armored brigades, plus a light armored brigade with wheeled armored cars, this under the command of a Spanish officer—Colonel Enrique Navarro[8]—and one independent tank battalion at Army level, four in total as the Popular Army was then operating four Armies, one per each front line where operations were taking place. So, by mid-1937, the Popular Army has a total strength of 12 tank battalions, a force substantially superior to the Nationalists, not only in quantity but also technically.

At the end of June 1937, General Pavlov was replaced by Major General Rotmistrov[9] and returned to the Soviet Union. Though a successful tank commander, Pavlov was relieved that summer, according to the Soviets' habit of repatriating even highly competent officers following a relatively short period of time in Spain. General Rotmistrov, nicknamed "Rudolf" in Spain, gave impulse to the creation of major armored units, and reorganizing once more the forces available, managed to create by October 1937 the first armored division of the Popular Army, the so-called *Division de Ingenios Blindados*. This division was a major achievement, integrating the two existing armored brigades, plus an independent tank regiment, equipped—as all Soviet armored divisions later were—with brand new BT-5 heavy tanks that were received in August 1937. The division was under the command of a Spanish officer, Colonel Julio Parra Alfaro, and General Rotmistrov was acting as kind of Inspector of Armored Troops at the Supreme HQ of the Republican Army. Colonel Rafael Sanchez Paredes[10] took over the training base and depot at Archena. The Republican Army carried on expanding its armored forces during 1937, and Republican armor grew from one tank brigade in early 1937 to two armored divisions by mid-1938. Nevertheless, brigades and divisions were just administrative units and never saw combat at that level.

General Pavlov,[11] nicknamed "Pablo" in Spain, would early in World War II become the commanding officer of the Northwestern Military District, but was executed subsequently, accused of negligence in the face of the German invasion in 1941. It was Pavlov who brought to Stalin first-hand evidence and ideas that large armored formations had no future, and that tank battalions should be incorporated into the rifle divisions and corps, with tank brigades organized independently but available to the rifle formations should the situation warrant their use. Nevertheless, after the fall of France in 1940, Pavlov, appointed as armored warfare specialist[12] at the Stalin Academy of Mechanization and Motorization of the Soviet Army, could no longer disguise that his ideas were ill-conceived and that large armored formations were necessary, thus reversing his earlier recommendations.

With armored wheeled vehicles delivered to Bilbao's port in the Cantabrian Sea, the Republicans formed the Northern Front Tank Regiment, the first such unit to be under the command of a Spanish officer, Lieutenant Colonel Anselmo Fantova. All these vehicles, plus apparently a very few T-26 tanks, were lost by October 1937 when the Northern front definitively collapsed and the whole region was taken by Nationalist forces. However, most of these tanks were Renault FT-17s, which were of little value.

The armored division of 1937 was integrated by two armored brigades, one motorized infantry brigade, one independent tank regiment, and one antitank company (with towed 45mm antitank guns), plus combat and service support.[13] However, despite its superiority, this unit failed to answer to the tactical requirements of the Popular Army. On the Nationalist side, the biggest armored unit to be employed by General Franco's forces never exceeded battalion size.

The division's independent tank regiment, also called the International Tank Regiment, was the last Soviet tank unit deployed to Spain. By the summer of 1937, the Soviet Union had shipped 256 T-26 tanks to Spain for the various tank battalions. The last major shipment of 50 tanks were the BT-5 fast tanks.[14] In contrast to the T-26 light tanks, the BT-5s were intended for deep maneuver operations rather than close infantry support. They were a license-built copy of the American Christie tank, but with the same Soviet-designed turret and gun as the T-26. They were considered by Soviet advisers to be the most modern and best tanks not only in Spain, but in the Soviet Union too, and were held initially in reserve, waiting for a major opportunity to exploit their capabilities.

From autumn 1937, all T-26 tank crews were Spanish. While Pavlov's 1st Armored Brigade had been recruited from a unit trained and equipped to conduct close infantry support, Colonel Kondryatev's International Tank Regiment had been raised from the Soviet Union's premier mechanized formation, the V *Kalinovskiy* Mechanized Corps from Naro-Fominsk, which had been the showpiece formation for Marshal Tukhachevskiy's experiments with deep maneuvering. However, in September–October 1937, the Republican 1st Tank Brigade was disbanded. Some volunteers returned to the USSR, while others joined the International Tank Regiment under Kondryatev.

As in the case of other Red Army units deployed to Spain, Soviet crews made up only a small fraction of the personnel in the regiment. However, the International Tank Regiment was allotted the cream of the Spanish trainees and the personnel from the International Brigades who had been sent to the Gorkiy Tank School in the Soviet Union in the spring of 1937. The training of the unit, though much better than any other Republican tank unit, was far from complete. In the hope of preserving the mechanical state of the equipment, training was limited to stationary exercises, and there were no opportunities for the unit to practice platoon or company field exercises. For many of the Soviet advisors in Spain, the International Tank Regiment was the last and best hope to display the power of tanks on the modern battlefield. At the end of March 1938, the Soviet advisors and instructors left the International Tank Regiment and its remains were incorporated into the Republican Army's tank forces. By that time, only 22 men were left from the original 85 volunteers and just 18 tanks from the initial 50 were put into service, using parts from the other vehicles. BT tanks, even if captured, were never used by Nationalist units.

Nevertheless, the armored division itself, as already mentioned, never entered combat. Its subordinate units always acted separately, or independently, on the various fronts. The tank's role continued to be considered as merely for infantry support. At the end of 1937, however, it was set to be employed offensively in a major operation on the Extremadura front, but this was canceled in favor of a dubious offensive in Aragon against the city of Teruel. By the spring of 1938, the Republican armored forces were exhausted and no longer a threat to the Nationalists.

By mid-1938, the armored division was split in two, being assigned to both the Madrid front—the Army Group Center[15] (*Grupo de Ejercitos de la Region Central*/GERC), still fighting around the capital—and to Catalonia, within the Army Group East[16] (*Grupo de Ejercitos de la Region Oriental*/GERO). The battle of the Ebro was the last major offensive involving Republican armored forces, and proved their swansong. For the Republic, it was the beginning of the end.

From the point of view of organizational effectiveness, the Republican Army, with the help of Soviet advisers, was much more innovative than the Nationalist Army. It was the first time the concept of an armored force was seen in Spain, even if it was not to much avail. Overall, the deployment of tanks and volunteers was considered a success. Crewmen received high state awards following their return to their homeland, and lectured about their experiences in military schools and to other units.

Several brigades, especially the armored ones, were directly commanded for months by Soviet officers, and since Spanish communist officers came to command many of the best Republican units, it meant the concentration of communist command in large parts of the Republican Army. However, one of the several ways in which the Soviet advisers constituted a problem rather than a solution lay in the autonomous control they exercised over key sections of the army, such as the armor. This gave them a dominant influence in the most important aspects of Republican strategy and helped to determine the way the war was fought.[17] To this problem must be added the strict military limitations and failures of some Soviet advisers, a few of whom were not even prepared for their roles.[18] The Soviets, as has been said, maintained control of their equipment and installations even when fighting for the Spanish government; therefore, access to such materiel required the permission of the Soviets. That permission was always difficult to obtain.

CHAPTER 11

The Opening Rounds:
The "Franco-Style" *Blitzkrieg*

The initial strategy of the military uprising had been to drive straight into Madrid after General Franco landed in southern Spain with the Army of Africa. General Mola raised troops in the north and trying to combine his efforts with Franco's, they advanced together to take the Spanish capital. Although they routed the Republican militias along their path, relieving the Nationalist troops besieged in Toledo—a movement not agreed with Mola—held up Franco's attack on Madrid by up to a month, giving the Republicans time to prepare their defense of the capital.

The Nationalists' attempt to capture Madrid had serious tactical drawbacks. For one thing, their troops were outnumbered more than two to one by the defenders, although the Nationalists were far better trained and equipped. Another problem was their inability to surround Madrid as soon they arrived and cut if off from outside help.

The first armored combat actions took place between Italian and Russian tanks. The first modern tanks entering combat were Italian, which were the first ones received by the Nationalists. As Italian troops were initially barred from combat, Italian crewmen began to train their Spanish counterparts on the operation and basic maintenance of the vehicles. Due to the intensification of hostilities, the first platoon delivered—still with a combined Spanish and Italian crew—was added hastily to the Nationalist army structure, and began its contribution to operations in the Basque Country, though without seeing any serious action as the Republicans had virtually no armor at all there.

Nevertheless, the first Italian platoon, with five tanks, under the command of a Spanish officer, was soon operational and participated successfully in several low-intensity combat actions immediately following its arrival, contributing to the conquest of the city of San Sebastianin the Basque Country on September 12, 1936. The platoon took part later in several battles on the Aragon front, also contributing to the conquest of the city of Huesca on September 20.

It was reassigned straight after to the Central front, where on October 19, it joined the next shipment of Italian and German tanks, at the castle of Arguijuelas de Arriba, near Caceres in northern Extremadura. Up to this point, the employment of Italian tanks had been solely to support infantry strikes, with no action against enemy armor of any kind having taken place.

A first Italian tank company with 15 Fiat L3 light tanks[1] was formed, commanded by Italian Army Captain Oreste Fortuna, and went into combat on the road to Madrid on October 21, 1936, when Italian ground troops were also rushed into action as part of the drive on the capital. The *New York Times*[2] of October 23, 1936, carried a report of the action under the headline "Italian tanks cut Madrid defenses. Whippet tanks rip barbed wire and smash trenches at Navas del Marques." The company of Italian tanks actually contained no Whippet[3] tanks, but they did rout the Republican forces, suffering one tank lost. During the following weeks, the Italian tanks were constantly engaged on the Madrid front, but would soon come up against Soviet tanks.

The Nationalist Army of Africa captured Navalcarnero, the largest town between Talavera and Madrid, about 30 miles southwest of the Spanish capital and a key junction with the road to El Escorial in the northwest. The Republican militias abandoned the heavily wired trenches in front of Navalcanero upon sight of the advancing Nationalist infantry of the Spanish Foreign Legion, which were well supported by the Italian tank company. Following the action on October 21, Captain Oreste Fortuna, who had been lightly wounded, was replaced by Spanish artillery Captain Guillermo Vidal-Quadras, a decision that would later have unforeseen implications.

On October 29, the 5th Republican Regiment, a fully communist unit, launched a counterattack against the advancing Nationalists but was beaten back at Parla-Esquivias-Seseña, barely 25 miles south of Madrid. On November 2, the small town of Brunete—later to become famous—fell to the Nationalists, leaving their troops already in the western suburbs of Madrid. Republican and Nationalist tankers saw their first tank-to-tank combat during the advance of Franco's forces towards Madrid and during the siege of the capital, where the Nationalist *Panzer Is* and Fiat L3 CV-33s suffered heavy losses to Soviet tanks armed with a 45/44mm cannon.

Soviet tanks saw action for the first time during the civil war on October 29, when a tank company team led by Soviet Captain Pavel Arman, a.k.a Major Greisser, met an advance guard detachment of General Franco's spearhead, mostly cavalry on horseback, then advancing at full speed towards Madrid. The encounter took place on the outskirts of the town of Seseña in the province of Toledo. The outcome of this first combat action was very disappointing for the Soviets and in the end served no purpose, apart from dramatically unveiling the arrival of Soviet equipment and military units to the Nationalist forces, while General Franco's troops continued unhindered their advance towards the Spanish capital.

At dawn, the Republicans counterattacked against the Nationalist right flank, from Aranjuez towards Seseña and Esquivias. This was the first venture of the new Popular Army with Russian equipment. Fifteen T-26 tanks,[4] driven by Russians, spearheaded the attack against General Monasterio's Nationalist cavalry. Infantry support was provided by one of the first Republican mixed brigades that had been recently organized.

Arman's company engaged in battle as 12 T-26s advanced 30 miles during a 10-hour raid, inflicting significant losses to the Nationalist forces. The tanks quickly outdistanced their supporting infantry, but still scattered the enemy cavalry in the narrow streets of Seseña and reached the town of Parla on the Madrid–Toledo road. During the battle, the Russians wiped out a whole platoon of Italian tanks. Although successful against both the Nationalist cavalry and their supporting Italian tanks, the T-26s were forced to retire when the Nationalists managed to set several of them on fire with hastily improvised "Molotov cocktails."

The first known instance of ramming in tank warfare was made that day when the T-26 tank of Russian platoon commander Lieutenant Semyon Osadchy encountered two Italian L3s from the Nationalist First Italian Tank Company *Navalcarnero* and overturned one of them into a small ravine. Crewmen of another tankette were killed by tank machine-gun fire after they abandoned their vehicle. The T-26 of Captain Arman was burned by a "Molotov cocktail," but although wounded, Arman continued to lead his tank company. Arman's T-26 destroyed one and damaged two L3 tanks by main-gun fire.

On December 31, Captain Arman was awarded the Order of Hero of the Soviet Union medal for this tank raid and his active participation in the defense of Madrid. However, on November 17, Arman's company had only five T-26 tanks left in operational condition from its initial 15 tanks.

On October 28, Nationalist horse-mounted cavalry and German *Panzer I A* tanks had also encountered Republican T-26 tanks, when the *Panzer I A* proved immediately to have insufficient armament when pitted against its Soviet opponent.

According to a witness who was among the Nationalist forces that intervened in the encounter on October 29 between Italian and Russian tanks, the events developed as follows:

> The advancing Nationalist forces, under command of General Varela, had Madrid as [their] ultimate goal, and were integrated by a total of some eight infantry brigades with the fire support of 23 field artillery batteries, but no tanks at all except one single light tank company

equipped with Italian Fiat L3 tankettes, armed only with machine guns and no guns whatsoever, recently supplied by Italy to General Franco. The advanced guard was formed by a horse-mounted cavalry brigade under command of Colonel Monasterio, supported by two Italian field artillery batteries equipped with 65/17mm light assault guns.

The Republican Army's concept of maneuver envisaged an encircling movement of the Nationalist advanced guard, to penetrate then in depth against the bulk of Franco's forces and recapture the town of Toledo, located 40 miles SW of Madrid. The main effort was to be carried out by the First Infantry Brigade of the Popular Army supported by the tank company team of Major Greisser (15 T-26B tanks). Overall command of the operation was to Soviet general Batov[5] and Republican artillery support was overviewed by Soviet Colonel Voronov.

It was the first action really undertaken by Soviet military in Spain and it clearly showed the involvement and commitment of the Soviet Union in Spain at such an early stage of the war already. While the concept of maneuver was appropriate and well planned, the execution was poor and the Soviets failed in their mission because inadequate arrangements were made to back the tanks with equally mobile infantry and artillery, and because fuel resupply broke down and tanks had to go back to their base for refueling.

Early in the morning of October 29, 1936, after the initial attack had been initiated by the Republican Air Force, also Soviet-equipped and led, the T-26 tanks began to move, taking profit of the morning fog that is typical of the southern Castile plains during early autumn. At the beginning, they managed to penetrate inside the Nationalist deployment, creating some confusion and disorder but soon, lacking infantry support and liaison with higher echelons due to poor communications, the tanks were brought to a halt. It is not difficult to imagine the Soviet tankers in inland Spain, facing a full new environment, not understanding a single word of Spanish, most likely without adequate maps and without communication with their superiors; they must have felt completely lost.

Still advancing but without clear references, they came under direct fire of the artillery howitzers attached to the Nationalist cavalry. One tank of the leading platoon was destroyed by a direct hit, and a second was damaged but managed to find a hull-down position from where it continued firing on the Nationalist forces. The third tank in the platoon started to withdraw from combat but made the mistake to enter through the narrow streets of the town of Seseña where it was soon destroyed by Nationalist cavalrymen with improvised 'Molotov cocktails.' What was left of the Soviet tank company disengaged from the action and withdrew towards the Republican lines, putting an end to the planned operation.

Back to the second tank of the unfortunate leading Soviet platoon, this one was immobilized in its hull-down position but continued firing on the Nationalist forces and with undoubted resolution and courage its crew rejected all Nationalist attempts to destroy it. The Nationalist cavalry commander decided to involve the Italian L3 light tanks available but they proved completely inadequate and soon one was damaged, being overturned by a direct hit from the T-26, its crew escaping miraculously alive, and another, of a flamethrower version, [was] totally destroyed and its crew killed also by a direct hit. After 40 minutes, the Soviet tank was finally destroyed by a direct hit of a Spanish 75mm field howitzer and its entire Soviet crew killed. Thus, during their first action the Soviets failed in their mission and lost three tanks out of 15 committed, destroying in exchange two light Italian L3 tanks. It was not a very bright start.[6]

The initiation of the T-26 tank in the Spanish war was, like that of the Soviet high-speed bombers, a dramatic if uneven performance: a triumph for Republican morale perhaps, but a tactical fiasco. For years, controversy and myth have surrounded this first entrance into the war of a Republican tank company. Given the large number of conflicting versions, it is probably impossible to accurately recreate the event. *Pravda* correspondent Mikhail Koltsov's account is perhaps the most enthralling, and, though dismissed by some as fictitious, has now been partly verified by recently declassified Russian after-action reports. The Russian journalist drew attention to a detail ignored by most other commentators: the broadcasting of the Republic's strategy on the eve of the battle. According to Koltsov, the night before the attack was due to start, Republican Prime Minister Largo Caballero inexplicably read the battle orders aloud over Madrid radio airwaves.[7] Virtually every detail, save the initial location of the operation, was revealed. The text of the battle plan was also sent to the press for inclusion in the morning newspapers. Whether this unorthodox strategy was designed to demoralize the enemy or was indeed a tactical blunder by the prime minister remains open to speculation. Fortunately for the Republicans, no more specific warnings on the use of the new tanks followed.

Although the action in Seseña sounded an alarm among Nationalist forces and convinced General Franco that Madrid was already well defended with Soviet troops, both on the ground and in the air, the failure of the Soviets in this clash led to Franco ordering his units to continue advancing towards the capital. The Nationalists soon obtained proof that Seseña had only been the result of bad luck and some hasty and poor planning on their part. However, two horse-mounted troops of Nationalist cavalry and two infantry battalions were halted, and it is estimated that two field guns, four Italian L3s tanks—a full platoon of three tanks plus one flamethrower tank—and some 20–30 trucks with their cargo were destroyed or damaged, for the loss of just three T-26 tanks to "Molotov cocktails"[8] and antitank artillery fire.

The Russians at Seseña woefully displayed the cloying limitations of their tank education. Trying to emulate British theory without possessing the proper means, they had thrust ahead with their tanks, leaving the infantry well behind. The tanks found it difficult to hold ground on their own, and soon had to turn back due to shortage of fuel, thereby forfeiting the advantage of mobility that alone could have brought them success. Yet the tactical shortcomings of the abortive Seseña operation were recognized by few save those who had made the attack.

On the other hand, Colonel Krivoshein's own assessment of the tanks' debut was adequately balanced:

> The main failure was in the area of tactical coordination between tanks and infantry. Neither the soldiers nor the commanders of the Republican Army mastered the use of tanks, staying with them and developing their success. The tankers, for their part, forgot the infantry behind

because they had been overcome by their desire to smash the enemy; the tanks often failed to orient properly on the terrain.[9]

The Nationalist command seems to have reached contradictory, and somewhat biased, conclusions following its troops' early experiences in fighting with or against tanks. The first operations of the Republican armor during the autumn of 1936 had been unsuccessful due to the lack of coordination with the infantry, and as a result, on the eve of the assault on Madrid early in November that year, the headquarters of the Nationalist Army of the North concluded that tanks required close support with solid and aggressive infantry.

The first two Nationalist *Panzer I* tank companies were also deployed on the Madrid front on October 29, and entered combat on November 1 and 2. By then, each tank company had one antitank platoon with 37mm guns attached, and they managed to destroy a Republican armored train on the railroad between Madrid and Aranjuez on November 2.

The Italian tank company had been so heavily battered on October 30—it had then only 11 tanks in service: nine battle tanks and two flamethrower tanks—that it had to be withdrawn from the front line back to the town of Yuncos, south of Madrid, where the Nationalists had established a logistical base. The tank company remained there until November 2, resting, and carrying out maintenance and hasty repairs.

On November 3, the Nationalists captured their first operational Soviet T-26 tank, almost in mint condition and fully in service, sending it to the rear support services. It is interesting to note that at this stage of the conflict, the Germans in Spain helping Franco began offering the sum of 500 Spanish pesetas (less than $5 at 2021 exchange rate) for each T-26 tank captured intact. This reward, proof of the German interest in Soviet equipment, attracted a lot of attention among Colonial Nationalist troops, mostly of Moroccan origin, who on many occasions managed only to get killed in their efforts to capture a Soviet tank regardless of the cost.

The Soviets lost about six more T-26 tanks in subsequent combats with the advancing Nationalist troops, and these destroyed tanks were carefully inspected and studied. Some of their main components were sent to Italy, where some of the knowledge obtained was used in the development of the Italian Ansaldo M-13/40 tank, which despite its poor design was employed with reasonable success in the North African campaign of 1941–43 alongside the German *Afrika Korps*.

Krivoshein's tank group[10] also took part in the fighting for Torrejon de Velasco and Valdemoro, near Madrid, on November 4–5, as well as in a counterattack in the suburbs of Madrid, in the neighborhood of the so-called

"*Cerro de los Angeles*"—a Catholic sanctuary also called the "*Cerro Rojo*" (Red Hill)—on November 13, and in the continuous fighting in the outskirts of Madrid until mid-December. Confined to a single road by steep hillsides, the Russian T-26s lost their freedom of maneuver, and two tanks were quickly destroyed by German *Pak 36* antitank guns deployed near the summit.

Krivoshein's formation, consisting of 23 T-26 tanks and nine BA-10 armored cars, attacked Nationalist forces on November 4, supporting the main Republican column retreating to Madrid. Prior to the attack, participating infantry battalion commanders received a briefing on tank–infantry cooperation at Colonel Krivoshein's request. Krivoshein now commanded four tank companies, after having incorporated Captain Arman's company, and ordered them all to act in strict cooperation with the infantry. That meant staying no more than 400–600 yards ahead of the infantry, no matter how light the resistance appeared at any given moment.[11]

The operation on November 4–5 was a failure, and the Republican units retreated to Madrid. During November 5 and 6, most tanks and armored cars of Krivoshein's group underwent much-needed maintenance, only to go back to the front to support the Republican forces wherever urgently needed. Whenever tanks were present, morale improved, and tank–infantry cooperation at tactical levels was better.

By mid-November, less than three weeks after arriving at the front, Captain Arman's tank company had lost half of its original tanks due to breakdowns and Nationalist action. Colonel Krivoshein not only ordered its withdrawal for a complete refitting, but arranged for a new service support facility to be established closer to the front.

During most of November 1936, Krivoshein's tank companies continued to shore up Madrid's defenses. Each company usually supported an infantry battalion, despite the terrain being poor for tank operations, and the tactical gains were minimal. By the last week of the month, they were fighting in the narrow alleys of the Madrid University campus, where the T-26s proved to be unusually easy targets for *Pak 36* antitank guns and direct field artillery fire. Tanks also fought on unfavorable terrain at the Casa de Campo, a hilly and heavily wooded park on Madrid's western perimeter.

Soviet military personnel of Krivoshein's group returned to the USSR by the end of November, but some tankers, mechanics from the Alcala de Henares tank maintenance and repair base, and instructors from the Archena training center remained. However, they were not retained long enough to impart their hard-earned knowledge to inexperienced replacements, and newly arrived commanders such as Koniev and Rokossovsky repeated the same tactical mistakes of October. When General Pavlov took over Republican tank operations, infantry support missions were more urgent, and the Soviet concept of "deep battle" and mobile warfare had disappeared into oblivion.

On November 5, the Italian tank company returned to Madrid's front line and entered combat in the neighborhood of Villaverde and Getafe—southern suburbs of Madrid—losing one tank. Their next step would be the first attempt to capture Madrid, following General Mola's plan.

Under the leadership of Mola, as C-in-C of the Army of the North, the Nationalists commenced their first attack on the capital on November 7 with 20,000 troops, mostly Moroccan *Regulares*[12] and the Foreign Legion, supported by Italian and German armor. At 0700, two platoons of the Italian tank company began moving forward from their Villaverde positions. On that day, the tank company commander, Captain Vidal-Quadras,[13] was killed in action when his tank was destroyed by Republican infantry attacking with hand grenades, although the tank was later recovered by the Nationalists. During this incident, the Republicans managed to seize the captain's maps and orders which contained full details of the Nationalist plan to take Madrid. Spanish infantry Lieutenant Daniel Gómez Pérez, from the Foreign Legion, replaced Captain Vidal-Quadras.

Forest and built-up areas helped strengthen the fortifications in the outskirts of the city, where the assault troops also faced better-organized Republican forces. The assault on Madrid revealed the limitations of the Nationalist armor and prompted the Nationalist general headquarters, *Cuartel General del Generalisimo* (CGG), to send instructions to the Army of the North on the tactical use of tanks. Tanks were said to be unsuitable for street-fighting, where they were too exposed to enemy weapons, while their own field of fire was more limited and they could not provide mutual support. It was felt better to keep them outside towns as a reaction force against enemy counterattacks. The CGG said tanks should not be scattered among columns, as their effectiveness lay in mass use. The battle for Madrid had also proved that Nationalist tanks were no match for the Republicans' Soviet armor.

On November 12, the whole Italian tank company went into action again in the neighborhood of Usera, another southern suburb of Madrid, losing one more tank, again the company commander's tank, that of Lieutenant Daniel Gómez, who was severely wounded and permanently blinded.[14] The company was left with just eight operational tanks, and once more underwent major maintenance and repairs until November 19, when infantry Captain Vicente Gomez Salcedo took over as the new company commander. On November 26, the tank company assembled in Caceres and was being prepared to join the tank battalion of the new Italian CTV. A total of five L3 tanks had been lost in combat.

The following report by a member of the Soviet staff in the International Brigades, Manfred Stern[15] (a.k.a. "Kleber"), recalling the mid-November battle at the Madrid suburb of Carabanchel, summarizes the myriad obstacles confronting the Republican tank crews during their first weeks of operations:

> In one such battle, units of my sector were supposed to storm the Garabitas Hill. We had been given about two-dozen tanks. The time was set for the assault. The infantry was ready, and the tanks did not come. Finally, the tanks arrived.
>
> The infantry, having moved forward once, without tanks and having achieved nothing, did not want to go a second time, even with the tanks. An uncoordinated attack occurred where some took part, and others did not … And then the tanks stopped in front of the enemy trenches and did not move forward or backward. It turned out the tanks had gone into battle without filling up with fuel. The enemy antitank guns dealt with the immobile tanks as they liked.

In retrospect, it appears that, in its haste to dispatch the tanks to the Republicans, the Soviets had managed to provide neither the basic needs for tank support nor proper coordination with the rest of the Republican defensive forces. These types of mistakes were not uncommon.

However, early German combat experiences in Spain were even more frustrating. Although the Nationalists held the initiative by late 1936, their *Panzer Is*, under Spanish command, never exploited it. Nor would German leadership have made a tactically significant difference with just a battalion of light tanks in service for the whole front at Madrid. Like the Republican tanks, the *panzers* were employed in close cooperation with infantry formations on foot, whose training in combined-arms operations was nil.

The German Condor Legion also provided air support, which took a heavy toll on the buildings of Madrid's Moncloa western neighborhood. On November 20, the Nationalists made their final frontal assault and, under cover of a heavy artillery bombardment, Moroccan and Foreign Legion troops fought their way into the University campus in the northwest of Madrid. While their advance was checked, they established a bridgehead over the Manzanares River. Bitter street fighting ensued. Despite fierce counterattacks by the 11th International Brigade and Spanish Republican units, the Nationalists kept their toehold in the University campus, and by the end of the battle were in possession of three-quarters of the complex. However, their attempt to storm Madrid had failed in the face of unexpectedly stiff Republican resistance, and Franco stopped further assaults as he could not risk losing any more of his best troops there.

Both the Italian tank company and the first two German tank companies formed a single tank battalion on November 20, the first and only time such an event happened, under the command of Spanish Major Jose Pujales Carrasco, and participated in the combat around Madrid's University Campus. They lost one more tank on November 25, with its crew killed and the Republicans capturing the Italian L3.

The Nationalist German-supplied *Panzer I* tanks were gradually deployed into combat during the fighting around Madrid in November 1936, usually in at least tank company strength, to provide support to various infantry units, normally of battalion size. Their first encounter with Russian T-26s took place within the neighborhood of Casa de Campo and Ciudad Universitaria, in the outskirts of Madrid. Losses were significant, with no less than six tanks destroyed and 16 damaged. Although the *panzers* were used mainly for infantry support, they could not avoid confrontation with T-26s and BA-6 armored cars.

By the end of November 1936, about 36 German *Panzer I* light tanks out of a total of 48 were damaged, and during the fighting around Pozuelo de Alarcon, barely 10 miles northwest of Madrid, in December 1936 and early January 1937, at least 12 *Panzer I* tanks were knocked out while engaging Russian armor. Colonel von Thoma made the decision to assign five towed *Pak 36* antitank guns to each Nationalist *panzer* tank company. As early as December 6, von Thoma urgently asked[16] the German General Staff in Berlin to send cannon-armed tanks to Spain, at least the new *Panzer II* armed with the 20mm Kwk30 gun, that had already begun service with the *Wehrmacht*. Meanwhile, von Thoma remained in Spain for the duration of the war, but served increasingly only as chief instructor and chief advisor.

Far more important from von Thoma's perspective were the results of tank-versus-tank and armored car-versus-tank engagements on the Madrid front, both of which favored the Republicans. When the Nationalists again shifted their main efforts to the south of Madrid in early February 1937, at the battle of Jarama, the *panzers* met a similar fate. Operating against initially disorganized defenses, they proved effective enough supporting the infantry, but only until the Russian T-26s arrived.

On December 19, the Italian tank company, with only nine tanks remaining, was finally withdrawn from the front line and taken back to Yuncos—where a main repair and maintenance center and a logistics base were established—for a general overhaul of all vehicles. After that, the Italian company joined the other new tank companies sent from Italy and formed the Tank Battalion (*Raggruppamento Reparti Specializatti*/RRS) of the Italian Volunteer Corps, remaining under Italian leadership for the duration of the war. Their first action after being withdrawn from the Madrid front did not take place until February 1937, when the offensive to capture Malaga began.

From the very beginning, Soviet gun-armed tanks were superior to German and Italian machine-gun armed light tanks. Nevertheless, during the first days of combat, the German *Panzer Is* negated this disadvantage by using special armor-piercing ammunition whenever the Soviet tanks appeared. Due to their initial losses, the Soviets quickly discovered that their tanks were being penetrated at ranges up to about 150 meters. Countermeasures against the ammunition used by the Nationalist *panzers* were simple and immediately applied: the Russian tanks no longer advanced to close range. As soon as they noticed the *panzers*, they remained over 1,000 meters away, still firing very accurately with their 45mm guns.

The Nationalist Army's tank units were created in September and October 1936, and provided the armored support for the Nationalist armies in all the main campaigns and battles during the late autumn of that year. Despite their strength being insignificant during the early weeks of the war, the Nationalists realized that even a small number of tanks could mean a major tactical advantage, and tried to use them accordingly, though always in the infantry-support role.

CHAPTER 12

On the Move: Republican Armor is Never "Enough"

"There's a valley in Spain called Jarama,
It's a place that we all know so well.
For 'tis there that we wasted our manhood,
And most of our old age as well."

"VALLEY OF JARAMA" BY ALEX MCDADE, SUNG BY WOODY GUTHRIE

The front remained stabilized during the winter of 1936–37, but the new year saw the employment of armor on a much bigger scale than in 1936. During most of the winter, a stage of deadlock prevailed, hardened by the weather. During these months, the Republican forces remained on the defensive, and to a certain extent succeeded in frustrating the Nationalists' efforts to extend their gains.

The year 1937 saw two major battles in the immediate area around Madrid, the battle of Jarama (January–February) and the battle of Brunete in July. Two other battles were fought further afield as part of the Nationalists' campaign to take the capital: in March at Guadalajara and near the end of December at Teruel, both northeast of Madrid.

On January 5, 1937 German *Panzer I* tanks, preceded by air and artillery support, tried to break through the Republican lines, and at first it was like the World War I battle of Amiens all over again. The first echelon of *panzers* advanced under the supporting fire of field artillery, followed by infantry formed in line of company columns, then a second wave of more tanks and more infantry. The situation was further complicated by the surprise appearance of a company of Russian BA-10 armored cars. The Nationalists lost over a dozen tanks to them. Combat lasted for several days until the tiny *panzers* could take no more. By January 15, when both sides again dug in, their positions had changed little.

The 1st Republican Tank Brigade (*1ª Brigada Blindada*) first saw action near Las Rozas and Majadahonda, to the northwest of Madrid, in the beginning of January 1937, supporting the 12th and 14th International Brigades; an action that managed to break up the second Nationalist assault on Madrid. General Pavlov's brigade was prematurely pressed into action with only 47 tanks available. Nevertheless, contrary to whatever had happened before, cooperation between tanks and infantry was more successful. Russian tanks managed to overcome the Nationalist defenses, but after a while, the infantry was unable to keep up with them and the breakthrough came to a halt. The scourge of Pavlov's forces came to be the new German *Pak 36* antitank guns, and in just three days of fighting, the Republicans lost five T-26 tanks. However, the focus of the fighting soon switched to the southeast, along the Jarama River.

The deadlock was broken by the fall of Malaga in southern Spain, a Nationalist coup that was marked by good strategic judgment as well as Italian contribution on a new and important scale. The Republican resistance was slight, its moral stability easily shaken by the surprise attack.

Malaga was the culmination of an offensive between February 3 and 8, 1937, by the combined Nationalist and Italian forces to eliminate Republican control of the entire province of Malaga. The participation of Italian armor resulted in a complete rout of the Spanish Republicans and the capitulation of Malaga in less than a week. Following the failure to capture Madrid, the Nationalists had sought to regain the initiative. The arrival of Italian troops at the nearby port of Cadiz boosted hopes for a successful attack on Malaga. The Italians, led by General Mario Roatta,[1] formed nine motorized-mechanized battalions of about 5,000–10,000 men, equipped with L3 tanks and wheeled armored cars. One of the advancing columns was under the command of Colonel Carlo Rivolta, soon to be the commander of all Italian tanks sent to Spain. Three tank companies, all equipped with L3s, took part in the operation.

General Roatta decided to employ his forces for the first time to take Malaga as it was one of the few areas in which relatively favorable weather for an offensive could be expected in midwinter. The Italian General Staff approved the attack, which fitted perfectly with the outline of Mussolini's plans for Spain.

The operational plan called for an attack by three columns. Two tank companies[2] advanced, with a column on the right flank from Antequera to Malaga and one in the center, between Loja and Malaga, while the other tank company was kept in reserve. The left flank column had no armor. The main role—and therefore the main effort—involved the Italians; however, Spanish Nationalist troops also took part in the attack.

The Spanish Army of the South initiated the assault of Malaga from the west on February 3. Surprise was only partially achieved, but the Italians' rapid advance disoriented the defense. Attacking from the north on the night of February 4, the Italians—Colonel Rivolta's column—achieved a massive breakthrough due to the Republicans being unprepared for armored warfare, no matter how light the Italian tanks were. No Republican armor appeared on the battlefield. The Nationalists continued a steady advance towards Malaga, reaching the heights over the city on February 6. By the following day, all resistance had been overcome. On February 8, General Queipo de Llano and his Army of the South, together with the Italian tanks, entered Malaga. The battle of Malaga was over almost before it began.

At midnight on February 8, an Italian infantry battalion under Colonel Costantino Salvi of the Italian Blackshirts, supported by a tank company and an artillery battery, combined with air support from the Italian Air Force, set off in pursuit of the fleeing Republicans. However, with only one company of L3 light tanks, they only reached the town of Motril, some 50 miles up the coast, where they halted on February 14.

The Italians had employed their recently developed tactical concept of "*Guerra Celere*" for the first time in Europe. It was a sort of "*blitzkrieg*," in which motorized columns moved ahead very rapidly, spearheaded by armor. Little effort was made to protect the flanks of the attacking columns, despite the rugged terrain which facilitated defense. Their security was entrusted almost exclusively to the speed and mobility of their advance, which was expected to disorganize the defenders and prevent them from reacting.[3] Nevertheless, if the operation was successful, it was largely due to the weakness of Malaga's defenses and the lack of preparedness shown by the militia troops.

The fall of Malaga was a major failure for the Republicans. The occupation of the city shortened the front by about 150 miles, gave the Nationalists control of a Mediterranean port for the first time, and also had a significant effect on morale. The Republic was spurred to change its strategy and to attempt a widespread series of offensive actions. These, as expected, made no significant gains, and actually offered an opportunity for the Nationalist forces to renew their offensive.

The battle for Malaga was a disaster for the Republicans, and Mussolini[4] saw the success of the Italian troops as reason enough to continue and increase Italian involvement in Spain, despite having accepted the terms of the Non-Intervention Agreement.[5] Yet the Italian commanders failed to see that their rapid victory was achieved due to good weather and the lack of experience in armored warfare on the part of their Republican militia opponents. Afterwards, for nearly two months, the Nationalists' attention was focused on renewed attempts to capture Madrid. Plans were made to achieve a decisive victory by attacking and capturing the capital, this time maybe with the help of the Italians.

By the winter of 1936–37, the Nationalist forces, having failed to carry Madrid by storm in November 1936, resolved to cut off the city by crossing the Jarama River to the southeast and severing its communications with the provisional Republican capital of Valencia.[6] General Mola, rather than Franco, was in overall command of the Nationalist forces around Madrid, and planned an offensive across the Jarama about 7 miles south of the capital. The attack had been intended to coincide with an offensive by Italian troops, but the Italians were not ready in time and Mola decided to press ahead without them. The Nationalists had roughly 25,000 men for the operation, and Mola also had 10 squadrons of cavalry at his disposal. They were supported by the Condor Legion, including a light tank battalion under the supervision of Colonel von Thoma as well as some new 155mm artillery batteries and German 88mm antiaircraft *Flak* guns.

The battle began on the morning of February 6, 1937. Following the failure of the attempts on the west of Madrid in November and December 1936, Franco had prepared a new offensive to the south of the capital, aiming to cut the vital road that linked Madrid with Valencia. Initially intended to be part of a combined operation with Italian troops to the east of the city, Franco approved the decision to push ahead despite the Italians having been delayed by heavy rains.

The Nationalist offensive pressed forward quickly, and by evening that day, the Republicans had been pushed back to the Jarama River, with rebel troops within shelling distance of the Madrid–Valencia road. Over the next three days, the Nationalists continued to force themselves forwards, despite the Republican commander, General Miaja, committing three more infantry brigades to the defense of the city.

By February 7, Nationalist forces had reached the junction of the Manzanares and Jarama rivers, and the following day they captured the bridge across the Manzanares just south of Vaciamadrid and threatened to reach the Madrid–Valencia highway. At the same time, despite desperate defensive efforts by the Republican forces to the south, Nationalist troops managed to cross the Jarama River and prepared themselves for an assault on the Pingarrón Heights, an imposing ridge in front of them. At this point, the 15th International Brigade was thrown into the defense.

On February 13, the Nationalist Army, making one more attempt to occupy Madrid, embarked on an ambitious encircling maneuver from the southeast that led to what has been recorded in history as the battle of Jarama, pretty well described by Hemingway and perpetuated by many songs of the time, even many years later by American folk singer and activist Pete Seeger. It was the largest operation of the conflict to date and, for the first time in the Spanish Civil War, large units met in the field in open battle.

Even after the losses suffered in previous weeks, the Republican tank and armored forces managed to recover, as more crews became available and tanks were repaired. By February 1937, Pavlov's brigade had around 60 tanks, and even if scattered, supported the initial offensive launched by the Popular Army, but was broken up into small company-size units of about 10 tanks to reinforce the Republican lines. The Nationalists had amassed close to 70 tanks around Madrid, between German and Italian types, but they were clearly inferior to the T-26s.

At the battle of Jarama, the 1st Armored Brigade of the Popular Army, commanded by General Pavlov, managed to delay the advance of General Franco's troops at the Jarama River, but as had happened at Seseña, the Soviet tanks acted without infantry support and remained in a defensive attitude, failing to exploit their success and technological superiority. The Republicans counterattacked twice with Soviet T-26 tanks, which in the end were beaten off by artillery fire from Nationalist batteries, but they managed to hold up further Nationalist advances.[7] On February 14, the Republicans counterattacked again with 50 T-26 tanks, supported by infantry, artillery, and air power. Although they did not retake any lost ground, the attack again bloodied the Nationalists and halted their advance, overtaking a major Nationalist force, and causing an estimated 1,000 Nationalist casualties.

For the next few days, until 16 February, the battle swayed to and fro, with gains for either side. Pavlov's tanks were being used more often as pillboxes from hull-down positions, using their mobility simply to move from place to place as the Nationalist threats developed.

Some lessons from the first months of the war seem to have been learnt more quickly by the Nationalist Army than its Republican foes. Peter Kemp,[8] a British volunteer who fought with the Nationalists at Jarama, recalled the lack of coordination of the Republican counterattacks in the La Marañosa sector on February 17 and 18:

> Despite their initial gallantry, the infantry alone were unable to reach the Nationalist positions. When Republican armor at last appeared—just a single unit of six T-26 tanks—the Republican infantry was too mauled to support its advance, and the unsupported tanks were driven off by artillery fire. Next day, the Republican infantry troops renewed their pressure, but they were surprised by a well-timed counterattack of Nationalist armor, when a full company, of sixteen Panzer I light tanks, charged from a flank and overran the enemy.

As shown by this account, the Nationalist command seemed to become more aware, probably due to German advisors, of the advantages of using tanks in comparatively large formations.

The overall balance of losses were again unfavourable for the Soviets and Republicans, as they lost 24 T-26s destroyed or captured, against 17 *Panzers Is* lost. Italian tanks did not take part in this battle as they were committed in the south to the conquest of Malaga. Nevertheless, following days of fierce fighting around the Jarama, no breakthrough was achieved. Republican counterattacks over the captured ground failed too, resulting in heavy casualties to both sides. On February 27, the Republican Tank Brigade launched no less than five attacks on Nationalist positions without infantry support, and took heavy losses from antitank guns, losing an estimated 40 percent of its tanks in the attacks.

The Russian evaluation report on the battle of Jarama was not a positive one. The fighting cost the Republicans 34 tanks—slightly above 70 percent of the force committed—mainly to Nationalist antitank guns. It was the result of the hopeless muddling of their logistics, their command structures, and even their faulty aims. The Nationalists lost 11 *panzers* destroyed, and their main lesson learned was that "to overcome a T-26 another T-26 was needed." The main problem for the Nationalists was how to get them, and it was then that the Germans offered a cash reward for every Russian tank captured.

The Republican Tank Brigade's poor showing at the battle of Jarama from February 6–27 continued the earlier negative trend, with a few notable exceptions. Although the Nationalist forces enjoyed numerical superiority in the engagement, quantity was of negligible importance, given the fact that the T-26 was so much superior to the German and Italian tanks. In several attacks at Jarama, the Soviet tanks were able to better coordinate their movements with the infantry. This tactical integration proved successful, and in one engagement on February 14, the combined Republican forces routed several Nationalist companies, claiming about a thousand enemy killed or wounded. Yet if some Soviet military analysts considered Jarama an improvement in terms of tactics, no one could deny the heavy price: of the 47 Soviet tanks that participated in the engagement, 34—or 72.4 percent—were damaged or destroyed, most of these by the superior German-made *Pak 36* 37mm antitank gun.

The battle thus ended in a draw, with neither side satisfied. The Republicans felt that the Jarama River was not in itself an effective defensive line, and in this they were right as the river could be crossed anywhere when its level dropped during the dry spring and summer months. For the Nationalists, the result was disappointing, as they had wanted to at the very least cut the vital roads leading to Madrid. It might be said that General Franco had expected too much with the forces at his disposal, but that was not the only factor. The Nationalists gained some ground, but they could not achieve any breakthrough. The newly formed Republican mixed brigades waged an effective battle, blunting a major advance by Franco in the open field.

At the end of February, both sides dug defensive fortifications and a stalemate ensued, which neither side was able to overcome. The positions remained virtually static for the rest of the war. Celebrated by the Republicans as a great victory over the Nationalist army, the battle of Jarama was, like the earlier battles for Madrid in November and December 1936, only successful in the sense that it stemmed the Nationalists' advance on the capital. But this was at great cost; the Republicans lost somewhere around 10,000 soldiers—while the Nationalists suffered only 6,000 casualties—plus 70 percent of the total armored force. This was not a good return for the Republicans.

Both Nationalist and Republican troops were now exhausted and low on ammunition and food. Although the Nationalists succeeded in crossing the Jarama River and resisted all attempts to dislodge them from their footholds, the Madrid–Valencia road remained out of reach and firmly in Republican hands. Consequently, the area lost much of its strategic importance and merged into the wider front.

While no Italian armor was committed to the battle of Jarama, the Italian Volunteer Corps was on the offensive in March with the battle of Guadalajara. The main effort of the Nationalist offensive was a stroke towards Guadalajara and Madrid, with a three-pronged advance following an axis from south to west, from Siguenza and southern Zaragoza. At dawn on March 8, 10 field artillery battalions of the Italian expeditionary force sent to Spain by Mussolini opened fire on the lightly defended positions of the 12th Infantry Division of the Popular Army that barred the avenues of approach to Madrid from the northeast. The battle for Guadalajara had begun. Four motorized infantry divisions of the Italian Volunteer Corps attacked on a wide front, one of them an elite division of the Italian regular army, the Infantry Division *Littorio*[9] under the command of Major General Bergonzoli,[10] who had previously been in the Ethiopian campaign under Marshal Graziani. A total of 35,000 men were committed by the Italians at Guadalajara, but armor was scarce, limited to a reinforced battalion-size unit of Fiat L3 light tanks.

The Italian High Command in Spain had established the main objectives for its offensive as the taking of the cities of Guadalajara and Alcala de Henares, the latter only 20 miles from Madrid. The ultimate goal was to achieve a crumbling of the entire front and the occupation of Madrid, forcing the surrender of the Republican forces and the end of the war. Such a victory would have been of immense benefit for the Fascist ideology, reinforcing the undisputed leadership of Italy in Southern Europe. However, several mistakes were made by the Italians: first, they underestimated the combat value of the Popular Army, failing to take into account the presence and reinforcement of Soviet-backed troops; second, they disregarded the weather forecasts, maybe thinking that Spain was as sunny as the tourism brochures advertised, while failing to carry out any in-depth reconnaissance of the terrain they were fighting over. While the concept of the operation guaranteed surprise and mobility, these advantages soon waned because bad weather gave time for resistance to harden and be reinforced. While the result was a disaster for the Italians and the Nationalist forces, it is difficult to understand why the Popular Army and the supporting Soviet forces that withstood the Nationalist attack failed to exploit their success and pass over to the offensive.

In a severe windstorm, freezing temperatures, and heavy snow—typical of a late winter in the northern part of Spain (some years in mid-March, there are even snowstorms on the hills and mountains close to Madrid)—the Italian forces began their attack with visibility sometimes limited to only 3 or 4 yards, yet managed somehow to penetrate some 15 miles into the Republican lines. Due to the adverse weather, the air support committed to the operation by the Nationalists—the entire Italian expeditionary air forces in Spain, plus some units of the *Luftwaffe*'s Condor Legion and the Spanish Air Force—were unable to take off, leaving the ground forces on their own. After two days, the Popular Army managed to reorganize the front and stop the Italian offensive, as a result of help provided by the 1st Armored Brigade of General Pavlov and the air support of the Spanish–Soviet Republican Air Force, which was able to conduct operations from airfields unaffected by the weather.

On March 9, Republican General Miaja ordered to the Guadalajara sector "all currently available reserves and any that can be quickly constituted," including all available tanks. Initially, about 80 Italian Fiat L3 tanks supported by motorized infantry managed to advance more than 20 miles inside the Republican defenses, but were quickly counterattacked by the Popular Army with two International Brigades and an armored task force made up mainly of Russian T-26B tanks. On March 10, in an isolated event, a single section of two T-26 tanks led by a Spanish Republican NCO destroyed or damaged several Italian tankettes. The Soviet tanks made short work of the smaller and much lighter Italian tanks, forcing the Italian infantry to withdraw, but the Republican forces lost their tempo and were unable to exploit their success.

The battle of Guadalajara provided several lessons, and the Italian High Command took them seriously, however, most were wrongly interpreted, and not much was done to correct the mistakes anyway. An Italian assessment of the fighting established the events in Guadalajara as follows: "A Mobile Division of the Italian Army had conducted a mechanized attack; had been blocked by infantry on the defense, had been taken out of combat by air attacks and then annihilated through a combined attack of enemy tanks and infantry," which for the Italians meant that "independent armored forces could not survive in the modern battlefield, that antitank technology was superior to armored vehicles, and that tanks supported by infantry could overtake and win over mechanized forces."[11]

Guadalajara was the first major armored operation which took place on a European battlefield before World War II. The first encounters between tanks at the battle of Madrid in the autumn of 1936 had seen tanks employed just as infantry support. But at Guadalajara, the battle turned out differently from what had been expected. Some have treated the battle of Guadalajara as a trial of mechanized and armored forces and an exposure of their defects. Yet we should take into account that the bulk of the attacking Italian and Spanish forces was composed of infantry who were merely carried to the front in trucks and had to dismount before attacking. They should be more precisely described as "motorized infantry," and even then, few of their vehicles could be used effectively off-road. The inability of this temporarily truck-borne infantry to attack effectively after they had dismounted provided a reminder that weather can be a barrier to men on foot just as to men on wheels, especially if under enemy fire.

The implementation of the German *blitzkrieg* would soon prove the Italian evaluation to be wrong, but at the time, in 1937, not many dared to challenge it. The Italian defeat at Guadalajara was actually due not only to the inferior performance of the L3 CV-33/35 tank, but to the slow rate of advance of the motorized columns due to heavy rains and snow, lack of experience of tank crews, and the lack of air support. At Guadalajara, the Italians lacked most of the elements and procedures necessary for an effective employment of an armored force. It also became obvious that the Italian L3 light tank[12] had no possibility of success when facing heavier and better-armed tanks with guns; it was outpowered, outgunned, and outclassed.

Combat around Madrid during the winter of 1936 had already proven that Italian armor was clearly inferior to that of the Soviets. But after Guadalajara, L3 tanks were limited to creating diversionary attacks or keeping under fire those Republican tanks which were either immobilized or brought to a halt, but not attacking them directly. In addition to their technical inferiority, the Italian armored forces lacked the tactics to exploit their speed and agility. The battle of Guadalajara is a clear example of how not to use tanks. Italian tankers should have gained from it.

Regarding the L3 tank's employment, Colonel Carlo Rivolta, who was in command of the armored detachment (RRS) at Guadalajara, was very clear in his report:[13] "Our tanks are not good for a breakthrough. Their efficiency depends on speed, mass employment and close support of the infantry."

It also came to light that, in some cases, Italian crews dismounted and used their tanks to block roads, which led to them being blown up by enemy fire. Tanks were sometimes used to bring ammunition under cover to the front line too. Amongst common faults in the employment of tanks, Colonel Rivolta also made reference to the lack of assembly areas for them before attacking, but especially the absence of specific zones and pre-planned areas for refueling, maintenance, and recovery; all aspects that seriously complicated the task of tank commanders. A tactical problem was the eagerness of Italian commanders to commit the tanks into battle too early; the tanks' combat range was established at around 100 miles, but it was actually less than that. Committing the tanks into battle too early, as Rivolta said in his report, "did nothing more than reducing the tanks' range, their capabilities and the strength of the units."

Colonel Rivolta explained why these problems arose: "[A]ll these mistakes took place because the infantry commanders didn't pay any attention at all to the rules and procedures established in the field manuals of the Italian Army regarding the employment of tanks." Another mistake was the lack of training for tank crews. Rivolta also talked of columns of tanks blocked on the roads, poor combat deployment in wide formations, and lack of cooperation between tanks at either platoon or company level, all of which translated into a lack of expertise.

Furthermore, the L3 tank had a very limited performance, Colonel Rivolta pointing especially to very little room for armament and ammunition, and the need for a turret able to move around 360° and better armor, as in some cases the tanks were even pierced by infantry rifle rounds. The light Italian tanks simply could not stand and fight against the heavier Russian armor.

This made the absence of adequate antitank weapons even more critical at Guadalajara, the infantry having to rely on regular artillery guns or howitzers for antitank defense. It could take hours for a gun to be dragged into position and put into action, meaning an entire column could be held up by an enemy section of just two tanks.

The Italian Corps lost almost two divisions, with some 1,400 killed, 4,500 wounded, and 500 missing. Losses on the Republican side were higher, but the Italians were forced to withdraw to their departing positions. Incredibly, the Popular Army that had performed so well, with brilliant coordination of close air support, artillery, tanks, and infantry in defense, lacked the spirit to go on the offensive, never exploited their success, and allowed a neat and tidy withdrawal of the *Littorio* Division, which saved the Italians from total disaster. Armor losses on both sides at Guadalajara were only moderate, the Soviets losing just eight T-26 tanks destroyed—five of those being captured by the Nationalists—and the Italians a total of 19 Fiat L3s, several of which were recovered later and just nine being declared fatal losses, with some being taken by the Republicans.

Pavlov's tank brigade had received a major infusion of new equipment and manpower between March 6 and 8, with the arrival of 100 new T-26 tanks. This was nearly as many as the total figure since the beginning of the Russian intervention, and apparently had not been detected by the Nationalist command, and henceforth neither by the Italians.

When the Italian offensive stopped, the Republican Army did go onto the offensive, with Pavlov's tank in the lead. On March 18, three Republican brigades with tank support routed the Italians and seized the town of Brihuega. But by the end of the day, the Republican tanks had suffered so many casualties, to both enemy antitank fire and mechanical problems, that from the initial 72 tanks deployed, they could muster only nine to chase the Italians. The Republican Army was thus unable to exploit its victory, which had undoubtedly been achieved thanks to Russian tank support. Tank losses amounted to about 40 percent of the total force, with 28 tanks out of order in just three weeks of combat.

During two weeks of fighting, the Republican tank brigade operated in close concert with the infantry and artillery. Platoons of three to five tanks were attached to each infantry brigade, and this effective combination helped decide the outcome of the battle, which was a major defeat for the Italian Volunteer Corps. For the Russian brigade, however, it was a Pyrrhic victory, and the final Republican losses appear to have been heavier than those they inflicted on the Italians.

Italian planning for the attack had been hasty, incomplete, and based on inadequate information. The successful execution of a *blitzkrieg*-style attack such as General Roatta had planned required absolute superiority in aviation and armor, and highly trained troops. The Italians had none of those, which had a decisive impact as Guadalajara and Malaga were the only two battles of the civil war in which the Nationalists—meaning Franco—allowed the Italians to play an independent role.

Guadalajara was a major defeat for the Nationalist forces and dealt a severe blow to Italian prestige, yet it was not a complete victory for the Popular Army. The most important strategic consequence of the battle of Guadalajara was the abandonment of the goal of conquering Madrid by the Nationalist forces, at least for the time being. Madrid remained in Republican hands until the end of the war on April 1, 1939. Franco had shown the same obstinacy with Madrid as Lincoln had with Richmond during the American Civil War, and both only achieved their prize at the close of the war.

The obstinate repetition of the same mistakes on the Republican side was unquestionably a major problem for them, but the reaction, when it came, was even worse, for Pavlov and other officers who returned to Russia spread the impression that modern theories had failed. The French, for instance, subsequently claimed that only when tanks attacked with infantry close behind were they likely to prevail.

Italian captain Oreste Fortuna, the officer who came to Spain leading the second Italian arms shipment, and first commander of the initial Fiat Tank Company, was severely wounded at the battle of Guadalajara. He returned home, where he was awarded the Italian Gold Medal for Military Bravery for showing great courage in the face of battle. His military record reads as follows:

> Company commander of assault chariots, of tried courage, repeatedly decorated for bravery, in the vicissitudes of an uphill battle, where acting on his own initiative, he dispersed enemy units easily, in a decisive way, to fulfill the task the column was assigned. Wounded by an explosive bullet to the face, despite copious bleeding, he continued to fight until the conquest of the objective and managed to capture several prisoners, including two enemy officers. Even more seriously wounded a second time, with four fractured vertebrae and six more bruised, despite his desperate physical condition, he maintained control of his unit and repelled an enemy counterattack. Fighting with the infantry, not listening to the calls of his subordinates who implored him to get treated, he stood at the head of the surviving tanks, with one hand clutching his head and maneuvering a machine gun with the other, and led a surprise attack, putting to flight a whole opposing division. Only at night, once he was within our lines, and having reported to his superior, did he allow himself to be treated and evacuated.
>
> (Road to Trijueque and Guadalajara, March 9–12, 1937, Spain)

Guadalajara was the last Nationalist attempt to outflank the capital. The battle on the Central front became a stalemate. The defense of Madrid between November 1936 and March 1937 was probably the most notable—indeed the only—accomplishment of the Popular Army. It was only a temporary defensive victory, and would not be repeated. Defense does not win wars, and the attention of the Nationalists then turned to the industrial northern Republican zone, a move that would work decisively in the rebels' favor.

In April 1937, after the Republicans had received a large new shipment of T-26 tanks from the Soviet Union, they planned an attack west of Madrid. Tanks were to be used independently, following General Pavlov's ideas, breaking through the Nationalists positions, with the infantry following close behind to occupy them. Fifty T-26s began the operation, but only 14 returned[14] from a classic example of independent tank action against well-prepared defenses. After this failed operation, Republican tanks were never again used independently. Nevertheless, fighting continued around Madrid, but during the next two major engagements, Republican tanks again recorded high losses. At Casa de Campo—between May 5 and 12, 1937—23 of 84 active tanks, or 27.4 percent of those deployed, were damaged or destroyed.

Republican tank actions were greatly hindered by the poor training given by Soviet instructors to the Spaniards. Many tanks were lost through mechanical troubles before they reached the battlefield. How much of this was deliberate is unknown, but it is suspected that either cowardice or defection played a large part. Tank crews needed to be men of great courage besides mechanical ability. Nationalist tank crews were far better trained and achieved better results, despite the technical inferiority of their vehicles.

On May 25, 1937, the U.S. Army attaché in Paris, Lieutenant Colonel Sumner Waite, sent a report to Washington stating that it was possible to evaluate the type of tanks used so far in Spain and the method of employment, mentioning the Nationalist *panzers* and Fiat L3s, as well as the Republican T-26s. Colonel Waite concluded that since December 1936, no attack had been launched without the support of tanks, and their number had increased steadily, which, in his view, indicated the value attributed to tanks by both warring parties. At first, he said, both sides parceled out all available tanks and therefore, their mass employment was impossible. The few tanks engaged in local actions rarely left the road and were soon destroyed by either antitank weapons or even field artillery, he said. The superiority of antitank guns on both sides was even more evident due to insufficient artillery. At the same time, Waite[15] emphasized that the Spanish Civil War appeared to have demonstrated the need for a heavier tank for close-combat operations.

French military assessment also emphasized the insufficient armor protection of Soviet tanks, not only regarding thickness but also the lack of protection for vital parts. The conclusion was that the armament and armor of the tank were no less important than speed, questioning the idea of speed to the detriment of armor.

CHAPTER 13

Stalemate and Attrition

"To combine tanks and infantry is tantamount to yoking a tractor to a draught-horse. To ask them to operate together under fire is equally absurd."

COLONEL "BONEY" FULLER, BRITISH ARMY,
LECTURES ON FIELD REGULATIONS (1929)

Following the poor results at Guadalajara, the whole Italian Volunteer Corps, including especially the armored RRS, was withdrawn from operations and underwent a major reshuffle and retraining.[1] Colonel Carlo Rivolta returned to Italy, becoming a scapegoat for Guadalajara, and was replaced by Colonel Valentino Babini on April 25, 1937. The entire spring and early summer following the battle of Guadalajara was a quiet period for the Italians, and no additional Italian shipments of troops and equipment took place. However, Italian tankers went back into action again in the offensive against the Basque Country and Santander.

The general trend in the war, until one side became exhausted, was always to fight for the stabilization of the battlefield. Fronts were broken through and rebuilt again and again, and there was a strong possibility of a reversion to the slog of trench and positional warfare. However, once Franco realized that Madrid was not going to be conquered quickly, he started looking north. This area had been isolated from the rest of Spain by the Nationalists since the beginning of the war, being attractive to them due to Biscay's industrial production and Asturias' mineral resources. To conquer and control this area would be profitable due to its valuable resources, while at the same time expelling Republican forces and allowing the concentration elsewhere of large numbers of Nationalist troops to dictate a two-front war for the Republic.

The main objective on the Northern front was clearly Bilbao, but before the heavily fortified city could be attacked, the Nationalists needed to penetrate far enough into the Basque Country to establish themselves in striking positions. The Italian General Bastico insisted that the CTV be employed to break the front here.

The tank battalion of the Condor Legion was also transferred to the Northern front by late March 1937. The experience of previous operations had provided the basic principles for the use of tanks. It had been shown that once the element of surprise had disappeared, the static use of tanks over several days was unsuitable, since the means of defense were quickly strengthened. The need for cooperation with motorized antitank units was also stressed. Moving in successive, concealed bounds, antitank guns provided a defensive screen against enemy armor. Both tanks and antitank guns, therefore, were integral parts of armored units. These guidelines had been obtained as a result of operations during the early months of the war.

Nationalist armor lacked the capacity to exploit in depth any initial successes, and the Republican forces had proved in the battles around Madrid their defensive resilience; therefore, it made no sense to insist on using tanks in sectors where the enemy could be reinforced. On the other hand, the tanks supplied by Germany were no match for the Republican armor in terms of firepower and protection, so cooperation with antitank units became essential. The Nationalist field commanders were provided with these guidelines, but do not seem to have paid much attention to them. Colonel von Thoma wrote to General Mola, C-in-C of the Army of the North, that the Spanish commanders' determination to issue orders of their own to the tank units prevented the Nationalists from being more successful. Nationalist commanders on the Northern front also had the tendency to over-use armor.

The Nationalist offensive began on March 31, and on the same day, Condor Legion aircraft bombed several towns. On April 6, the Nationalist government announced the blockade of Basque ports, and on April 20, the Condor Legion carried out the infamous bombing of the town of Guernica. The Basques retreated to the "Iron Belt"[2] line, and on April 30, the Italians occupied the suburbs of Bilbao with the support of L3 light tanks. For several days, the fighting was heavy and the Italians suffered substantial losses. On June 12, the Nationalists began the assault of the "Iron Belt," and following heavy aerial and artillery bombardment, they entered Bilbao on June 19.

Following the fall of Bilbao, the Republican government decided to launch an operation to stop the Nationalist offensive in the north. In the summer of 1937, one of the bloodiest battles of the whole Spanish Civil War took place; the battle of Brunete. Brunete is a small town about 15 miles northwest of Madrid, and by mid-1937, it was viewed by the Popular Army High Command as the best spot to create a diversionary maneuver to distract the attention of General Franco, and consequently alleviate the pressure by Nationalist forces in northern Spain that were committed to the conquest and occupation of the entire Basque region. The initial planning and concept of the Brunete offensive is today attributed to the late Soviet Marshal Rodion Malinovsky. The Brunete operation was designed as a pincer movement to cut off Franco's forces west and northwest of Madrid, but the southern wing never got started, which made the plan impossible to carry out. Superior Russian tanks, even if assisted by air control, proved of limited value as the Republican forces lacked training and coordination in combined-arms operations.

On July 5, three Army corps supported by 250 artillery guns and 300 aircraft began the offensive against General Franco's six divisions on the Madrid front. A total of 125,000 men with 130 tanks—the biggest military force ever assembled in Spain—attacked 50,000 men and 50 light tanks on the Nationalist side. Four brigades preceded by tanks carried out the main effort. From the outset, the Republican forces managed to advance and penetrate between 10 and 15 miles inside the Nationalist lines, but again with such caution and prudence that they lacked audacity and initiative, allowing the Nationalists to restore their lines. From July 7, the battle of Brunete transformed into a battle of attrition instead of a battle where decision was most sought and needed by the Popular Army. General Franco showed at Brunete a good grasp of the situation and achieved almost full control of logistics, being able to move his reserves to the right spot at the right time. Nevertheless, the Nationalist offensive on the Northern front was paralyzed for a while, as they were forced to devote all their attention to events at Brunete.

The battle of Brunete was nicknamed the "battle of thirst" (*la batalla de la sed*), due to the hot summer weather wreaking havoc among the troops on both sides and the lack of water, temperatures reaching 102 degrees Fahrenheit or even more. Many cases of foolishness, suicide, and collective panic took place, especially among the soldiers of the Popular Army, which, on July 12, stopped the offensive and reverted to the defensive to consolidate their lines. In the skies over Brunete, the German Condor Legion employed for the very first time Messerschmitt Bf-109 fighters, along with Heinkel He-111 bombers and various other modern aircraft, which swept from the skies the previously dominant Soviet/Spanish Republican Air Force. The Republican forces lost near 30,000 dead and 61 T-26 tanks destroyed or damaged at Brunete, while the Nationalists suffered 20,000 dead but only lost two *Panzer I*s. No Italian armor was committed, as the CTV remained on the Northern front for the entire duration of the battle.

Armor was very badly employed on the Soviet side, who split units and even assigned tasks to tanks as if they were just assault guns whose purpose was only to provide fire support. Lack of initiative combined with inability to exploit their initial success led the Popular Army to a major disaster. Brunete can be compared with the demise of the German *panzer* formations after the battle of Kursk in 1943, as following Brunete, the Popular Army was never again a coherent force capable of matching the capabilities of the Nationalist Army, nor were their superior armored forces able to present a real threat to the technically inferior armored forces of General Franco. By the last days of the battle, the Nationalists even employed for the first time their captured Soviet T-26 tanks, committing to the fight a fully operational company-size unit with 16 tanks; however, even they also employed their tanks mainly for infantry support.

The battle of Brunete was the first major strategic offensive by the Republican Army employing a sizable tank force, but the Republicans failed to take advantage of their superiority, weighed down by insufficient training. A few days before the battle, the headquarters of the Republican Army of the Center (*Ejército del Centro*) ordered[3] the Tank Brigade[4] to provide some tanks in order to carry out tactical exercises with the units spearheading the offensive. However, the order was canceled two days later. The source does not provide any clear explanation of the cause, so it is not possible to judge fairly the soundness of this decision. However, it seems reasonable to believe that the Republican troops' later performance was damaged by their lack of training.

On July 19, the headquarters of the Republican Army of Maneuver[5] issued instructions on the use of armor following the experiences of the first stage of the battle. The instructions listed the mistakes made by Republican forces: the tank commanders had been too independent, while the infantry failed to keep contact with the tanks when the latter gained temporary advantages during the fighting; there were no efforts to achieve tactical surprise; and the tank units engaged in frontal assaults on defended villages which caused too many casualties. The report urged field commanders to adopt a closer liaison between tank and infantry units, better and more secret preparation of attacks, and the use of enveloping maneuvers whenever villages were attacked.

The instructions' spirit generally followed the pre-war doctrine, since armor was subordinated to infantry. Tanks were simply a complementary means of this branch, temporarily attached to its units, whose orders the tanks should obey. However, the report recommended tanks not to be used in numbers below company strength (10 tanks minimum). This last point was a change from the pre-war regulations, which reckoned the platoon—three to five tanks—as the basic fighting unit. The instructions also emphasized the effectiveness of using tanks in comparatively large masses. This was without a doubt a necessary reminder to correct the tendency shown during the battle of Brunete by the Republican commanders to retain tanks temporarily attached to their troops. Such conduct led to the fragmentation of armor, which rendered it less effective.

At Brunete, Republican forces employed the tanks leading the infantry. They were entrusted the main role; that of carrying out the breakthrough, of opening the road, and the infantry needed only to follow. Yet the tanks were decimated by the Nationalist defense, which quickly acquired contempt for them, learning that isolated tanks were weak. If the infantry had followed the tanks closely, they would have made impossible many of the attacks on isolated tanks.

In the full heat of the Spanish summer at Brunete in July 1937, despite gaining territory at first, Franco's locally superior forces and complete air domination soon stemmed and pushed back the Republican advance. After Brunete, the Popular Army never again tried to employ its armored units to their full advantage, losing whatever technical and tactical edge they had obtained, and not making any use of their initial impetus in creating major armored units. Nevertheless, during the battle of Brunete, Republican tanks, used defensively as mobile artillery screens, were a serious obstacle for the Nationalist troops. Since the range of their antitank guns was too short, the Nationalist units demanded Italian 47mm antitank guns, which were reckoned more effective than the German *Pak 36*.

At Brunete, total Republican losses were 47 tanks destroyed out of 130, or about 35.5 percent of the original force. The Republicans remained incapable of neutralizing the rebels' antitank guns and, according to research by Steven Zaloga, a single German *Pak 36* antitank gun was credited with crippling a dozen tanks. Military theorists were later at pains to point out the tactical significance of the battle of Brunete for the use of the tank. According to Hugh Thomas, Czech captain and military thinker Ferdinand O. Miksche—who fought on the Republican side—later reflected in his theoretical study *Blitzkrieg* that Republican tanks were unsuccessful as they were used spread out in support of infantry, mostly following French theories, whereas the Nationalists, on German advice, concentrated their tanks to find a tactical thrust-point, and so gained the day at Brunete. As a matter of fact, the Republicans always used all their armor fully dispersed and the Nationalist–German experiment could only be conducted on a small scale since they had no more tanks than a reinforced tank battalion.

On August 14, the Nationalists launched their offensive against Cantabria, in the north, with the 90,000 men—including 25,000 Italians[6] of the CTV—and 200 aircraft of the Army of the North. The Italian attack was spearheaded by three divisions but only two L3 tank companies. On August 17, the Italians occupied the El Puerto del Escudo pass and encircled 22 Republican battalions at Campoo in Cantabria. There were numerous clashes against light enemy armored vehicles, among them obsolete Spanish Trubia A-4 tanks, which were built near Oviedo. There was heavy attrition of men and equipment, but on the following day, August 16, an Italian tank company supported by a motorized machine-gun platoon helped to isolate a Basque strongpoint at Reinosa, near Santander.

After the Italian CTV forces broke the Republican lines near Soncillo, El Puerto del Escudo, and penetrated deep into the Republican rear—resulting in a decisive victory for the Nationalists—they were transferred to the Aragon front. On August 24, the Basque troops surrendered to the Italians and the Republican troops fled from Santander. Italian tanks were the first Nationalist troops in the center of Santander, and the city was taken without a fight on August 26. By September 1, the Nationalists had occupied almost all the province of Cantabria, capturing 60,000 prisoners in the greatest victory of the war so far, losing only a single Italian L3 tank in the process. The Italian CTV did not participate in the rest of the campaign in the north against Asturias and went on to prepare for the next offensive.

The fall of Santander, coupled with the earlier capture of the heavily fortified Bilbao, tore an irreparable gap in the Republic's Northern front. The destruction of their Army of the North marked another crippling blow to the Republic's sagging strength and definitively turned the war in Franco's favor. Italian troops and armor, having obtained the propaganda victory Mussolini so desperately wanted, would not see much more action until the spring of 1938.

A new limited Republican offensive had begun on August 24, aiming to break into the Nationalist rear and disrupt their final efforts against Santander. The Republicans also targeted Zaragoza, the communications center of the whole Aragon front, but failed to reach it, managing only to capture the ruins of Belchite, a small town of no tactical value in the middle of Aragon.

Along the Aragon front, the Republicans had deployed the Army of the East, along with about 200 aircraft, many T-26s, and some new BT-5 tanks. Once again, the Republicans suffered a considerable loss of much-needed armaments, tanks especially. The Republican attack had begun with no artillery bombardment in order to maintain the advantage of surprise, but within two days, delays in their advance had given the Nationalists time to bring up reinforcements, and the advance towards Zaragoza fizzled out.

The Republican Army tried to use mechanized forces, albeit in a limited way, for an advance in depth during the action against Zaragoza. It is believed that the plan was made by Colonel Vicente Rojo, chief of Army General Staff, who had planned some mechanized operations, following the ideas of Fuller. According to the Republican plan, once the enemy front was broken through on the north bank of the Ebro River, a motorized task force made up of one truck-borne brigade plus two tank companies and an armored car company would advance southwards to occupy the northern quarter of Zaragoza and the bridges on the Ebro, about 20 miles away. On the southern bank, another task force with two motorized brigades plus 40 tanks and 10 armored cars was to cover 30 miles in one day from its assembly area towards Zaragoza.

The ground was suitable for mechanized forces and the enemy front was a thinly held screen of isolated positions and fortified villages. The first attack was unsuccessful, while the southern task force was delayed in seizing small Nationalist positions on the first day, but the following day—when a fast advance to Zaragoza was still possible, according to Colonel Rojo—it became engaged in fighting for Fuentes de Ebro on its right flank instead.

The operational plan for the whole offensive was probably too ambitious for the Republican Army's capabilities, although a more resolute advance of the southern task force, bypassing the isolated points of resistance, might have brought them more success. Nevertheless, the episode is interesting as the most significant use of combined armor and motorized infantry by the Republicans, and shows that Colonel Rojo saw the potential role of mechanized forces.

With this latest Republican offensive another failure, the Nationalists continued their attack against the Republican-held zone in the north. The Republicans had only advanced 10 kilometers, taking a handful of unimportant towns. Furthermore, the Republican Army suffered a heavy loss of armament and tanks. Secretary of Defense Indalecio Prieto said:[7] "So many troops to take four or five 'pueblos', does not satisfy the ministry of defense." The Republican forces had again lacked coordination, logistics, and military intelligence, their commanders wasting troops, time, and energy to reduce irrelevant resistance points until the offensive ended on September 6 with no positive gains.

A Nationalist document written after the summer of 1937 concluded that the Republican armor's poor performance revealed limited technical and tactical training and a lack of offensive spirit. This, added to the Russian tanks' technical limitations, meant that their role depended heavily on their firepower, so they ended up being used as mobile guns. However, this role of mobile artillery was effective. The document also complained of the lightness and weak firepower of the German and Italian tanks, which had to rely too much on the close support of infantry to overcome enemy strongpoints.

The Republicans also assessed the performance of their armor in the battles of the summer of 1937.[8] In instructions on offensive operations written in late September 1937, Colonel Rojo stressed that armor had to avoid frontal attacks against strongpoints and use maneuver instead. Tanks must operate speedily, bypass points of resistance whenever possible, and advance deeply into the enemy's rear. Moreover, he said they must be supported closely by antitank guns. In these instructions, Rojo's thinking appears more open-minded about the capabilities of armor than the 1928 Army regulations, and perhaps his knowledge of Fuller's ideas was not unconnected with his stress on speed and deep penetration. The mention of close cooperation between armor and antitank guns, a feature of Nationalist doctrine, suggests that Rojo might have known, possibly through captured papers, his enemy's ideas on armor tactics, and thought it wise to follow some of them.

It appears that the Republican command continued advising the use of armor in larger groups. On the eve of the offensive against Teruel in December 1937, the Army of the East was ordered to always use tanks en masse, wherever possible in battalion strength. However, this went against the teaching being given at the Republican Army's Staff College, where students learnt that "the company was the tactical unit, but it does not fight as a single outfit under its commander, who has no responsibility for the actions of the tank platoons."[9] Yet the students were also taught that, "once the objective is reached, the tanks have to carry out a mopping-up operation and refrain from pursuing the enemy." This contradiction revealed problems of organization and doctrine within the Republican Army, leaving field commanders confused by the lack of a common doctrine on the employment of armor.

In operational terms, the summer of 1937 seems to have been the heyday of Republican armor. Tanks no longer played so important a role for the rest of the war. According to General Kindelan—the supreme commander of the Nationalist Air Force—the Republican armor force had lost its offensive spirit by the time of the battle of Teruel. The Republican tanks did not operate as aggressively as before, limiting themselves to the role of accompanying and supporting the infantry, though Kindelan said their firepower still intimidated the Nationalist troops.

In October 1937, in a further attempt to create a major diversion to alleviate Nationalist pressure on all fronts, the Popular Army attacked once more in southern Aragon. Here, for the first time, the heavy tank regiment which had recently been organized with the newly arrived Soviet BT-5 "fast tanks" saw action. The Republican objective was to take the fortified town of Fuentes del Ebro in order to reopen the road to Zaragoza. Fifty BT-5 tanks carrying Spanish troops were to cross the Republican lines and conduct a frontal attack against the town, supported by infantry of the 15th International Brigade, as part of the 35th Infantry Division. The BT-5 tanks tried to take advantage of their speed and, to benefit from infantry support, some also carried on their decks a full squad of infantrymen in the style later employed by the Soviets on the Eastern Front during World War II. However, many of these infantrymen were killed, especially by artillery fire. The attack was also ill-planned, as the tanks were not suited to carrying troops, little reconnaissance was carried out, there was virtually no artillery preparation, and the tanks soon became bogged down in the mud. The attack failed and the Republican Army lost 19 of its 50 new tanks, along with more than 300 men.[10]

According to Steven J. Zaloga in *Soviet Tank Operations in the Spanish Civil War*, preparations for employing the tanks were sloppy and incompetent.[11] The International Tank Regiment was only given its orders at 2300 hours the night before the attack, and had to conduct a hasty 35-mile road march that same night to reach the assembly area. Upon arriving and refueling near the front lines, the regiment learned just two hours before the operation's start that it was to carry infantry on the tanks during the attack. This decision was apparently opposed by the Soviet advisers as well as by the Tank Regiment officers, who felt that it would put the infantry at too great a risk. The BT-5 was not well suited to carrying troops, and there were no experiments in doing so prior to this battle. Although the men from the 15th International Brigade who would ride the tanks were regarded as good troops, the infantry unit that was supposed to accompany the tanks during the attack, the 120th Brigade, became notorious for refusing to leave its trenches. Furthermore, there was no infantry reserve. The mission was planned in such haste that the regimental staff had no time to conduct a reconnaissance of the battlefield, and the Spanish command did not provide adequate details of the battle area or the likely Nationalist antitank defenses, considering such issues as trivial, which would prove fatal to the operation. The lack of artillery preparation was caused by the two batteries assigned to the task being armed with 75mm howitzers captured only a few weeks beforehand and having little ammunition. A T-26 tank battalion was supposed to be used in one of the sectors, but it did not arrive in time to take part in the initial assault.[12]

The attack began shortly after noon. The 50 tanks of Kondryatev's International Tank Regiment began the attack with a salvo of their guns, and then set off at high speed "like an express train," with Spanish infantry clinging to their sides. In the clouds of dust raised by the attack, many of the infantrymen fell off the tanks, some to be run over and crushed by following tanks. Crossing the friendly lines also proved more complicated than expected, as the Republican infantry had not been warned of the attack and, in the confusion, there was some firing between the infantry and tanks.

Once clear of their own lines, the tanks continued to race forward, only to find that they were on a plateau some 9–10ft above the plains where they were to advance. The rushing tanks were brought to a halt, struggling to find passageways to the low ground. More discouraging was the fact that the terrain in front of the enemy positions consisted of sugar cane fields, criss-crossed with irrigation ditches. The tanks continued their charge but became bogged down in the cane fields and waterlogged soil. They began to take fire from Nationalist field artillery and antitank guns in nearby defensive positions. The advance could not press forward due to the terrain, and there was not enough infantry to hold any territory that had been gained. After using up their ammunition, the tanks slowly began to make their way back to the starting point with little direction or control, leaving behind several tanks stuck in the mud. The tanks rearmed and were instructed to return to recover their bogged-down compatriots. Instead, a T-26 tank battalion that was supposed to be employed in the original attack was sent out with some infantry support. The attempt to extract the tanks cost a further 80 troops. As well as losing 19 tanks in the fiasco, the International Tank Regiment suffered several more damaged and a third of its tank crews were killed or wounded.

An American member of the International Brigades said of the operation:[13] "Courage and heroism are plentiful in Spain and the Spanish people have no lack of it. What they need is tactics. And as for tactics, on October 13, the Regiment of BT tanks was bankrupt." In his report to Moscow, the commander of the Republican 35th Infantry Division, General Karol ("Walter") Swierczewski, exonerated Colonel Kondryatev and his tank regiment, and placed the blame squarely on the Republican Army commanders.

This small battle is undoubtedly the best documented of the entire war,[14] with nearly a hundred pages of testimony being sent to Moscow by the regimental commander, his assistants, company commanders, and even several tank crewmen. Colonel Kondryatev was spared from political recriminations due to their testimony, but unlike most other leading Spanish Civil War commanders, was denied the Hero of the Soviet Union medal. He was severely wounded during later fighting in the Teruel campaign. The great expectations for the BT tank regiment were foiled by the friction of war. The fiasco at Fuentes de Ebro was the swansong of the Soviet tank force in Spain. While Soviet tankers would continue acting as advisers, the number of Soviet tank crews diminished and the force became mostly Spanish by the end of 1937. The Soviet Union ended the sending of large shipments of tanks following the delivery of the unsuccessful BT-5 tanks.

The Nationalists had succeeded due to well-established fire planning and good employment of well-positioned and camouflaged antitank guns. The graveyard of wrecked BT-5 tanks was left in place for a long time afterwards, and was shown frequently to the international media as a clear example of the extent of Soviet intervention in Spain.[15] Today, with the available information, it seems that the Soviets tried to obtain some experience for their BT-5s without much coordination with the Spanish Popular Army Command.

Events like those at Brunete were repeated in Aragon during the autumn and winter of 1937. During Christmas 1937, in one of the worst Spanish winters in many years, Republican supporters around the world viewed the capture of the remote provincial capital of Teruel as "the turn of the tide." The area chosen was the weakest point of the whole Nationalist front, near the town of Teruel in southern Aragon. But while initially the weakest point, it ended up being far stronger than expected and the Nationalists put up a vigorous fight. The Republicans deployed some 40,000 men in the operation, but the armored force was again inefficiently used, split up among the attacking units. The Nationalist defenders consisted mainly of the 52nd Infantry Division, with less than 10,000 men, so it was unsurprising that the Republicans managed to obtain some early local success.

On December 1, 1937, at a lecture on the ongoing Spanish Civil War at the U.S. Army Command and Staff School at Fort Leavenworth,[16] it was concluded that so far tanks had been used in numbers too small to furnish conclusive lessons as to their effectiveness. In general, whenever attacking tanks had met with antitank guns, they were either destroyed or immobilized before they had accomplished their aims; without such defensive means, they had usually been successful. Tank obstacles were considered to have been effective, but apparently antitank mines had not been employed.

The last major campaign in which Soviet tank crews participated was the bitter fighting for Teruel from December 15, 1937, to February 22, 1938. The first of the new tank divisions was committed to the fighting, consisting of two T-26 tank battalions, the BT-5 survivors of the International Tank Regiment, and other supporting units. A total of 104 tanks took part in the operation. They were not used as a unified force, nor had they ever been intended to be used as such. Instead, small units were assigned to support the various attacks. The fighting took place under difficult circumstances, with extremely cold weather, heavy snow, poor roads, and mountainous and hilly country. However, the tank units were praised for their efforts by the infantry they supported. While the Teruel campaign has seldom attracted much attention, it was nevertheless carefully studied by the Red Army.

The Republicans' decision to move against Teruel was motivated by several strategic priorities. First, Republican military leaders thought that Teruel was not strongly held and sought to regain the initiative through its capture. Second, the Teruel salient was similar to what Kursk would be on the Eastern Front in 1943, a piece of Nationalist territory inserted into Republican Spain, and its capture would have shortened the lines of communication with the capital of Valencia on the coast.[17] Lastly, Republican intelligence learned that Franco's intentions were to launch another major offensive against Madrid around mid-December, leading the Republicans to try again to divert the Nationalists away from the Madrid area.[18]

The main attack began on December 15, 1937, just three days before the intended Nationalist offensive in the Guadalajara sector, the Republicans obtaining almost complete surprise, partly as a result of the weather, but also by foregoing any preliminary artillery and air support. Snow was falling heavily and weather conditions were almost Russian-style. On December 19, the Republicans reached the outskirts of Teruel, and by December 25, they proclaimed victory. However, the city did not surrender completely until January 7, 1938. At Franco's headquarters they decided to maintain the front line and recapture Teruel. Franco canceled the Guadalajara offensive on December 23, but the relief force could not begin its attack until December 29. Franco's forces soon retook Teruel and the Nationalists were able to use the success as a springboard for a colossal offensive in the spring of 1938. During the entire battle, the Nationalists used the Italian CTV artillery and aviation, but held Italian troops and armor in reserve, much to the Italian High Command's discomfort.

The Republican tanks were deployed in urban areas in street fighting during the battle for Teruel, which cost them 15 more tanks, most falling victim to "Molotov cocktails" dropped from above. The BT-5 tanks did, however, claim a couple of armor kills—two Fiat L3 light tanks—but the Republicans paid with the lives of 37 tank crewmen and the loss of 16 tanks. With temperatures around 5 degrees Fahrenheit, conditions were not much better than those of Stalingrad in the winter of 1942–43 and precluded the Nationalists from launching a counterattack until December 29. Ten Nationalist divisions then attacked the Republican lines, supported by all available artillery and aircraft. Combat continued throughout January 1938, and the battle did not end until February 22 with the final liberation of the city. The battle of Teruel, with its harsh weather and street fighting, was one of the most terrible struggles during the entire civil war. While the Nationalists suffered around 40,000 casualties, the Republicans lost about 60,000 men and no less than 40 tanks.

Soviet advisors[19] with the Republicans reported to Stalin that the defeat at Teruel was due to "the erroneous and treasonous leadership of the Republican General Staff, especially due to General Vicente Rojo."

Teruel was a decisive battle, the Nationalists' use of their superiority in men and equipment in regaining the city making it the military turning point of the war.[20] The battle depleted the resources of the Republican Army, which could no longer replace the men and arms lost in combat.[21] Franco's act of retaking Teruel was a bitter blow to the Republic after the high hopes engendered by its capture, and removed the last obstacle for Franco's breakthrough to the Mediterranean. British poet Laurie Lee, who, by his account, served with the International Brigades, summed up the Republican strategy of attacking Teruel: "The gift of taking Teruel at Christmas had become for the Republicans no more than a poisoned toy. It was meant to be the victory that would change the war; it was indeed the seal of defeat."[22]

From the end of 1937, tanks continued being employed in a secondary role until the end of the war, acting only in support of the infantry or as mobile assault artillery. The Popular Army usually assigned one tank battalion to each infantry division and each army corps. Its armored brigades and the armored division were never employed as such, the war becoming a simple succession of infantry battles. The Nationalists also employed their armor mainly in support of the infantry, but were forced to use it in an antitank role due to their technical inferiority. During the Aragon offensive, German Colonel Ritter Von Thoma convinced General Franco for the first time to concentrate his tanks rather than spread them out among infantry formations.

Wasting no time, Franco began the Aragon offensive on March 7, 1938. The battle of Aragon, or the "March to the Sea," was launched to split apart the Republican-held zone and isolate the central and eastern regions from Catalonia in the northeast. The Nationalists were able to concentrate some 100,000 men, with the best troops in the lead. Even though the Nationalist army was numerically inferior to the Republican forces, the Nationalists were better equipped and had almost 950 aircraft, 200 tanks, and thousands of trucks. The Republic was still rebuilding its strength following the loss of Teruel and offered little resistance. The Nationalists rolled through southern Aragon, entered the provinces of Catalonia and Valencia, reached the sea, and by April 19, they controlled 40 miles of coastline, thereby effectively cutting the Republic in two.

Responding to Italian Command requests, the CTV was given a prominent position in the offensive, forming the center column that advanced on Alcaniz. Italian troops pushed ahead rapidly, aiming to be the first to reach the Mediterranean, but were held up at various points both by the difficult terrain and the dogged resistance of Republican troops. As usual, the Nationalist offensive opened with massive artillery and aviation support, notably with German Ju-87 *Stukas* for the first time. Air operations were at their most heavy, with effective interdiction of the whole Republican battlefield. The Republican retreat was more a rout than a withdrawal. During the first 10 days of the offensive, the Nationalists penetrated to depths of between 50 and 100 miles. On April 3, the city of Lérida—a Republican strongpoint—fell to the Nationalists, and on April 15, they captured the seaside town of Vinaroz, thereby separating Catalonia from the rest of the Republic.

The early stages of this offensive witnessed the most successful operations by mechanized forces in the entire war. The bulk of the Nationalist armor supported the attack against the Moroccan Army Corps, which was led by General Yagüe. British volunteer Peter Kemp, who took part as a Spanish Legion infantry platoon commander in the breakthrough and early pursuit, recalled that "each rifle company of his battalion (*bandera*) was preceded in the initial assault, on March 9, 1938 by a composite platoon of six *Panzer Is* and two T-26 Russian tanks." The armored support force comprised 24 tanks—a reinforced company—for the three rifle companies of the battalion. This was an impressive increase in the strength of armor attached to infantry units when compared with the 1928 Spanish Army regulations, which proposed a lower ratio of one tank platoon—just five tanks—per infantry battalion.

After breaking through the Republican lines, the tank companies—followed by fast-marching infantry task forces of up to four truck-borne infantry battalions, one artillery battery, and the essential engineer and logistical units—advanced fast along roads deep into enemy territory. Under aircraft support, these troops deployed in fighting order behind a line of tanks whenever they encountered organized local resistance. Although it was no *blitzkrieg*, the outcome was remarkable by the current standards of the war; for instance, the army corps to which Peter Kemp's battalion belonged advanced more than 30 miles on foot in a single day.

The Italians made a major contribution to the Aragon campaign. The CTV succeeded in advancing rapidly against the Popular Army's best units, and particularly during the early stages of the offensive, it helped to establish a swift pace of advance. Only 13 Fiat L3 tanks were lost. On March 10, Captain Paolo Paladini, one of the longest-serving Italian officers since the early days of the war in 1936 and a veteran from Malaga, Guadalajara and Santander, was killed in combat. In the fighting around Aragon, Paladini once again displayed his spectacular organizational skills and fighting qualities during a dangerous operation with his tank company. While conducting an attack from his tank, he was first shot in the arm and then severely wounded in the stomach, dying soon after. Another act of courage was displayed by Italian Corporal Renato Zanardo, who was honored for continuing to drive his tank despite being badly wounded during fighting on the Aragon front on March 11.[23]

Russian Lieutenant Razgulyayev also showed outstanding skill and bravery when his BT-5 was surrounded by five Nationalist *Panzer Is*. The crew of the BT-5 managed to destroy one *Panzer I* by gunfire before the Nationalist tanks' machine-gun fire destroyed the BT-5's optics. Undeterred, Razgulyayev decided to try and break through by ramming the closest *Panzer I*. The German tank tipped over and burst into flames as fuel from its damaged fuel tank leaked onto the hot engine. It was the first-ever documented ramming of an enemy tank by a Russian BT tank. The remaining *Panzer Is* retreated.

On April 25, just 10 days after reaching the Mediterranean, the Nationalists began an offensive towards Valencia, but bad weather forced them to suspend the operation. On May 4, the offensive recommenced and the Nationalists launched attack after attack, but could not break through the Republican front. Progress was slow and painful, with little that the tanks could do, although three Italian L3s were lost on the road to Sagunto. It is interesting to note that by late May 1938, of the two tank battalions equipped with German light tanks in the Nationalist Army, one was left with just 16 *Panzer Is*, highlighting that German equipment suffered just as badly as did the Italian.

At the beginning of July, Franco ordered the Italian CTV and several newly formed infantry divisions to reinforce the front and continue the offensive on July 138. The Nationalists tried in vain for 10 days to overcome the Republican defenses. The Republican slogan "to resist is to win" was finally starting to have some meaning. Then, something unexpected happened: the battle of the Ebro, which was about to begin, changed the whole picture of the war and ultimately paved the road to its conclusion.

CHAPTER 14

The End: The Battle of the Ebro and the Catalonia Offensive

"Men of my generation have had Spain in our hearts. It was there that they learned that one can be right and yet be beaten, that force can vanquish spirit and that there are times when courage is not rewarded. It is this, no doubt, which explains why so many men, the world over, feel the Spanish drama as a personal tragedy."

ALBERT CAMUS, *ETAT DE SIEGE*, 1948

In the summer of 1938, the Republican Army launched a huge offensive back across the Ebro River, the biggest operation of the entire war. The International Brigades were involved in the crucial battles around the Aragon town of Gandesa in July and August, and in the mountains of the Sierras, Caballs, and Pandols in September. The plan conceived by Republican General Vicente Rojo was to launch an attack against the main Nationalist forces trying to advance towards Valencia to relieve the pressure on the city and show European governments that the Republicans were still a viable entity and could go onto the offensive.

On July 24, 1938, the battle of the Ebro—named after the Ebro River—began. It was the main and final battle of attrition of the war, and while armored units had not played a key role when the battle ended four months later, the Spanish People's Army had by that time ceased to exist as an organized military force. From December 1938 until April 1939, the Republican forces were only able to conduct a disorganized and hasty defense that would culminate in their unconditional surrender and the end of the Second Spanish Republic. Stalin and the Soviet Union were the main losers with regard to the outcome of the Spanish Civil War, but this is often overshadowed because World War II was about to begin with a rage and fury that had never been seen before.

The battle of the Ebro was the longest and largest battle of the Spanish Civil War. It was known as "the battle of the 100 days," with fighting mainly concentrated in two areas on the lower course of the Ebro. These sparsely populated areas were fought over by the largest array of armies in the war. The results of the battle were disastrous for the Republicans, with tens of thousands of dead and wounded, while the advance of the Nationalist Army continued unabated.

A total of 80,000 men—with nearly all the armor, artillery, and aircraft then available to the Republic—were committed to the battle. The Nationalists facing them initially comprised just three infantry divisions. Lacking intelligence, the Nationalist High Command had considered it unthinkable that Republican forces would be ready to undertake any offensive operation after having been so severely mauled in Aragon, especially now having to cross the Ebro , one of the biggest rivers in Spain.

The Republicans had prepared the crossing of the Ebro in detail, with mockups, training, and even practicing all kinds of water crossings, from small ravines, creeks or small rivers even to beaches along Catalonia's coasts. Early in the morning of July 25, six Republican divisions began the crossing of the Ebro River, spearheaded by units in assault boats, the bulk of forces using 12 pontoon bridges in an area lightly defended by the Nationalists—about 100 miles from the sea—close to the rural town of Gandesa. At the center of the attack, the Republican troops advanced rapidly and overwhelmed the Nationalist 50th Infantry Division, capturing some 4,000 prisoners. In less than 24 hours, the Republicans seized almost 200,000 acres of land, but the Nationalists reacted immediately, sending a fresh division to help close the breach.

It has been said that the attack caught Franco's forces totally unaware, although Italian sources claim that the CTV's military intelligence had provided full information on Republican preparations and troop movements.[1] Eight Nationalist divisions were turned around to march against the Republican bridgehead. All available air forces were also tasked immediately for operations on the Ebro, and by the early afternoon of July 25, Nationalist aircraft were already attacking the crossing points, giving the highest priority to the pontoon bridges. More than 250 aircraft, including 100 fighters, went into action. The Republican Air Force was nowhere to be seen.[2]

Meanwhile, the Nationalists managed to open up the dams on the Ebro up in the Pyrenees and the flooding swept away the bridges, with the result that only 22 T-26 tanks and a handful of artillery units managed to cross the river and Republican troops soon began running low on supplies, ammunition, and drinking water. The Nationalists were able to hold the front around Gandesa with the help of their air force. All the Republican tanks that crossed the Ebro were lost, with 11 being captured by Nationalist troops, nine destroyed, and two missing, probably lost in the Ebro, where they still remain.

The Nationalists launched six counteroffensive operations in a row against the Republican positions to recover the ground lost and destroy the Republican force. The Italian CTV artillery was placed directly under the command of Nationalist forces, which used it for concentrated attacks against specific areas. The first counterattack began on August 6, and the last one started on September 3, supported by German *Flak 18* 88mm guns, but fighting continued until November 14, the final Republican soldiers crossing back over the Ebro two days later. Casualties were horrific: while the Nationalists lost 60,000 men, the Republicans lost 75,000, of whom 30,000 were killed. Apart from the terrible loss of life, all equipment and armament—that was sorely needed now to defend Catalonia—were lost. Furthermore, in October 1938, the Republican government agreed to withdraw the volunteers of the International Brigades.

The key factor in the battle of the Ebro was the Nationalist air superiority, provided by Italian and German aircraft. The overall Nationalist superiority in terms of manpower and equipment meant they were better able to withstand their losses and grind down the Republicans. During the battles at the Ebro between August 17 and November 8, the Italians lost a total of 13 Fiat L3 tanks, although some of these were soon repaired. Thanks to the efforts of their maintenance service, on October 6, in the middle of the battle of the Ebro, the Nationalists managed to get into active service a total of 64 *Panzer Is*, plus 32 Russian T-26 tanks. After the battle, most of the Nationalists' tanks and trucks needed repairs[3] or spare parts, but the Republican Army had lost most of their weapons and experienced units. The Ebro saw the Republican army destroyed as an effective force, while the Republican Air Force was no longer capable of offering further resistance.

The Republicans were unable to accomplish any of their strategic goals and, according to historian Antony Beevor,[4] were unwilling to apply the Russian theory of "deep battle"[5] into their attacks, meaning their forces spent a long time clearing Nationalist secondary defensive positions, allowing their opponents time to quickly deploy sufficient forces in strong defensive positions. However, operations would prove that the Nationalist infantry still fell short of being trained sufficiently in cooperation with tanks.

During the defensive operations in the Serós sector in November 1938, Nationalist tank units carried out support missions. However, after each day's fighting was over, the infantry withdrew in such a way that the tanks often remained isolated on the battlefield. Nine *Panzer I* tanks broke down, and although five were recovered during the night, it involved a number of casualties. The Nationalist headquarters urged the Army of the North's command to draw the field commanders' attention to the misuse of armor by punishing those responsible for leaving behind so many tanks on the battlefield.

After the battle of the Ebro, the Popular Army looked beaten even before the last battle began, having little equipment left. It was unquestionably broken and would never recover. Its estimated strength of around 250,000 men had no more than 100 pieces of artillery, only 40 tanks, and less than 100 aircraft. The morale of the government troops and civilian population in the Republican area was at its lowest. People only wished for the end of the war: "[J]ust let it be over, it doesn't matter how it ends, but let it end now."[6] Six months later, the beleaguered Spanish Republic would finally collapse. The conclusion of the battle of the Ebro reopened for the Nationalists the issue of whether to attempt a new attack in central Spain, aimed at Madrid or Valencia, or to turn north towards Barcelona. Franco, under pressure from many of his own generals as well as from the Italians, eventually decided to attack Catalonia.

By December 10, the Nationalists had deployed 340,000 men, almost 300 tanks of various types—including those captured from the Republicans—more than 500 aircraft, and some 1,400 artillery guns all along the front lines in Catalonia. General Franco had concentrated the Army of the North, led by General Fidel Davila, to conquer the province. The Nationalists assembled their best divisions, plus the entire Italian Volunteer Corps (CTV) of four divisions (55,000 men) with 100 Fiat L3 light tanks, along with the German Condor Legion. Nationalist armor was organized for tactical purposes into three tank battalions, two of them German-equipped, also integrating some captured Russian tanks, and one Italian heavy tank task force with all the Fiat tanks.

The Catalonian offensive was finally launched on December 23. An over-whelming barrage of about 500 artillery guns along a 3-mile front supported the offensive in the Italian sector. Using their initial surprise, superiority in artillery and air support, together with their mobility, the Italians pushed ahead more than 20 miles. On January 3, 1939, the Nationalist troops penetrated about 50 miles into enemy territory, and by January 15 had taken Tarragona, capturing 23,000 prisoners and inflicting more than 40,000 casualties on the Republicans. Even though the Popular Army had established several fall-back lines of resistance, they were more theoretical than practical; once Tarragona fell, Barcelona was almost unprotected and defenseless.

The Republican government tried to organize Barcelona's defense and ordered the general mobilization of all men, while also militarizing its industry, but it was too late. In the early evening of January 26, Barcelona fell and the Nationalists entered the city without any real opposition. On February 2, Gerona also fell and all fighting stopped on February 9. The Republican-held area had been

The Renault FT-17 light tank was the Spanish Army's standard light tank on the eve of the civil war. The tank shown is armed with a 37mm cannon. (Photo taken at the Spanish Army Tank Museum in Madrid)

The Spanish Trubia A-4 light tank, illustrating the improved turret concept, produced in the Trubia Artillery Works (Fábrica de Artillería de Trubia), near the city of Oviedo.

The Italian Fiat L3 CV-33 light tank. The Italians successfully tested the L3 tank in Ethiopia. The outcome of tests in Spain would prove to be different.

A side view of an Italian Fiat L3 CV-35 at the Spanish Army Tank Museum in Madrid. See behind a German *Panzer I A/B* and a Russian T-26B.

A Fiat L3 CV-35 flamethrower variant ready to enter combat.

Italian 47mm M-35 antitank guns were supplied for the use of the Italian Volunteer Corps only.

A platoon of Italian Fiat L3 CV-35 flamethrower tanks in combat. They were effective but vulnerable.

An Italian L3 tank captured by the Republican People's Army (note the machine guns have been removed).

After fighting on the Northern front, Italian L3 tanks did not enter combat again until the major offensive on the Aragon front in the spring of 1938.

Italian L3 tanks of the Littorio Division entered victoriously into Santander, northern Spain, on August 26, 1937.

A mass of Italian L3 light tanks after the battle of Guadalajara. Following the battle, the whole Italian Volunteer Corps (CTV) was reorganized, and especially its tank unit. Colonel Valentino Babini took over command of all Italian armored forces in Spain. He was a true believer in armored warfare.

An Italian L3 flamethrower tank displayed at an Italian military establishment near Rome in 2010.

Nazi Germany sent to the Nationalist Army the *Panzer I* light tank, armed only with two 7.92mm MG-34 machine guns in a revolving turret.

The *Panzer I* was a training tank but ended up becoming the workhorse of German armor until 1939–40.

There were three variants of *Panzer I* deployed to Spain: a *Panzer I Ausf A*, with a four-cylinder air-cooled Krupp engine, quickly named the "Krupp tank" by the Spaniards, is seen here.

Front view of a *Panzer I A/B*, at the Spanish Army Tank Museum.

Side view of a *Panzer I A/B*. This is one of the few Nationalist *panzers* which survived the war—a *Panzer I Ausf B* "Maybach"—preserved in good condition at the Spanish Army Tank Museum in Madrid (note that the symbols of the Spanish Foreign Legion can be seen painted on the tank).

A *Panzer I* in the outdoor display of the Spanish Army Tank Museum, wearing a different camouflage pattern.

Following the initial confrontations with Republican armor, the situation became so critical that Nationalist German tanks were ordered to avoid direct engagement with Soviet tanks.

Nationalist *Panzer I* tanks entering a small Spanish town.

A German *panzer* in the Spanish countryside. German *panzers* adapted quickly to the Spanish landscape.

Among the *Panzer I* tanks sent by Germany was a single driver training tank, basically a *Panzer I* without a turret and armament.

Spanish Nationalist soldiers training with a *Panzer I* tank (a German instructor can clearly be seen on the left side).

Spanish recruits and their German instructors seemed to get along very well (here while training on the *Panzer I*).

A Nationalist *Panzer I Ausf A* "Krupp" tank on the outskirts of Madrid in early November 1936, with pet included.

A knocked-out Nationalist *Panzer I* in the vicinity of Madrid, late in the winter of 1936 (Republican soldiers can be seen in the background).

Side view of the *Panzer I* command tank at the Tank Museum, Bovington, UK. The command tank had no combat role and hence only had one machine gun for self-defense and no revolving turret.

A close-up view of the linking system of the road wheels and tracks on the *Panzer I Ausf B* "Maybach" tank.

A detailed view of the suspension system of the *Panzer I Ausf B* "Maybach" tank.

Due to the efforts of Lieutenant Colonel Walter Warlimont of the German *Wehrmacht*, the small *panzer* tanks came to Spain in the company of several antitank batteries with the excellent 37mm *Pak 36* gun, which saved the day on many occasions and became the scourge of Soviet tanks. Photo taken at the Spanish Army Tank Museum.

Another view of a German *Pak 36* antitank gun. Photo taken at the Military Museum of Finland in Helsinki.

A *Flak 18* 88mm gun of the Nationalist Army manned by German Condor Legion soldiers, somewhere at the front during the war.

The commanding officer of the German tank group sent to Spain was Colonel Wilhelm Ritter von Thoma. On November 4, 1942, von Thoma—by then a general—was captured by the British at El Alamein. Here he is saluting his captor after surrendering. That evening, von Thoma dined with British General Montgomery at his headquarters to discuss the battle.

The Tank Badge (*Panzertruppenabzeichen der Legion Condor*) was created in September 1936 by Colonel von Thoma and was recognized as an official award of the German state on 10 July, 1939. It was awarded to tank crews who had served for at least three months in the Spanish theater of war. Spanish soldiers used to wear it too.

A German Stuka Ju-87B dive bomber. The Spanish Civil War saw the beginning of ground–air liaison. Stukas operated in coordination with German *panzers* by mid-1938.

A Nationalist *Panzer I* at a parade before General Franco after the war.

A Nationalist *Panzer I* before General Franco (note the tank commanders giving the Fascist-style salute).

A column of *Panzer I*s entering a town (note how they run with all hatches closed, probably to avoid enemy snipers).

Panzer I tanks crossing an urban area.

A Nationalist tank unit preparing for battle (note the mixed composition of German and Russian tanks).

A Nationalist *Panzer I* right after the war (note the ruins of Madrid's outskirts in the background).

After the end of the war, a *Panzer I* command tank passes before General Franco (note the line of Moroccan soldiers in the background).

First casualty: a Soviet T-26B tank undergoing repairs on the battlefield.

The T-26B was a formidable opponent for the Nationalist forces. Its weakness was the poor employment the Republicans made of it. This T-26 tank was placed near a memorial for the battle of Ebro, in the middle of a field close to the Ebro River where Republican forces launched their last offensive of the war in July 1938.

A T-26B tank in Russia today. This tank was lifted from the bottom of a river in 2003. Photo taken at the Kirovsk Museum near St Petersburg in 2006.

The Republicans achieved limited success when they managed to capture the town of Teruel in Aragon. At least a platoon of T-26s are shown in the vicinity of the bullring in central Teruel.

A Republican T-26 tank during the battle of Brunete, near Madrid, waiting at the Villanueva de la Cañada, which was almost destroyed in the fighting.

View of the main 45mm gun inside the turret of the T-26B tank.

Loader's position and ammunition storage inside the turret of the T-26B tank.

After the battle of the Ebro in 1938, the remaining Republican tanks (mainly just T-26s) gathered to repel the final Nationalist offensive against Catalonia.

A Republican T-26B tank destroyed and captured by the Nationalists near Madrid on October 29, 1936. These tanks came as a big surprise for General Franco's troops.

A captured Nationalist T-26B at the battle of the Ebro in 1938.

A full platoon of captured Nationalist T-26B tanks.

A captured Nationalist T-26B displayed in an unknown Spanish city during the war.

Three T-26B tanks captured by Nationalist troops on October 29, 1936, were taken to the town of Yuncos, on the Madrid front, where the Nationalist Army had established a logistical base and field workshop.

Spanish Nationalist officers inspecting a captured Republican T-26B tank at the front.

God on the Nationalist side: a captured T-26B tank being used as main altar for a Catholic field mass at the front.

By mid-August 1937, the Republican Army had received 50 brand-new Russian BT-5 tanks. These were the heaviest, fastest, and most modern tanks used in the Spanish Civil War. However, the main 45mm gun was still the same as in the T-26B. Photo taken at the Kirovsk Museum near St Petersburg in 2006.

The Nationalists captured some BT-5 tanks in working condition, but they never integrated them into their own units.

A Nationalist armored column on the move. It is possible to identify at least two T-26B tanks and several *Panzer I*s behind (see the contrast between those who appear to be Spanish soldiers and a clearly identifiable German officer on the left-hand side) The foremost T-26 appears to have an additional Maxim heavy machine gun on the turret.

An armored column of the Nationalist Army in the streets of Barcelona at the end of January 1939. Note the mix of German *Panzer I* and Russian T-26B tanks.

A Nationalist T-26B entering Madrid at the end of the war. Madrid had been dealt much devastation by Nationalist aircraft and artillery).

With the war over, two captured T-26B tanks of the Nationalist Army enter Madrid at the end of March 1939. The front tank is an updated variant with a new hatch and equipped with an auxiliary machine gun.

reduced to just central Spain, with the loss of the eastern coast virtually cutting off any land means of communication with the outside world. Republican armor had proved futile, and the few tanks that were left escaped into France with the remaining Republican forces. The French government eventually returned 10 working T-26 tanks to the Nationalist forces once the war was over. The Italians, meanwhile, lost only four tanks during the whole offensive.

With the fall of Catalonia and Barcelona, the Republic had lost the country's second largest city, the Catalan war industry, and a large part of its army (more than 200,000 soldiers). On February 27, President Azaña resigned and on the same day, France and the United Kingdom acknowledged the Francoist government. Further military resistance became impossible and the war was over for the Republic, despite 30 percent of Spanish soil still being under Republican control. Prime Minister Negrín insisted that the Republic could not continue its resistance.

All Italian tanks were then relocated to Toledo, from where they took part in the final skirmishes of the war, mainly against Alicante. However, they were given the honor of entering Guadalajara at the end of March 1939 and raising the Italian flag, together with the Spanish Nationalist flag, at the city's Town Council building. Military operations thus came to a halt. A military coup in Madrid resulted in the Communists being defeated, forcing General Miaja to try to reach a compromise with Franco, who rejected his proposals. Miaja was obliged to accept unconditional surrender, but fled to Algiers. Nationalist troops finally entered Madrid on the morning of March 28, and on April 1, the war was officially over.

Italian support had undoubtedly been an essential element in the Nationalist victory. Italy and Germany were Franco's only significant sources of modern arms. However, Italian armor was inferior in quality to that provided by Germany. The distinctive element about Italy's intervention was the large number of men it sent, but despite their number, their armor was not a significant factor in Franco's victory. Italian tanks clearly demonstrated their inadequacy in Spain, with about half of the total number supplied being lost, but the Italian Army did not attempt to use the civil war as a proving ground, and no major efforts were made to substitute obviously deficient equipment such as the L3 light tank. Italy went away unprepared for World War II, its military leaders failing to respond adequately to the evolving situation, and did not make use of the opportunities offered by the war in Spain to improve its equipment and organization.

All surviving Italian L3 tanks were delivered to the Spanish Army, forming the Spanish Army Tank Regiment No. 4 at the town of Estella, near Pamplona.

By 1943, there 60 Fiat L3 light tanks still operational in the Spanish Army within armored cavalry units, and they remained in active service until the late 1950s.

German tanks performed little better during the civil war. A total of 125 tanks were rebuilt or repaired, meaning that some underwent serious repairs more than once as the total number of tanks supplied by Germany to Spain was 122. Thus, all German tanks supplied had suffered some damage or breakdown. On May 12, 1939, the final figure of German *Panzer I* tanks in active service with the Spanish Army was 84, meaning 38 had been lost. This means that some 31 percent of the total force of *Panzer I* light tanks supplied had been destroyed after three years of almost continuous combat. Considering that the war was over and won by the Nationalists it was not a bad outcome, but in absolute terms, the results were appalling and should have made the German High Command think twice about its armored forces and implement some changes.

Soviet tanks were far better than Italian and German ones, but almost 50 percent of the total supplied ended up in service with the enemy. Curiously, the Nationalists had increasingly turned throughout the war to the Russian T-26 tank as their tank of choice, and these were gradually integrated into the Nationalist Army's armored units, eventually becoming the backbone of the new Spanish Army following the war.

Arrival of equipment to the warring parties had been too irregular to allow for the organization and planning of the employment of tanks as anything more than an ancillary weapon. Tanks were employed in battle, from time to time, insofar as they were available. Whether there were many or few tanks present in combat did not matter much in the end, and their effect was almost negligible. According to French General Maurice Duval,[7] tanks were just an additional weapons system included in combat of infantry against infantry.

The war had become almost exclusively one of opposing infantry armies, supported by an even limited number of automatic weapons and some artillery and air power. One could almost be tempted to say that any other element was superfluous.

CHAPTER 15

Antitank Warfare

"Out-gunned, out-maneuvered, and hard-pressed, the Spanish had no effective answer to the tank, in desperation they resorted to hand-to-hand fighting"

JOHN WEEKS, *MEN AGAINST TANKS: A HISTORY OF ANTI-TANK WARFARE*, 1975

The Spanish Civil War was the war which produced the "Molotov cocktail," but Spain also witnessed the first widespread use of antitank weapons, especially guns and most notably the German Rheinmetall 37mm *Pak 35/36* and its Russian copy, the Model 1932 45mm antitank gun. These weapons, when skillfully used, proved very effective against tanks. The light tanks were extremely vulnerable to them, and learning from this lesson, production of medium and heavy tanks began in several major European armies. Combat in Spain proved that better armor was needed, even if the main tank contributors—Germany, Italy, and the USSR—did not initially show much haste when it came to making new and more effective tanks.

Since the early days of armored warfare, improved artillery was seen as the quickest solution for antitank defense. In Germany, the Rheinmetall corporation commenced the design of a 37mm antitank gun in 1924, and the first guns were produced in 1928 as the 37mm *PanzerabwehrkanoneL/45*, later adopted by the *Wehrmacht* as the *Pak 35/36*. It made its first appearance during the Spanish Civil War, and the Soviet Army soon upgraded the design to a higher-velocity *L/45* Model 1935, while also making a licensed copy of the German gun. However, the Red Army was taught several hard lessons about antitank warfare when many tanks sent to aid the Republican Army were destroyed in combat engagements with German guns.

At the time, the predominant ammunition used against tanks was the armor-piercing kinetic energy shell that penetrated armor by direct pressure, spiking or punching through it. In Spain, the antitank defense of the Nationalists was organized by German Condor Legion officers. The antitank guns were incorporated into a system of obstacles created to stop an armored attack, slowing tanks down, isolating them from the supporting infantry with machine-gun and mortar fire, and forcing them to conduct deliberate head-on assaults with engineer support or to seek a less-defended area to attack. The time thus gained for the defenders meant that Nationalist field artillery could also engage the Soviet tanks.

The only change to German World War I antitank tactics was that an effective antitank weapon was now available to support the defending infantry. However, the Soviet tanks armed with 45mm guns easily destroyed the German light tanks in Spain, establishing an urgent need for antitank guns to be included in mobile tank-led units due to the strong possibility of encountering enemy tanks. To many analysts, the Spanish Civil War reconfirmed the importance of defense over the offensive and of antitank weapons over tanks.

Poorly trained Spanish tank crews among both Nationalist and Republican forces proved undisciplined and prone to attacking heavily defended positions even when equipped with antitank weapons. Tank attacks occurred with little prior reconnaissance and without coordination with supporting infantry and artillery. Too often, tanks made themselves vulnerable to destruction by moving on their own through village streets or remaining on open roads. It was the poor tank tactics that made antitank warfare so successful.

A report presented in Berlin on September 12, 1936, by Lieutenant Colonel Walter Warlimont pointed out that antitank defense was one of the main weaknesses of the Nationalist Army. Consequently, the first German antitank guns came with the first tank shipment the following month, comprising 24 *Pak 35/36* 37mm guns. An antitank company with 15 guns was formed immediately, with the remaining nine guns kept for training purposes under the supervision of the *Drohne* group at the German base in Cubas de la Sagra.

A further 28 guns of the same model arrived with the second shipment of tanks in November. With these new guns and four more from the *Drohne* group, making a total of 32 guns, the Nationalists organized their first three antitank companies. At the end of May 1937, another shipment of 100 37mm *Pak 35/36*s arrived at Vigo's harbor for the Nationalist Army, which organized 10 antitank batteries with 10 guns each within the artillery branch, while 50 more guns were delivered in August. On April 14, 1938, the last shipment of antitank guns was received by the Nationalists, with 100 more *Pak 35/36*s delivered at Cubas de la Sagra, making a total of 352 *Pak 35/36* antitank guns supplied to the Spanish Nationalist Army by Germany.

A problem arose when it was established that the antitank gun supplied by the Germans to the Nationalists had a maximum range of 900 meters, whereas the guns in Russian tanks could engage targets at up to 3,000 meters.

The Nationalists, under German guidance, were forced to attach at least five antitank guns to each light tank company to provide some effective protection against Soviet tanks. However, the effect was minimal as understanding and coordinating the new tanks and antitank guns proved extremely difficult for the Nationalist forces. Despite much training, and to the dismay of German instructors, Nationalist troops often began shooting wastefully at targets far over 1,000 meters away.

The Condor Legion also made extensive use of the excellent 88/56mm *Flak 18* antiaircraft gun in the civil war, where its usefulness as an antitank weapon and general artillery gun exceeded its antiaircraft role. The first four of these guns came to Spain even before the formal organization of the Condor Legion on August 6, 1936, landing with the first shipment of aviation equipment from the *Usaramo* cargo ship at Seville. They were part of the first heavy air defense artillery battery and arrived with a full complement of men and accessories. The battery was under the command of *Luftwaffe* First Lieutenant Aldinger, and the guns were to be used in Spain for the first time. The battery was soon combat-ready and was deployed at Seville's military airfield as protection against Republican raids.

The air defense artillery unit of the Condor Legion was named *Flak Abteilung 88* and was commanded by Lieutenant Colonel Hermann Lichtenberger,[1] with Lieutenant Colonel Georg Neuffer[2] as second in command and chief of staff. All air defense artillery personnel belonged to the *Luftwaffe* and not to the Army. Initially, four batteries—16 guns—of *Flak 18* 88/56mm guns were sent to Spain as air defense artillery for the Condor Legion in 1936, but they were soon used in antitank, antibunker, and even antibattery roles. Further guns were sent later, and more 88mm guns were also supplied to Spanish units. At the end of the war, the Spanish Army took over five batteries— 20 guns—from the total of 71 *Flak 18* guns sent for the Condor Legion.

Soviet tank superiority was clearly shown in combat around Madrid, where, by the end of November 1936, the Nationalists lost a total of 28 *Panzer Is* plus several Italian L3s, resulting in a stalemate. Here, the Spanish People's Army made the major mistake of not going on the offensive but remaining in a defensive posture. It was here around Madrid where the Nationalist forces employed for the first time in an antitank role, and with great success, their *Flak 18* 88mm guns. Such was their effectiveness that the Germans later turned the "88," with some modifications made for ground-to-ground combat, into one of the most dreaded weapons of World War II. The "88" gun literally obliterated T-26 tanks in Spain at the first hit. Luckily for the Republicans, the 88mm guns were not supplied to the Nationalists in large numbers.

Not much is known about the first combat actions of *Flak* units in Spain, but unconfirmed reports point at 88mm guns entering combat in early 1937 during the fighting around Malaga, when a battery of *Flak 18*s was assigned to support an infantry column. Bad weather had grounded the main bomber force, but the assault succeeded, mainly because of the concentrated and accurate fire of the supporting 88mm guns.

The *Flak 18* guns were deployed mainly to protect airfields and bases used by the Condor Legion. However, the nature of war in Spain, with its wildly fluctuating front lines and the presence of Russian tanks, forced the Germans to employ the *Flak 18* guns in a direct-fire role against ground targets. Furthermore, the initial scarcity of Nationalist Spanish artillery and the general low proficiency of its crews soon forced the use of the *Flak 18* gun as a direct-fire infantry support weapon. The *Flak 88* group fought at the battle of Jarama, in February 1937. The following month, the unit moved northwards and took part in all the battles along the Northern front, where their tasks were divided between antiaircraft duties and field artillery employment. *Flak 18* guns took part in the assault against Bilbao's line of fortifications, the so-called "Iron Belt" (*Cinturon de Hierro*), and following the battle of Brunete, went north again to contribute to the Santander and Asturias campaign.

Flak 18 batteries were also employed by the Nationalist Army in the Aragon offensive and at the battle of Ebro in 1938, being used for direct fire against pillboxes and indirect fire in the advance towards Barcelona during the final campaign in Catalonia. During the battle of Ebro, *Flak 88* batteries took up positions in the neighborhood of the main bridgehead as direct support to the ground forces.

By the end of the war, the 88mm guns had performed far more missions as an antitank and direct-fire field artillery gun than as an antiaircraft gun. In total, German 88mm guns were involved in 377 combat engagements, and only 31 were against enemy aircraft. On the other hand, the use of the 88mm guns in close vicinity to the enemy made them vulnerable to infantry fire. Casualties among the Legion's 88mm gun batteries in the Spanish Civil War were second only to those of bomber pilots and crews. According to two different sources, which provided information to U.S. Army Lieutenant Colonel Waite, the Germans alone manned their antiaircraft weapons. No one was allowed within a few hundred yards of them, especially the Spanish soldiers. The French War Department verified that "great secrecy surrounded the operation of these weapons."

In May 1939, the *Flak 88* unit returned to Germany, leaving practically all its equipment in Spain for the Nationalist Army. After the civil war, in 1943, more improved *Flak* models were sent to Spain—almost 90 88/56mm *Flak 36s*—and in the same year they were manufactured under license by the Spanish artillery factory at Trubia, near Oviedo, under the name FT 44. These remained in active service with the Spanish Army until the early 1980s.

Italy also sent various antitank guns to Nationalist Spain; however, these were only used by the Italian Volunteer Corps. They were mainly the *Breda* 47mm Model 35 antitank gun, but there were also some 37mm Models 36 guns, a copy of the German *Pak 35/36* made in Italy under license from Rheinmetall.

The Republicans used a similar antitank gun to the German *Pak 35/36*, the Russian Model 1932[3] 45mm gun. The first shipment of these guns took place on April 29, 1937, when the Republicans received just 15 guns. However, they later received 100 additional guns in May that year, and another 20 in December. In January 1939, the Republicans received through France the last three Soviet guns. The total number of Model 1932 guns delivered to the Republican Army was 138; however, throughout the war, the Republicans received a total of 494 guns of various calibers capable of antitank use. The Soviet Model 1932 45mm gun was a copy of the German *Pak 35/36* after the Soviet Union purchased the rights for production from Rheinmetall in 1930 and began a small-scale procurement for the Soviet Army. However, the Soviet General Staff wanted a more "universal" gun able to fire both antitank and high explosive rounds, so the gun was scaled up to 45mm, entering production in 1932,[4] created by Soviet artillery designer Loginov. Towards the end of 1937, the Model 1932 was pushed out by the Model 1937 45mm antitank gun. The new gun had better ballistics, a higher rate of fire, and was more reliable. The new wheels were also made of metal rather than wood (the Model 1932 also received metal wheels in 1937). However, due to insufficient armor penetration against the newest German tanks, it was subsequently replaced by the long-barreled Model 1942.

The Italian M35 47mm gun was a dual-purpose gun able to fire a high explosive round as well as an antitank projectile. It was originally an Austrian artillery piece produced under license in Italy. It was used both as an infantry assault gun and antitank gun, proving to be very successful, especially when equipped with HEAT (High Explosive Antitank) rounds. Due to its shape, the 47mm gun was commonly called the "*elefantino*" (little elephant) by Italian troops.

The British Major General Fuller wrote an interesting letter[5] published in the London *Times* following a visit to Spain:

> I have referred to the antitank gun several times. On the Nationalist side, the German 22mm gun, mounted on a small wheeled vehicle, has proved to be very useful. It is the gun that I saw in use with the German Army. Other German models are also reported to be in Spain, a 37mm and an Italian 47mm. From all the information that can be gathered, the German antitank gun is a very efficient weapon.

In May 1937, U.S. Army Lieutenant Colonel Lee quoted an article by Liddell Hart, who said that "the defense against tanks has been developed and perfected more quickly and more effectively than the tank itself." The antitank weapons used in Spain were clearly a threat to the tankers. As Colonel Fuqua, the U.S. Army attaché in Madrid, concluded, an infantryman with an antitank gun had no need to fear tanks.

The British antitank battery was formed within the International Brigades in May 1937 from 40 volunteers and was issued with three Soviet Model 1932 45mm guns, capable of firing both armor-piercing and high explosive shells that, at the time, represented state-of-the-art of military technology. Well led, trained by Russian instructors, and comprising a high proportion of students and intellectuals, they represented somewhat of an elite unit, and quickly became a highly efficient force in the 15th International Brigade.

After cutting its teeth at Brunete in July 1937, the battery was heavily involved in the battles at Belchite in August, where, according to Bill Alexander, the battery's political commissar, the antitank guns fired 2,700 shells in just two days. During October 1937, the 15th International Brigade took part in the disastrous operation at Fuentes de Ebro, where the new BT-5 tanks were mauled. Initially, the antitank battery was held back from the main battle until the panicked brigade staff ordered it to advance on the Nationalist lines. None of the guns were able to fire and the battery's second in command, Jeff Mildwater, was injured before the battery was eventually wisely withdrawn.

During the Aragon front retreat in the spring of 1938, the antitank battery was virtually surrounded and forced to fall back swiftly from Belchite, to avoid being cut off. The battery had to destroy one of its guns that could not be moved, while low-flying Nationalist aircraft destroyed another. With the battery no longer in existence, the men were incorporated as riflemen into the British battalion of the International Brigades.

The remark that antitank weapons had surpassed tank development was perhaps the most important conclusion reached about the use of tanks and antitank weapons in Spain. And if the trend was toward heavier tanks trying to overcome the threat of antitank weapons, there was also a trend for more powerful antitank guns.

In an article sent by American Lieutenant Colonel Lee to the Military Intelligence Division in the spring of 1937, Liddell Hart had argued that light antitank weapons had the advantage of being easily shifted from location to location and quickly brought up to the front lines. Other sources observed that antitank defense needed to be coordinated and that antitank guns were only part of the defensive plan. The U.S. Army attaché in Paris, Lieutenant Colonel Waite, commented that antitank weapons worked most effectively when they were used in combination with obstacles.

All tanks employed in Spain often faced antitank weapons that could immobilize or destroy them at any moment. The tank, that was supposed to return maneuver and offense to the battlefield, was countered with modern antitank weapons that gave the advantage back to the defense. To overcome the threat of antitank weapons, military attachés, observers, and their sources stressed the need for tanks to be employed en masse, not as separate weapons or in small groups. They also recommended that tanks be combined with infantry, which could hold the ground gained, and with artillery and aviation, that could protect the tanks by destroying or suppressing enemy antitank fire.

Although little technical data about antitank and antiaircraft weapons was gathered, there was general agreement on antitank weapons being effective in meeting their enemies in Spain. However, with the trend toward heavier tanks, there was an implied corresponding trend toward more powerful antitank weapons, as has been mentioned. With clouds of war gathering all over Europe, some countries looked to Spain to see what, if anything, they could learn. Unfortunately, most of the lessons were misleading, especially those relating to tanks being defeated. The issue seems to have been that whereas the designers of tanks saw clearly that they had to improve armor and gunnery, those whose specialty was antitank weaponry were quite happy with what they had achieved and took few active steps to improve anything. Such thinking was to work to the detriment of the German *Wehrmacht* when World War II began, as the *Pak 36* was no longer as effective.

Regarding the war in Spain, when expectations about tank performance was not met, it was concluded that circumstances were so specific to the Spanish situation and its kind of war that battles fought there were unlikely to provide useful lessons for most European armies. Others, who had their predictions fulfilled, pointed to specific incidents as evidence that the testing ground of war had proven them right. Nowhere was this more apparent than regarding the efficacy of antitank weaponry. Officers who did not like the tank argued that combat in Spain clearly demonstrated the superiority of antitank guns over tanks. Tanks in Spain had proven themselves as less than the decisive force that some battles of World War I had promised, while antitank weapons now had an advantage in development over tanks.

Yet while the war on the ground was similar in its trenches and infantry battles to World War I, it was also a signal of changes to come in a future European war. Each country was confident that it had in service an adequate antitank defense. Yet, by 1939–40, before a year had passed, each was to find how over-optimistic these predictions had been, how vulnerable troops were, and how poorly the designers had prepared for the onset of the German *blitzkrieg*.

CHAPTER 16

Logistics

Spain had been in the backwater of European military developments for more than a century. Economic conditions affect the development and outcome of wars. In particular, the amount of resources available to warring parties is usually a determinant in the outcome. An advantage in resources can be readily transformed into military superiority to better meet the needs not only of the war effort, but also of the rear areas, which is essential for keeping up the population's morale.

A superiority in resources usually reflects a higher level of economic development, which in turn allows for greater flexibility in adapting the productive structure to the necessities of the war. However, the Spanish Civil War seems to contradict this general conclusion. When civil strife began in July 1936, and the Spanish economy was divided in two, most of the industrial base and the financial wealth were concentrated in the area controlled by the Republican government.

And yet the Republicans lost the war three years later, with General Franco claiming a total victory over a demoralized and defeated Republican Army in March 1939. The prevailing explanation for this apparent contradiction is that the Republican defeat was partially due to a gross mismanagement of the resources at its disposal. Neither army, though, ever fully attained their requirements of arms and ammunition, a deficit in the latter explaining certain lulls in campaigns and even in daily combats.

The Spanish Civil War was a "pauper's war," which is often forgotten in simplistic comparisons with both World War I and II. Both armies lacked weapons, ammunition, clothing, and food, but Republicans especially suffered from the dearth of basic supplies. Nationalists joked that emaciated Mahatma Gandhi felt admiration for Republican Prime Minister Juan Negrín, who "forced millions of Spaniards to fast for 28 months." As inflation increased in the Republican area, its soldiers' willingness to sacrifice declined. The daily needs of Republican soldiers were often unmet, and they lost faith in the credibility of their institutions. Nationalist soldiers received steady wages and subsidies for their family members; compared to the enemy, they possessed an abundance of water, soap, and tobacco.

On the eve of the war, Spanish industry, armed forces, and diplomacy were entirely unprepared for any kind of war, whether civil or international, short or long. In 1935, the level of public expenditure stood at around 13 percent of GDP. Reported military spending was low, and the quantity and quality of military equipment and supplies was clearly insufficient to wage a long confrontation. It was nothing new for the country, and indeed the situation is very similar to this day in Spain. By European standards, Spain was a particularly backward country in 1936. There had been little industrial development and 70 percent of people still lived from the land, with almost 52 percent of the workforce employed in agriculture, which accounted then for between half and two-thirds of Spain's exports. Again, this is not much different to today's situation, where only between 5 and 10 percent of Spanish exports can be considered high tech.

On paper, with more developed markets and an industrial base that could ultimately produce the goods needed for war, the Republican government was in a better position to face the challenge of mobilizing resources and defeating the military uprising. The Republican territory encompassed 60 percent of the country's population (around 14 million inhabitants), the main commercial cities (Madrid, Barcelona, Bilbao, and Valencia), practically the entire industrial base concentrated in Catalonia, the Basque country, and Asturias, and the main agrarian exporting area on the Mediterranean coast.

The Nationalists, on the other hand, had virtually no manufacturing industry to produce military supplies and, without any initial financial resources, relied entirely on private donations and funds borrowed from abroad to purchase foreign supplies. The only initial advantages Franco had were the control of large grain-producing regions and the support and aid of many entrepreneurs, business managers, and lenders who jumped into the Nationalist area immediately following the outbreak of war due to lack of trust in the Republican government's policies.

At the time of the military uprising in Spain, less than 2 million out of a total population of 24 million worked in industry, 70 percent of which was concentrated in a single area within the Republican area: Catalonia. There, within hours of the uprising, workers seized control of some 3,000 enterprises. This included all public transportation services, shipping, electric and power generation companies, gas and water works, engineering and automobile assembly plants, mines, cement works, textile mills and paper factories, as well as electrical and chemical suppliers.

It was in the Republic's industrial areas where some of the first Marxist–Socialist collectivizations took place. However, once the initial period of fighting was over, it became clear that the next vital step was to ensure the continuation of production. Factories and workshops were immediately seized and run by the workers. Other sections of the bourgeoisie were reluctant to keep the factories going, and by closing them, attempted to indirectly contribute to Franco's cause. Closing factories and workshops would lead to higher unemployment and increasing poverty that would play into the Nationalists' hands. The workers understood this instinctively, and established control committees in almost all workshops to keep a watch on the progress in production, and to keep a check on the financial position of the owner of each establishment. In many cases, control was quickly delegated from the control committee to the management committee, where the employer was drawn in with the workers and paid the same wage. Certain factories and workshops in Catalonia thereby passed into the hands of workers who were engaged in them. However, the results were not impressive.

Also of the utmost importance and urgency for the Republic was to create a war industry in order to supply the front and to get the transportation system moving again so that the Republican militias and supplies could be sent to the front. Thus, the first expropriations of industries and public services took place in a bid to guarantee victory over the Nationalists, with anarchist militants taking advantage of the situation to push immediately for revolutionary goals.

Factories in northern areas of Spain produced a fair number of armored tractors and trucks. Trubia Artillery Works, a military industry in Asturias near Oviedo, manufactured some light tanks known as the "Trubia-Naval" model, a local version of the Renault FT but only armed with machine guns. However, most construction revolved around armoring trucks that became known as "Tiznaos" (dark) due to the grey color of their steel armor. Yet as a result of the armor's weight and the low power output of their engines, many were not able to move more than 20 yards before breaking down. These were mostly built in the heavily industrialized regions in northern Spain and in the northeast in Catalonia. The factories of the Valencia region made, under Soviet guidance, what was to be one of the best armored trucks of the war, the UNL-35. These vehicles were based on the Soviet ZiS-5 truck, and were built between early 1937 and March 1939, at a rate of five vehicles per month, but not every month. Some 120 additional UNL-35s, based on other chassis such as Ford's model 817T truck, were also built.

The Nationalists sponsored at least two tank-production projects, the Carro de Combate de Infanteria Ansaldo in 1937, with Italian industry and technical support, as well as the Spanish Carro Verdeja designed by Nationalist Army engineer Captain Felix Verdeja. However, the latter never materialized and only a few single prototypes were built.

On August 7, 1936, the Generalitat of Catalonia (a local autonomous government) established the Comissió D'Industries de Guerra (Commission for War Industry), headed by Josep Tarradellas—who would later play a key role in Spain's political transition to democracy following Franco's death—with a view to adapting Catalonian industry to the war effort. Great innovations were created in these factories. Many workplaces, once in control of the workers, were converted to the production of war materiel for Republican troops. This was also the case with the metal industry in Catalonia, which was completely rebuilt. Only a few days after the start of the war on July 18, 1936, for example, the Hispano-Suiza Automobile Company was converted to manufacture armored cars, ambulances, weapons, and ammunition for the fighting forces.

Another example was the optical industry, which was virtually non-existent before the war. The small scattered workshops that had previously existed were voluntarily converted into a collective enterprise that became a new factory. In a relatively short time, the factory produced telemeters, binoculars, surveying instruments, industrial glassware in various colors, and certain scientific instruments. It also manufactured and repaired optical equipment for the Republican Army.

However, George Orwell highlighted the way his fellow Republican soldiers were inadequately equipped despite being funded by Spain's official government. Indeed, Republican forces suffered numerous problems with logistical supplies that impaired their abilities as an army. The civil war also disrupted Spain's local industries and trade, making the production of vital supplies difficult. This disruption also weakened the Republicans' ability to import supplies from abroad. As a result, the logistical dilemmas of the Republican forces were the direct result of lacking materiel support, raw materials, and the ability to produce their own supplies in the quantities needed.

On September 22, 1936, at a Comintern meeting, it was reported that the shortage of weapons was the Republic's most serious concern; consequently, the most immediate problem was to get arms to the Republic as quickly as possible. It was not "only arms," but "arms above all else." The arms problem was particularly critical because the Nationalists had already begun receiving substantial aid from Italy and Germany, while what the Republicans had received was insignificant. However, the Soviet Union contributed a great deal to changing this situation.

The Republicans' continuous military setbacks during the first two years of the conflict reduced their economic power and tilted the economic balance in favor of the Nationalist administration and military forces. The collapse of the whole Northern front in June 1937 caused the entire Basque and Asturias armaments industry to fall into the hands of Franco. Trained workers lucky enough to be evacuated in time were sent to work in the arms factories that the Republican government hastily set up in the province of Valencia. However, when the Nationalists then occupied the northern provinces—with the largest coal deposits, iron and steel industries, shipyards, and merchant fleet—the economic balance shifted permanently in their favor. It was astonishing, indeed, that the Republican armored force was thereafter able to function at all.

From the outbreak of the war, the Nationalists had control of the arms factory at Oviedo. Besieged by forces loyal to the Republic, during the first two years of the war the factory was partially transferred to Corunna, in Galicia, where a new arms plant was established. Once Oviedo was liberated from the Republican siege, both factories and the artillery workshops at Trubia, also near Oviedo, worked together to provide substantial help to the Nationalist war effort. The Nationalists also had also received war materiel from the artillery workshops at Seville, as well as the powder and ammunition factories in Granada.

After the battle of Teruel, Franco had the edge on resupply as his Nationalists now controlled the efficiently run industrial might of the Basque country. The Republican government had to leave the armaments industry in Catalonia in the hands of anarchists. One anarchist observer reported: "Notwithstanding the lavish expenditures of money on this need, our industrial organization was not able to finish a single kind of rifle or machine gun, or howitzer."

Spain was also backwards in the automotive field, with maintenance and repair workshops for automobiles and trucks being scarce, especially in the military field where there were virtually none. Only the Army of Africa had a primitive automobile service, which became the nucleus of future and more complex support services.

With tanks and armored vehicles, their most vital requirements are maintenance and logistics. Lack of these, and of an industrial and technology base in Spain in the 1930s, were an obstacle that both sides faced. Tanks are complex weapons systems that require a number of sub-systems, as well as the appropriate crew, to function properly and provide the vehicle with its key characteristics: firepower, protection, mobility, and communications. Tank crews in Spain varied in size, with an average of two people on the Nationalist side for the Italian and German tanks, and three for the Republicans' Russian tanks. Casualties—combat and non-combat—sometimes reduced crew numbers to the point of making it impossible to operate a tank. Nonetheless, it was essential that each member of the crew perform his designated task well for the tank to achieve its full capability.

The Nationalists also gave priority to equipping their military. At their largest city, Seville, during the crucial first few months of the war, the ammunition factory was increasingly able to furnish both the southern and northern forces with almost all their needs. At the same time, General Queipo de Llano led an effort to create several industrial areas and joint ventures. Many entrepreneurs who fled Republican-held territory were encouraged to regenerate the industries they had abandoned. With their assistance, workshops began to fill the Nationalist quartermaster's requests. The engineering company Hispano-Suiza repaired aircraft and tanks, while some Italian firms also set up shop in Seville. Labor productivity was also generally greater on the Nationalist side than in the Republican area.

Industrial production jumped in the Nationalist area, where as a rule the workforce had been fully militarized, taxes had been established, and even some fixed delivery quotas had been enforced. Production of steel recovered tremendously, while the amount of iron and steel from the Asturia region at least doubled under Nationalist control. Copper and brass production climbed too, although some of the increased production went to Nazi Germany as payment for the help being received.

The Neutrality Act[1] prevented American companies from selling any weapons of war to the Spanish Republic or the Nationalists, but did not apply to other materials such as food, commercial vehicles, or oil. Regarding fuel supplies, massive quantities of oil were sent to the Nationalists by the Texas Oil Company (Texaco). Several U.S. companies—such as Texaco, Standard Oil, Ford, General Motors, and Studebaker—exploited this loophole to sell such items to General Franco under credit. By 1939, Franco owed more than U.S. $100 million to these and other American companies.[2]

Neither did the Neutrality Act forbid the import of goods from nations involved in a war. The United States imported $4 million worth of olives and olive oil from Nationalist Spain, which helped finance Franco's war effort. The end of the neutrality policy came only with the Lend–Lease Act of March 1941, which allowed the U.S. to sell, lend, or give war materiel to nations that the administration wanted to support. Great Britain also imported a great deal from the Nationalists, further contributing to their war effort.

During the war, the Canary Islands remained firmly in the Nationalist camp, and Spanish oil company CEPSA's refinery there became an asset of significance to Franco's cause. Refinery production there, denied to Madrid and out of bombing range of the Republic's air force, helped earn foreign exchange and fuel Franco's success. To gauge some idea of their needs, the Nationalist Army's consumed 1.2 million liters of gasoline, 200,000 liters of diesel fuel, and 80,000 liters of oil per combat day in 1938. Between them, Texaco, Shell, Standard Oil, Socony, and the Atlantic Refining Company sold about U.S. $20 million worth of oil and gasoline to the Nationalists, Texaco alone shipping 1.886 million tons. Without these deliveries Franco's war would have come to a halt in days, as at that time he had no other suppliers and the Soviet Union was supplying to the Republic. By the end of July 1936, and before committing to providing arms to the Republic, Stalin had given orders to the NKVT (the People's Commissariat on Foreign Trade of the Soviet Union) "to sell fuel oil to the Spaniards, at reduced prices, on most favorable conditions, on any amount they need."[3]

Spain had historically been very dependent upon imports, so diligently maintained sea lines of communication with a relatively strong navy. When the government was not quickly overthrown in a coup, the rising degenerated into a war of attrition. Accordingly, each side quickly became dependent upon the imports of war materials. Should either the Republicans or Nationalists not be able to maintain their sea lines of communication, the war would be lost despite the valiant efforts of the soldiers on land. Fundamentally, the Republic lost the civil war as they were unable to control the seas and maintain the sea lines of communication.

The war was first and foremost one of logistics and lines of communication. The Nationalists had comparatively short lines of communication (from Italy and Germany), whereas the Republic relied extensively, often solely, on supplies provided from the Soviet Union. The equipment from the Soviet Union had to transit the Black Sea and the Mediterranean or be transported to France and then across the Pyrenees. Given that 80–90 percent of all supplies to participants in the war went by sea, anything that could be done to interdict the supply lines would have a significant impact on the conflict. During the last year of the war, supply lines through the Mediterranean were so untenable due to Nationalist submarine warfare activity that the Soviets ceased shipping supplies on that route altogether. The Soviets instead used French ports on the Atlantic and the French rail system, but the cargo could only cross the French–Spanish frontier with the permission of the French government. As a result, the border with Spain was not always open. During the final battle for

Catalonia between December 1938 and February 1939, large stockpiles were held up on the border because France would not agree to open the frontier. Undoubtedly, if Republican forces had secured access to these supplies, the war could have been prolonged.

The Nationalists gave a high priority to transportation. Whereas the Republicans attempted organizational innovation, the Nationalists maintained the pre-war enterprises that were able to accommodate their military and civilian needs, especially with the railroad. Nevertheless, trains were often incredibly slow and could take several days to move only a few hundred miles, although troop trains had priority over civilian rolling stock. Road transportation was usually the most effective way to move troops and supplies, but the Spanish road network was very poor. Usually, the movement of large number of trucks indicated that an offensive was being prepared.

To help minimize wear on the tanks, both sides turned to the use of commercial trucks to move them between battles and to the front lines. Nationalists preferred American trucks to German and Italian ones. Acquisition of trucks from U.S. manufacturers was vital for the Nationalist victory, and in some way conditioned the postwar influx of American capital into Spain. As many as 12,000 trucks were procured from Ford and GM, as opposed to only 1,800 German and 1,200 Italian ones; however, some estimates point to the Italians having supplied at least 5,000 trucks. Without reliable vehicles, the Nationalists would not have won the war so soon as they did. After the war was over, José Maria Doussinague, who was Under-Secretary of State at the new Spanish Foreign Affairs Ministry, said: "Without American oil and American trucks, and American credit, we could never have won the Civil War." When the war ended, American companies recovered and repaired a large number of Spanish vehicles.

At the beginning of the war, the Republicans purchased about 7,000 trucks from the Soviet Union and relied mainly on Russian vehicles. The Republican Army, to help extend the life of tanks, also used trains or heavy trucks to transport the tanks to their combat positions whenever the units had to move more than a few miles. This was a practice also adopted by the Spanish Army after the war.[4]

Tank Maintenance of the Nationalist Faction and the War Equipment Recovery Service

Due to the scarcity of weaponry and ammunition, at least initially, a key asset in the logistical management of the Nationalist Army was the recovery throughout the conflict of enemy war equipment, either abandoned or captured. During the Spanish Civil War, losses of major items of equipment were substantial in many battles. Due to the expense of producing and procuring such equipment, the Nationalist Army made a substantial effort to recover and re-use all enemy materiel that fell into its hands. The recovery effort led to the update, repair, and maintenance of much equipment. Equipment deemed useful was then classified and distributed to the appropriate front-line units.

As well as its use on the battlefield, captured materiel was also of value to the Nationalists as a source of intelligence on Russian equipment capabilities and for identifying weaknesses of German and Italian equipment. Use of captured equipment has obvious benefits and less-obvious drawbacks. When Russian tanks were captured and could be repaired for use, they were often immediately used in operations. However, the drawbacks of using enemy equipment were significant too. First, captured vehicles were often mistaken as the enemy and subjected to friendly fire, which was why huge Nationalist flags were painted on both sides and on top of such vehicles. Sometimes it was also difficult to repair or maintain them unless resorting to cannibalizing other captured vehicles, and the simple act of obtaining ammunition or minor engine parts proved at times to be almost insurmountable. Furthermore, troops did not always understand the maintenance requirements of the unfamiliar captured enemy equipment, despite training and familiarization procedures provided by the specialized recovery service.

At first, the recovery services were organized within the Artillery Combat Service Support and were named the *Servicio de Recuperacion de Material de Guerra* (War Equipment Recovery Service), directly under artillery command at the Supreme Nationalist Headquarters located in Valladolid, northern

Castile, with delegations at army, corps, and divisional levels. The Recovery Service comprised the following:

- recovery battalions,
- specialized classification battalions,
- recovery detachments for tanks and artillery guns,
- special units for artillery ammunition,
- transportation units,
- training services.

The efficiency of this special service was clearly shown, as captured Republican equipment became a main source of supplies for the Nationalists. No other army in history had ever used captured enemy equipment in combat to such a great extent.

To get a comprehensive idea of the quantity and size of armored equipment captured by the Nationalist Army at the end of the war, we must take into account the work of Spanish historian Lucas Molina Franco, *Las Armas de la Guerra Civil Española*, published in Madrid in 2006, with an introduction by Stanley G. Payne, who clearly considers the employment of T-26 and BT-5 tanks by the Republicans as a failure; not due to the quality of the tanks but to other reasons never before fully analyzed. No less than 350 different tanks and armored cars were captured by the Nationalists, most of them being re-used and sent into combat against their original owners.

Based on the Army of Africa's automobile services, in December 1936 the Nationalist Army created a full Automobile Recovery Service at the main logistical base in Seville that became the central and main workshop for all motorized vehicles of the Nationalist Army. By 1938, on the Aragon front alone, there were no less than 43 main workshops and six mobile workshops integrated into the major combat units. The main central headquarters of the service was located in Bilbao, in the Basque region, and one mobile workshop was attached to the Army of the South, under General Queipo de Llano, for the final operations of the war.

Although tank maintenance and sustainability were a nightmare on the Nationalist side, Franco's tankers generally fared far better than their Republican counterparts. The Italian Fiat L3 light tank, even though considered technically almost perfect when the crewmen were trained experts, required high-intensity maintenance, sometimes up to 14 or 15 hours a day, for field repairs, resupplying, and tuning up. Such demanding issues put such heavy stress on crewmen that they sometimes required medical attention or transfer to rest areas. There were other worrying issues, such as the air intake systems on the tanks, which were not equipped with appropriate filters to protect the engines or crewmen from the fine dust so prevalent at times in the Spanish countryside. Such a feature would be improved later for vehicles sent to North Africa.

For the Italian tanks, refueling while in combat was a problem, mainly due to their limited range. Refueling became an issue and a special organization was set up by the Italian command to refuel either individual tanks or whole platoons. However, the Italians were a meticulous people, with organized and efficient logistics from the early days of armored combat in Spain. Even the first platoon of five tanks which arrived in August 1936 had a full combat support service section structured into a mechanical support squad, a service squad, a POL (petrol, oil, and lubricants) squad, and a field repairs and maintenance squad, all of them with Italian staff, plus a total of seven support vehicles, including five special trucks to transport the tanks.

The German *Panzer I* had several design flaws too, including suspension problems—which made the vehicle pitch at high speeds—and engine overheating, although this issue was basically corrected with the *Ausf B* model. Based on the judgment of the Nationalist troops and their achievements with the *Panzer I Ausf A "Krupp"* variant (that covered between 4,000 and 7,000 miles per tank during the war) and the *Ausf B "Maybach"* (1,500–3,000 miles), both tank variants were considered a success in terms of mechanical reliability.

Nevertheless, Colonel von Thoma often complained about the misuse of tanks that in his view sometimes fought on too-rugged ground and were forced to cover long distances from one place of intervention to another. The latter wore tanks down and forced long repair and maintenance periods. Therefore, the Nationalist general headquarters reminded its commanders that armor had to be preserved to operate on ground suitable for the tanks' tactics and mechanical performance.

The Spanish Nationalist command's neglect was not limited to doctrinal issues, sometimes also paying little attention to logistical matters, especially to maintenance problems, much to von Thoma's chagrin. In January 1938, the general headquarters sent a message[1] from von Thoma to the Army of the North to remind the Nationalist command of the need to withdraw the tanks from the front line by nightfall. If this was not done, mechanical maintenance would prove impossible and fuel supply would be difficult as the trucks had to stop several miles away from the front. Nevertheless, each tank company had one mechanical service support and maintenance section, each tank battalion one maintenance platoon, and there was one mobile workshop company to meet all the needs[2] of the two battalions.

Probably even more than the Italians, the Germans demonstrated great care in maintenance and sustainability of armored equipment. The first shipment to the Nationalists in early October 1936 came with full logistical support: no less than 10 Bussing NAG 80 tank transporters, six repair and maintenance mobile workshops, 45 cargo trucks—including 14 more transporter and tank recovery Vomag vehicles—19 tank trailer platforms, and a substantial stock of spare parts and special tools. Colonel von Thoma established his main logistical base at the town of Cubas de la Sagra, near the Madrid front, by the end of October 1936, where it remained for the duration of the war.

At some time during the war, one command and control tank from the four supplied, a *Panzer Befelhswagen I B*, was converted into an armored recovery vehicle (ARV or *Bergepanzer*) to be used by the Nationalist mobile workshops. This was undoubtedly a pioneering project, the first time an armored recovery vehicle based on a combat tank was used to recover vehicles in the field. It was fitted with a light crane that allowed the crew to remove the engine from a broken tank. Unfortunately, there are no surviving examples of such an original but primitive vehicle.

Despite these developments, the administrative management of the Nationalist armored force was severely criticized by the Germans. Colonel von Thoma affirmed,[3] in a report dated April 29, 1938, that supervision of personnel and training was very deficient. He said training periods were too short, given the continuous need for replacements at the front line, especially the training of tank drivers, who needed several months of tutelage.

On the other hand, separation of tank companies was not desirable because it complicated the logistical support. The knowledge of crews about mechanical matters was so poor that breakdowns which could have been solved at the front often required moving the tanks back long distances for repair because there was just one mobile workshop available.

Despite operational success, von Thoma later emphasized the poor maintenance skills and training of Nationalist armor at the battle of the Ebro. He sent a memorandum, dated September 13, 1938, to General Franco and General Orgaz, head of manpower and Ordnance Support Command. Von Thoma stated that no decision had been made about the proposals he put forward in his April report, as the tank units had been continuously in action. As a result, it was now almost impossible to supply enough spares, while replacement personnel were untrained as nobody had been sent to the armor school in half a year. Von Thoma proposed to withdraw one tank company at a time from the front line, in rotation, to follow a short course and some overhaul. During the 12 days of the course, von Thoma emphasized, officers as well as other ranks would be taught the essentials of tanks. Furthermore, he said the tank school needed to train replacements continuously in one-month courses. Von Thoma proposed that the school should have 25 drivers and 25 gunners, including officers, in training at any time, plus 15 drivers and 15 gunners under reassessment to relieve those who had lost proficiency.[4] It was the German way of training.

On October 3, 1938, von Thoma sent another report on the strength of the tank battalions to General Orgaz, providing further evidence regarding previous German statements. Eleven out of 64 German tanks were being repaired, and with another nine not able to be used because there were no drivers for them, nearly one-third of German tanks were out of service. The situation with captured Russian tanks was slightly better, though one-sixth—five out of 32—were under repair. The reasons for this situation, he stated, were poor maintenance—as time was insufficient and crews lacked necessary training—and the use of armor on unsuitable terrain due to the incompetence of senior commanders.[5]

The tactical misuse of armor had been pointed out by von Thoma in his September memorandum. He openly disapproved of the use of tanks on the Ebro battlefield. Despite the losses suffered in exchange for no gains, the Nationalist forces carried on resorting to armor on unsuitable ground. Von Thoma attributed this to the Nationalist commanders' limited knowledge of tanks. The presence of enemy tanks was no argument, as the Republican Army used them as artillery pieces in fixed positions, not for attacks on rocky ground. Lieutenant Colonel Pujales, in his introductory note to von Thoma's memorandum, also complained about ground unsuitability, which forced tanks to move forward along paths in single file, without any possibility for deployment. Pujales[6] concluded his note by asking General Davila, chief of the Northern front, to withdraw his battalion from the Ebro sector.

CHAPTER 18

Tank Combat Service Support in the Spanish Republic's People's Army

During the early days of the conflict, the Republic had already begun to study how to produce weapons and not have to procure them abroad. They tried it in the north and studied the possibility of building weapons factories in Barcelona and Madrid. The outbreak of the war led to the building of hundreds of armored trucks, especially by Republican militias in industrial areas. Factories under Republican control built at least 400 of these, and no fewer than 150 were produced in Catalonia between 1936 and 1937. However, they were often poorly designed and were prone to breakdowns. Excess weight led to engine overheating and failure. Their narrow tires tended to mean that they had a high ground pressure and could not be used off-road. They were also prone to overturning.

The need to buy arms-building machines abroad was discussed. However, as this would have taken a long time, it was necessary to procure arms from abroad. The safe transit of weapons from the Soviet Union to Spain presented numerous difficulties. The obstacles included the great distance involved in the journey, the large volume of arms being delivered, and the inherent risks of the sea and land routes. All that made the logistical flow of supplies very difficult.

The safe arrival in Cartagena of ships carrying weapons did not solve the problem for the Republicans. Unloading the vessels presented considerable risks and logistical problems. This was in part due to the half-hearted security measures implemented by the Soviets, who usually communicated in Spain using open telephone lines. From the moment a ship arrived in port, if not before, the news quickly spread throughout the city and beyond. Among those who learned of the arms shipments were often Nationalist agents operating around the port, who wasted no time in alerting Salamanca or Burgos. As a result, the Nationalist air force routinely bombarded the port of Cartagena.

If Soviet reports are to be believed, the ships ferrying arms to Spain were met by sloppy, inept, or even negligent Republican dockworkers. According to Soviet naval attaché Kuznetsov,[1] these workers carelessly handled barrels of gas and tossed around boxes of ammunition, disregarding the dangerous consequences. The naval attaché was dismayed that the unloaded shipments of fighter aircraft, tanks, cannons, and rifles often sat exposed on the docks with little or no protection. More than once, Kuznetsov claimed to have witnessed anarcho-syndicalist groups absconding with parts of weaponry. Even once unloaded and placed aboard rail cars, the Soviet hardware was rarely expedited to where it was needed as the Republic did not possess enough locomotives to carry the rolling stock to the front.

The Republican Army nevertheless managed to establish an acceptable network of logistical centres where maintenance and major repairs could be provided for armored units. By the end of the war, the main logistical bases were located around Valencia: headquarters, support bases, stock depots, mobile workshops, and transportation units. Some workshops were based inside tunnels to protect them from air attacks. Albacete—around 200 miles to the southeast of Madrid—was also a key logistical center, with some workshops at La Roda, an important communications network on the main road from Madrid to Valencia. The main Republican armored force training school at Archena—in the province of Murcia—also housed the maintenance training center, together with some workshops and a mobile workshop unit, providing support as far as to the Toledo front.

Logistical nightmares often occurred during the early days of the civil war. A recently published Soviet document reports that during the battle of Madrid—in combat to the west and south of the city—the newly delivered Soviet tanks ran out of fuel at times and were easy prey for the Nationalists; "about two dozen tanks had gone into battle without filling up with fuel." Nationalist antitank guns dealt with the immobile tanks at their leisure.[2]

Almost from the outset, a main logistical maintenance and supply center was established at Alcalá de Henares, about 30 miles northeast of Madrid, on the main road from Madrid to Guadalajara and Barcelona. The main service support center was located in abandoned cavalry barracks from the pre-war Spanish Army that ended up being used again by Franco's army after the war, becoming a main logistical base for the new Spanish Army and still currently active.

It was only after the battle of Jarama that Soviet commander General Dimitry Pavlov established a special reinforced recovery unit to avoid damaged T-26 tanks being captured by the Nationalists. This unit was equipped with several caterpillar tractors fitted with steel wire cable to tow damaged or broken-down tanks from the battlefield. However, they were not very effective and Franco's troops ended up being equipped with more Russian tanks than either German or Italian ones. Pavlov, in a report to Soviet Defense Minister Voroshilov on August 31, 1937, also complained that the organization of the rear area and logistics was inadequate.[3]

Compounding the issues presented by enemy mines, antitank guns, and "Molotov cocktails," there were endless mechanical and technical problems that frequently led to breakdowns in Republican armor. These maintenance issues were worsened by a lack of spare parts, established repair facilities, trained mechanics, and even fuel. Also missing from the first shipments of Soviet tanks to the Republic were trained mechanics, spare parts, and mobile maintenance equipment, an oversight that would seriously weaken the effectiveness of Soviet armor in the Spanish war.[4] Nor was this the only blunder associated with the arrival of Colonel Krivoshein's group. Indeed, the integration of armor into the Republican war effort was poorly planned and chaotic from the start.

Republican tank units were not in good shape by the end of 1936, as the inexperienced Spanish crews were unable to carry out field repairs and their unfamiliarity with driving tanks led to high rates of clutch and powertrain failures. There were no established maintenance facilities in the Madrid area yet, while spare parts were almost non-existent, apart from an initial batch brought in by Krivoshein with the first tank shipment. While Krivoshein's tank force succeeded in its immediate mission of bolstering the Republican forces during the defense of Madrid, this was no way to operate an armored formation for prolonged campaigns.

By the end of 1937, the Republican tanks had exceeded their mechanical lifespan, yet tank units were able to maintain a respectable amount of their equipment in combat on a daily basis and overall losses were relatively modest. A total of 63 tanks, mostly T-26s—more than half the force available then—required a full overhaul, which was hastily done in the field by the units. It was remarkable they managed to do this, which reflected some growing skills on the part of Spanish crewmen, maintenance units, and the improvised tank support infrastructure created by Republican industry.

The Russian T-26 tank required an intermediate overhaul at workshops after 150 engine working hours, and a full factory overhaul after 600 hours of use. The T-26's engine did not have a speed limiter, which often resulted in overheating and engine valve breakage, especially in summertime. Furthermore, the engine required top-grade gasoline as the use of second-rate fuel could cause damage to valve units due to engine detonation. The poor quality of fuel in Spain at the time led to engine carbonization, fouled sparkplugs, and other issues that ended up immobilizing tanks.

The transmission of the T-26 consisted of single-disc main dry clutch, a gearbox with five gears in the front part of the vehicle, steering clutches, final drives, and band brakes. The gearbox was connected to the engine by a drive shaft passing through the vehicle. A gear change lever was mounted directly on the gearbox. Tracks and track pins began to wear out after 500 miles, whereas side clutches became worn out and the powertrain was gradually knocked out of alignment from hard cross-country movement. In the fighting during the defense of Madrid, Captain Arman's hastily arranged company accumulated over 800 operating hours by mid-December 1936, far beyond the regulations, leaving many of his tanks completely inoperable and out of service.

The newly trained Spanish tank crews initially performed poorly for the Republicans, while the Soviet practice of assigning a junior crewman to driving duties usually left tanks in the hands of inexperienced Spanish tankers.[5] This led to abnormally high breakdown rates and forced the Russians to reorganize crew tasks, with tank commanders sometimes shifted to the driver's position in the hope of keeping the tanks in operating condition. However, this had an adverse effect on the combat capabilities of the tanks, as the more experienced Soviet commanders were thus unable to command the tank and aim gunfire from the driver's position.

On the other hand, the driver's ability to efficiently drive the tank and maneuver over rough terrain, in addition to making use of cover and concealed approaches, was critical for its survival. In the autumn of 1936 and into early 1937, most Spanish Republican tank drivers still had very little practical experience, whereas the Italians were pretty used to their tanks and the Germans had properly and sufficiently trained Spanish Nationalist drivers for their *Panzer Is*. Tank driver training continued to be a weakness for the Republican Army throughout the war.

Immediate lessons for the Republicans from the early fighting during the autumn of 1936 concerned technical issues, mainly in order to keep the armored force in a fighting state. The Soviet Army had never conducted any prolonged tank operations away from its peacetime training bases, so combat experiences in Spain were an eye-opening introduction to the day-to-day technical realities that had plagued tankers since World War I. It was clear from the initial fighting in Spain that tank units should not be employed non-stop, day-and-night, like infantry; they had to be carefully preserved for the most important missions.

The main technical problems with the T-26 tank were related to its engine: a Russian 90hp air-cooled four-cylinder GAZ-26 gasoline unit, which was a Soviet-made near-copy of the British Armstrong-Siddeley Puma engine.

However, the manufacturing quality of this Soviet engine was nowhere near as good as that of the British original, while cooling problems inherited from the Puma engine had not got any better. As a result of these cooling problems, the practical sustainable maximum road speed for all T-26 tanks was only about 25mph. Due to poorer manufacturing quality, oil leaks and starting issues were more common in GAZ-manufactured engines. Average fuel consumption was estimated as above 4 gallons per hour and average consumption of oil and grease 1.4 liters per hour. Transmission of this engine had a single-disk main dry clutch. This main clutch was not as strong as in Vickers engines, and thus had some tendency to burn. Also, likely due to poor manufacturing quality, the service life of the GAZ T-26 engine was remarkably short, requiring an extensive overhaul after every 250 hours of use.

And if these problems were not enough, the GAZ-26 engine had starting difficulties in cold weather. The main reason for this was the weak magneto that the Soviets used with the GAZ-26, which was found to be not strong enough to give a proper spark and therefore often failed to start the engine in cold weather. To fix the problem, the Russians had given the driver an additional magneto, which could be used to assist it, but even this solution was somewhat unreliable. Therefore, it could also be started with a winch.

The BT-5 fast tank was the other main battle tank employed by the Republicans during the Spanish Civil War. One of its basic attributes was the ability to run either on tracks or just on road wheels, but this advantage was never made use of by the Spanish People's Army. The tank running system proved to be unreliable, and due to mechanical failures and bad employment, almost all tanks of this type were lost by mid-1937 and were never replaced.

Evaluations of the T-26 in Spain concluded that if well maintained, the tank performed well, but a variety of shortcomings were noted. The most common problem during movement was track breakage. The engine spark plugs needed frequent attention, but it was difficult to get access to remove the plugs. The radiator was also easily damaged by artillery fragments and even by light weapons fire.

The poor durability of the Russian-made T-26 tank was a perennial problem, exacerbated by the lack of trained mechanics and repair facilities. During the battle of Teruel, from December 1937 to February 1938, the 104 T-26s involved in the Republican offensive required repairs 586 times over the 65 days of fighting, roughly once every 11 days for each tank. Most of these were just ordinary field maintenance repairs involving tracks and minor engine adjustments. However, there were 63 medium and heavy repairs which required 58 engine replacements, six new gearboxes, 15 main clutches, and 22 side clutches. In other words, every other tank had its engine replaced after only about two months of combat use. Thus, of the total number of tanks employed by the Republicans at Teruel, more than half needed an engine replacement, which gives an idea of the rate of mechanical attrition suffered during the battle.

Early in 1938, the Republican Army once more attempted to make up for its armor shortfalls by local production, starting to build true wheeled armored cars in cooperation with Soviet specialists. An efficient armored car called the UNL-35 began to make its way out from the factories in Valencia. This was a copy of the Russian FAI armored car and was usually built on Soviet Zis-5 or Ford Model 85 trucks. About 200 were eventually completed.

Another 275 armored cars based on the Soviet BA-3 armored cars were built at the Hispano-Suiza plant in Barcelona, using Ford SD 1.5 ton trucks and Chevrolet Series S Model 1937 and 1938 commercial trucks. In May 1938, the Republican Army had 176 tanks and 285 armored cars, while in December that year, it had just 126 tanks but 291 armored cars.[6] The nature of the Republican armored force thus shifted in the direction of a road-bound force tied to armored cars and protected trucks as the inventory of tanks shrank due to combat and mechanical attrition.

Logistics constrained and hampered tank operations throughout the Spanish Civil War. The tanks employed were not very technically advanced compared to their World War I predecessors, and often proved mechanically unreliable. However, it was noted that "they must be built as mechanically perfect, yet as simple, as technical science could make them; they had to be regularly serviced and overhauled; must be handled by expert personnel; and must be conserved for their most effective use."[7]

Inadequate tank maintenance and recovery systems, combined with an inherent unreliability of the armor used, resulted in the abandonment of many of the tanks that broke down during operations. This was unquestionably a more significant issue for the Republicans than the Nationalists, as is proven by the fact that the Nationalist Army ended up having more operational captured Russian tanks than the Republican People's Army itself. Indeed, the issue happened rarely on the Nationalist side. By 1939, when the war ended, few of the Soviet tanks still in service with the Republican Army remained operational.

CHAPTER 19

A Key Feature: The Republican Tank School at Archena

In 1936, Archena was a little town of no more than 8,000 inhabitants in the southwest of Spain, within the province of Murcia. It was home to a hot mineral-medicinal water spring spa, dating back to Roman times, and had three small hotels built around it. (While undergoing a recent development, further Roman ruins have been found on the spa's site.) Archena remained in the hands of the Republican forces from when the war began until March 22, 1939, a few days before it officially ended. Curiously, it was neither attacked nor conquered by the Nationalist forces; it simply fell into their hands when the Republic finally surrendered.

Apparently, it was Soviet military attaché Vladimir Gorev who decided the location of the main training and logistical center for the Republican Army at Archena in late September 1936. He did so mainly on the grounds of the place having railroad communications with the main harbor where the logistical flow of supplies from the Soviet Union was arriving, Cartagena, which was barely 65 miles far away, and being sufficiently away from main cities and roads. Archena also had decent medical facilities—there was a hospital nearby—and it had a strong local Communist presence. Furthermore, the landscape allowed easy camouflage of military installations and infrastructure. Almost at the same time, in August 1936, the Republican Air Force had decided to build with the utmost urgency a training airfield in the neighborhood of Archena that often ended up being used by some of the Republic's fighter aircraft, supplied by the Soviet Union.

The decision to establish a tank logistics base and school for the armored forces of the Republic at Archena was probably taken in September 1936, when the Spanish commandant of the base was Colonel Rafael Sanchez Paredes, who left his previous assignment as military commandant of the city of Malaga in southern Spain on September 22. He was fortunate to leave Malaga when he did; otherwise, he would probably have been captured and executed following the Nationalist attack in early February 1937. Colonel Sanchez Paredes arrived in Archena on September 29 and began making arrangements for the future tank base and accommodation of Soviet personnel.

Sanchez Paredes, who had only been promoted to colonel on August 6 that year,[1] came to Archena with four other professional Spanish Army officers who had remained loyal to the Republic.[2] Their orders were to establish adequate infrastructure and carry out a first selection of future crewmembers for the tanks due to arrive. However, they had no idea how many or what type of tanks would arrive.

Colonel Sanchez Paredes went to Barcelona and Madrid in early October to find potential tank crews among cab drivers and bus and truck drivers, but was told that all personnel chosen would need positive vetting by the trade unions and Communist Party. On October 12, the first Soviet tanks arrived at Cartagena harbor, and while they were being unloaded, Soviet colonels Gorev and Krivoshein went directly to Archena. Apparently, Colonel Krivoshein was satisfied with the selection of Archena as a training base, well protected and almost hidden from view from the ground or the air.

The main existing installations at Archena integrated into the tank base were a high school, a food warehouse, the spa station, and the hospital. At the high school, Colonel Sanchez Paredes, in agreement with Krivoshein, established training rooms for the tank school (driving and gunnery), as well as workshops for maintenance and repairs. The food warehouse was used as a warehouse for spare parts and equipment, and also as barracks for soldiers.

Accommodation for officers was provided at the spa center hotel (which still exists nowadays), as well as for the school headquarters staff and personnel in training. The installations continued to be used at least until February 1939. Early in March 1939, all military personnel were evacuated to Cartagena.

Among the first provisions taken at Archena by Colonel Krivoshein were the building of air defense shelters, still visible today, as well as the camouflaging of all buildings' roofs. A new bridge was also built to make the base more accessible. Several fixed basic training simulators were also provided for the tank school and installed at the warehouse, while a movie theater was established for training use and leisure time.

Strict security measures were enforced around the base, and prominent leaders from the Republican government occasionally went to visit it. Apparently, the base was also used at times by the Soviet NKVD to provide training on special warfare and counterespionage techniques.

Driver training and even gunnery practice with live ammunition were conducted outside the base at ranges carefully chosen and forbidden to civilian personnel. The 1st Armored Brigade of the Republican Army, led by Soviet General Dimitry Pavlov, was created at Archena on December 6, 1936. About 60 percent of the personnel were Russian, while the rest were Spanish.

Practically all tanks received from the Soviet Union went first to Archena, even the BT-5 tanks in the summer of 1937, but these were swiftly sent to Alcala de Henares, and from there to the Aragon front. The Soviets were satisfied with the provisions taken by Colonel Sanchez Paredes, who was awarded distinctions by General Pavlov at Alcala de Henares by the end of February 1937. The Nationalist Army never had a similar training center. After the war, Colonel Sanchez Paredes went into exile in Mexico. Today, a street in the town of Archena still bears the name "Comandante Sanchez Paredes."

CHAPTER 20

The Experience Reconsidered: Conclusions

The Spanish Civil War was the scene for the first encounter between tanks in combat, although only in a limited way. Nevertheless, the employment of tanks on Spanish battlefields allowed for many aspects and possibilities of armored combat to be witnessed that would later help make it a key tool in modern warfare.

Each nation that provided armor to the Spanish Civil War harbored specific views about how to employ tanks in operations. The Germans were still developing their thinking and the Soviets had already embraced concepts stressing "deep battle" by offensive actions—even codifying them in their army regulations of 1936—while the Italians were committed to their theory of "*Guerra Celere*," so far experienced only in Ethiopia against a much weaker foe. However, the circumstances of the war made it impossible for these ideas to be fully tested, except on a few limited occasions. Tanks thus became tactical weapons normally employed in support of offensive operations or to bolster defenses.

Neither the Nationalists nor the Republicans employed *blitzkrieg* tactics, for the simple reason that German doctrine at the time was purely theoretical and had not been fully worked out, even for the German Army, much less for the rudimentary Spanish Nationalist forces. Combined-arms operations involving air-to-ground support became important for Franco's offensives during the last two years of the war, despite the opposing armies being inadequately developed to create any other forms of combined-arms operations. Much of the time, the defense enjoyed an almost World War I-level of effectiveness, and though Franco was successful in most of his counteroffensives, they foreshadowed those of World War II only to a limited degree.

The *blitzkrieg* theory was only fully embraced following the campaign in France in 1940, leading to unforeseen consequences for the German Army. The word "*blitzkrieg*" was expressly mentioned in a 1935 article in the professional magazine *Deutsche Wehr*, which stated that "countries with a rather weak food industry and poor in raw materials should try to finish a war quickly and suddenly by trying to force a decision right at the very beginning through the ruthless employment of their total fighting strength." This was unquestionably not what happened with a poor Spain in 1936. A more detailed analysis of the term was published in 1938 in the official German magazine *Militär-Wochenblatt*, but such references are rare and the word "*blitzkrieg*" was also practically never used in the official military terminology of the *Wehrmacht* during World War II.

If the hope of military thinkers was that the Spanish Civil War would bring a return to maneuver on the battlefield by using tanks, the actual experience there was clearly a disappointment. Not much has been written about the employment of armor during the Spanish war, and undoubtedly, in comparison to what soon happened during World War II, it was easy to overlook.

Nevertheless, the Spanish Civil War was a kind of prologue for what was to follow, the lessons obtained in Spain confirming what we know today as essentials of armored warfare. The presence in Spain of key officers of the armored forces from Germany, Italy, and the Soviet Union, who during World War II acquitted themselves extremely well and even faced or fought alongside each other on some occasions, adds more interest to this chapter of Spanish history.

In 1936, the United States Army shared with the armies of Europe a special interest in the onslaught going on in Spain. It was the first time since the Great War that European weapons were used again by Europeans, against Europeans. Although most of Colonel Stephen Fuqua's[1] reports—as U.S. Military attaché in Madrid throughout the war—concerned the non-technical "infantry war" of individual soldiers, antitank and antiaircraft weapons became the focus of interest for most of the American military attachés. Even though they were not involved in the fighting, the attachés in Paris and London, and to a lesser extent in Rome and Berlin, provided information that supplemented the sketchy technical and tactical data sent from Spain to Washington by Colonel Fuqua.

The main conclusion reached by the attachés and their sources was that the tanks used in Spain were inefficient. They lacked the necessary armor and armament to successfully meet an enemy equipped with heavy machine guns and antitank weapons, and were continually plagued by mechanical malfunctions. U.S. Lieutenant Colonel Raymond Lee—military attaché in London—submitted a report in the spring of 1937 that contained an excerpt from an article by tank warfare advocate Liddell Hart. In this article, Liddell Hart stated that tanks used in Spain were "obsolescent and of poor quality."

In a certain sense, Liddell Hart was correct. With the rapid technical development taking place during the 1930s, much equipment was soon displaced by more advanced technology. Yet it would be wrong to assume from his statement that all tanks used in Spain were old and discarded models, as they were not. Although Liddell Hart may have been theoretically correct in arguing that these tanks were obsolete, in a practical sense tanks used in Spain were the standard weapons of their respective armies at the time. The information gathered by the attachés on Nationalist tanks appeared to be relatively accurate and consistent. Although the attachés never mentioned the German *Panzer I* by name, they provided an early description of its basic characteristics.

Meanwhile, U.S. Army Lieutenant Colonel Sumner Waite—military attaché in Paris—submitted a report at the end of January 1938 that stated: "Regardless of the type of tank, all tanks sent to Spain by the Soviets seemed to share an unfortunate flaw." Various attaché reports state that Russian tanks were susceptible to destruction by fire, apparently more than Italian and German tanks. According to an article written by Captain Ed Bauer of the Swiss Army, forwarded to the Military Intelligence Department by U.S. Lieutenant Colonel John Magruder, from the U.S. embassy in Bern, the part most likely to combust was "the rubber sheathing covering the roller bearing which supports the caterpillar drive." Another report from Lieutenant Colonel Raymond Lee, early in 1937, made a similar observation about how easily the synthetic rubber used on the treads of Soviet tanks burned. The Nationalists soon discovered this and exploited the flaw.

The tactical employment of armor during the Spanish Civil War reflected, for the most part, the contemporary doctrines of the nations providing materiel and training assistance to each side. Accordingly, the Nationalists used either a peculiar version of German *blitzkrieg* tactics or an Italian method of combined-arms operations integrating infantry and armor. Much has been said of the role of military intervention in Spain in testing and evaluating new weaponry and tactics, especially in the case of the German Condor Legion, which came to play such an important part in the Nationalist forces. What has not generally been appreciated is that this sort of advantage applied much more to the Soviet military command than to the Germans. Whereas the Germans were skeptical and carefully selective with the lessons they chose to draw from the Spanish conflict, the Soviet approach was much more extensive—and more credulous too.

Italian tankers in Spain faced radically different conditions from those of the Ethiopian war of 1935–36, where the poorly equipped Ethiopians were overwhelmed by a relatively modern Italian Army. The Italians found the tables turned against them in Spain, which was reflected in their relatively high level of casualties. Even more significant, however, was that the Italian General Staff failed to draw any useful lessons in tank warfare from the Spanish experience. Indeed, when Italy entered World War II in June 1940, its armored units—still including many L3 CV-33/35 light tanks—would face heavier tanks even more formidable than the BT-5 or the T-26B, and the results on the battlefield would be disastrous.

The first Italian mechanized unit which met such a fate in World War II, in North Africa in 1940, consisted of organic assets organized in a hurry and in a situation already seriously compromised. These Italian mobile units—with inferior means and scant logistics—fought the British troops by trying to employ mobile tactics within the limits of what was possible. Their use, fragmented and with little strategic policy, negatively influenced the results of the disastrous campaign, and all Italian mechanized units ended up being needlessly sacrificed in the battle of Beda Fomm on February 7, 1941.

The Italian Special Armored Brigade (also known as the "*Babini*" Special Armored Brigade after its commander, the then General Valentino Babini, who had fought in Spain from April 1937) was a mechanized unit of opportunity, quickly established in North Africa in November 1940 by the High Command of Marshal Graziani in Libya. Upon Babini's request, it was decided to group together the various operationally separated armored units in the theater, so as to constitute a sufficiently powerful and mobile unit that could thwart the efficient and dangerous mechanized units of the British Western Desert Force. Nevertheless, the Special Brigade was virtually destroyed and most of the Italian troops taken captive, including Babini, who had fought bravely and was captured on the battlefield of Beda Fomm.

In Spain, following the capture of Santander (on the Northern front), the commander of the Italian RRS—then Colonel Babini—drafted a special report[2] to the Italian High Command, from which we can assume that the intensive training program undertaken by all Italian crewmen following Guadalajara had provided good results. The Fiat L3 light tank was considered technically excellent, Babini stating that "when crewmen were expert and ready, the tank became almost perfect, achieving optimum results." However, it was clear that that the L3 tankette was not up to the task of making a breakthrough of the front, and that above all, a cannon-armed tank was necessary. For that reason, and while waiting for a much better tank, he said antitank guns must be towed, at least one per platoon.

In May 1938, the Italian War Department published an information booklet with titled *Notice on the employment of small infantry and artillery units in the*

*Spanish Civil Wa*r.[3] This paper was relevant for two reasons: first, it was about the employment of tanks; second, it was mainly addressed to the Italian military command in North Africa. In one of its chapters is the following statement: "First of all, it is important to take into account that the Spanish Civil War is quite different from a major conflict between great armies, especially regarding the figures of tanks and artillery. The experience obtained is of some use though, for the employment of major units, equipped with powerful combat means and it must be valued accordingly." The Spanish experience made the Italian War Department acknowledge that a future high-intensity major war would be different from World War I. When analyzing the employment of tanks, the paper brought into light two main issues: cooperation with infantry, especially considering the cross-country speed of tanks, and the refueling and resupplying of tanks in combat.

Cooperation between tanks and infantry was considered an issue by the Italians, as in Spain they were never able to achieve simultaneous efforts when tanks and infantry were on the attack. Requesting the tanks to restrict their movement in the open to the pace of the infantry was almost suicidal. Italian tanks in Spain often continued on their own until they ran out of fuel, when, without infantry support, they were sitting ducks for Republican antitank and other heavy weapons. The Italian War Department document didn't take into account Colonel Babini's proposal following his return from Spain—to organize combined assault task forces made up of light infantry (*bersaglieri*) and engineers together with tanks—but limited its scope to requesting the infantry to speed up its movement.

Nevertheless, full cooperation was always lacking between tanks and infantry. Combat in Spain proved there were rivalries between tank unit and infantry commanders, to the extent that "before the battle everyone was asking for the other's support, especially the need for tanks, but on the following day nobody wanted to admit that the other's cooperation had been essential."[4] Whatever the case, there were many mistakes when employing tanks, and they were often used simply as supply trucks carrying ammunition or to block road crossings in static positions. Italian tank officers sometimes complained about a lack of clear missions for their units.

The need to refuel while in combat was mainly due to the technical performance of the Fiat L3 CV-33/35, which had a limited range for operations. A special organization was set up to refuel either individual tanks or whole platoons.

The Italian War Department paper also spoke of the appropriate armament for assault tanks. Superiority of cannon-armed tanks over machine-gun versions had become evident in Spain. The usual procedure of towing antitank guns with some tanks while in combat was considered slow and unpractical when challenging the heavier and better-armed Republican tanks. According to the document, this solution lacked the mobility needed in battle. The need for cannon-armed tanks together with light assault tanks armed only with machine guns was a demand that could no longer be ignored, and the proposal was to organize mixed tank platoons of four tanks, with one cannon-armed tank for every three machine-gun tanks.

However, nowhere in the paper is any reference made to the light machine-gun tank being an obsolete vehicle. Light tanks such as the Fiat L3 were still considered useful for scouting and reconnaissance purposes, as infantry support platforms, and to achieve surprise against enemy forces, even if they were inferior when facing heavier tanks. Neither is any mention made of armor penetrating the depth of the enemy's deployment. The main idea still was that of tanks cooperating with the infantry. Nevertheless, an alarm bell went off in the minds of Italian tank officers. They realized the lack of capabilities of their means and the absence of organizational effectiveness for the employment of tanks in the thinking of the Italian High Command. Yet there were no Guderians, Fullers, or Hobarts in the Italian Army. They should have taken into account the experience and lessons learned in Spain, but they did not.

Almost all Italian commanders of tank units in Spain tried to present to their superiors the lessons learned during the civil war. For them, it was crystal clear that any future conflict would require a good understanding on how to employ tanks and armor on the battlefield. For these officers, the Italian Army, in the event of future major conflict, must count on modern armored cars with high firepower, medium tanks cannon-armed with 360° turning turrets (replacing all the Fiat L3s, that could still be used for reconnaissance purposes only), modern trucks, armored self-propelled artillery, good command, communications, and control assets, as well as efficient logistics.

The Italian High Command missed the opportunity to learn lessons from Spain, and consequently of improving their armored forces. Looking at how Italian armor performed in its first months of World War II, it is easy to see how the Spanish experience had been almost completely forgotten. Initially, Italian armored forces were still equipped with the Fiat L3 light tank, even though it was totally inadequate to break through enemy positions. The Fiat-Ansaldo M-11/39—the first Italian cannon-armed tank—first entered combat in September 1940 in North Africa, and the much better M-13/40 in October 1940 during the Greek campaign; however, both were inferior to tanks being used by the Allies.

Lacking adequate capabilities, Italian armor proved mostly ineffective. The Special Armored Brigade organized in Libya by Valentino Babini—despite achieving some limited success at first—was destroyed at Beda Fomm by the British Army when attacking in small detachments. The "*Centauro*" armored division took part in the Greco–Italian war and received its first M-13/40 tanks in December 1940, deploying them in January 1941, but many were lost to Greek artillery fire. With the experience obtained fighting in Africa, the Italian armored divisions were reorganized in 1942 into a three tank battalion and three infantry battalion structure, combined with a field artillery regiment that included two battalions of self-propelled guns and one antiaircraft battalion, plus reconnaissance and engineer battalions. Regrettably, such a move was too late.

If the lessons learned in Spain had been understood and implemented, later results at the operational level could have been different. Perhaps they would not have been as successful as the German *Panzertruppe*, but they would not have suffered such humiliating defeats as in Greece or Africa. There were lessons that should have been learned from the Spanish encounters. Valentino Babini said of the need for tanks and their role in modern warfare: "tanks for all, tanks spearheading, tanks for all missions." Therefore, there was a need for more and better tanks than the Fiat L3. The discourse was no longer about further cooperation between tanks and infantry, according to Babini, but about "tanks and their supporting infantry whose only mission was that of protecting tanks from assault weapons, antitank weapons and artillery." Colonel Babini went on to make a proposal for the future employment of armor: "All support means for the infantry, in the offensive, must be armored and must include heavy tanks for achieving a breakthrough, medium tanks for close support and for penetrating in depth, both cannon and machine gun-armed, as well as assault tanks machine gun-armed to go alongside the infantry."[5]

Even while the Spanish Civil War was still raging, Italian tankers continued implementing some of the lessons and experiences learned. At the end of April 1938, the Italian Tank Battalion (*Raggruppamento Carri*/CTV) drafted a special report on the results of recent operations on the Aragon front and the splitting of Republican-held territory into two. Signed again by Colonel Babini, the report confirmed all that was learnt following the capture of the city of Santander in northern Spain and opened the way for a new debate on tank employment procedures, an idea perhaps already grasped by the Germans.

In the chapter "Conclusions and Remarks" ("*Reflessioni e deduzioni*"), Colonel Babini's report mentions the "confirmed exceptional usefulness of high mobility units [*unita celeri*] when in battle," and, entering into details, states that if the tank battalion within the Italian CTV would have had the structure of a true high mobility unit, the outcome of the battle of Guadalajara would have been quite different.[6] Babini was clear on how armored troops should be organized: he mentions tanks suited to the nature of the mission, the need for tanks to be organized into tactical units, and the case for mass employment of armored forces. On the issue of infantry and tanks besides for reasons of mobility and speed, Babini's solution was that of creating heavy-tank task force units where infantry and combat engineers were integrated and subordinated to the tank force commander. At the same time, Babini spoke of the need for close coordination and support of tactical aviation.

To conclude, for the Italian military, the relative success of their small fast units, together with the mirage of the Nationalists' final victory, merely reconfirmed their own otherwise generally inadequate priorities and policies, as soon evidenced in World War II.

Perhaps the European military command that drew the best lessons from the civil war was the German command, which believed that the Spanish conflict was a special kind of war from which it would be a mistake to draw any major new conclusions. But even the Germans did not altogether draw proper conclusions about the need to improve their basic antitank weapons and speed up production of newer, more efficient, and better-armored tanks, as the invasion of Poland in 1939 proved, with most of the German armored units still being equipped with *Panzer I* and *Panzer II* light tanks.

According to reports sent to Germany by Lieutenant Colonel Von Thoma, the experience obtained by the Germans from the Spanish Civil War ultimately helped them in speeding up the production of gun-armed tanks, especially the *Panzer III* and *IV* types. Nevertheless, the misleading results of the Nationalist victory probably gave them some false reassurance, as even when Operation *Barbarossa* began in June 1941, the bulk of the *panzer* force still had more tanks of the *Panzer I* and *II* types in its inventory than the better-armed *Panzer IV*; the latter, though, was capable of confronting the new T-34 and KV-1 Soviet tanks that were far superior to anything within the German armory.

The Spanish Civil War also brought to the table the convenience of engaging enemy tanks at maximum range: some German reports mentioned no less than 3,000 meters, a distance that is considered more than adequate for today's standards but was out of the question then, unless they were thinking about the mighty 88mm guns. Further major conclusions were come to by the Germans regarding tank operations during the war. Von Thoma reported:

> The combination of tanks with motorized infantry qualified armored units to accomplish many combat tasks in which both types of units complemented each other [the failure to do so was the main reason for the Soviet mistakes] The speed of tanks, on the march

and in combat, made command and timely appraisal of the situation very difficult. Close cooperation with aircraft was therefore necessary for command, reconnaissance and combat [this was clearly understood by the Nationalists and the Germans from the very beginning of the civil war] Only the employment of tanks in depth promises success [a 2-mile wide front was considered as the smallest front for the employment of an armored division then] Employment of tank-only units was considered only suitable in rare cases and adequate mostly against limited objectives.

Von Thoma added that General Franco, as a typical general from the old school, always wanted to distribute the available tanks among infantry units, but most of the Nationalist victories happened when tanks were concentrated together, even if in close coordination with other arms. It seems that Franco and von Thoma were always at odds on this issue; the latter recalled: "the Spaniards learnt quickly but also forgot quickly."

How important the German *panzer* component was in the Spanish Civil War in terms of the final victory is hard to quantify. While it is true that the war gave the Germans an opportunity to see tank tactics practiced in a live situation, Franco and the Nationalist generals—veterans of the North African counterinsurgency campaigns of the Rif War—were fully conditioned to the requirements of a civil war where it was necessary to grind down local opposition thoroughly, territory by territory, rather than bypass it. Yet their interest in *blitzkrieg*-type mobile warfare was intermittent at best, leaving the *panzers* mainly confined to an infantry-support role.

Von Thoma's observations determined that, firing steel-core armor-piercing ammunition, the dual machine guns of the *Panzer I* could disable a T-26 or BT-5—which were scarcely better armored than the *Panzer I*—at short range. However, the Soviet tanks all carried the excellent 45mm Russian cannon; all the Spanish/Soviet gunners had to do was to open fire at the longest ranges possible to destroy a *Panzer I*, allowing the latter no opportunity to do more than merely scratch their paintwork. No wonder that captured Soviet tanks were greatly prized on the Nationalist side. Captured T-26s that the Nationalists managed to return to action ended up constituting the most potent component of Franco's armored force. Then again, the *Panzer I* was undoubtedly quite effective in an infantry support role, as long as it didn't encounter any Soviet tanks along the way.

Despite the important lessons learnt, the Germans did not plan the development of the *Wehrmacht* around their Spanish experience. They failed to draw proper conclusions about the need to improve antitank weapons and protection. Nor can it be said that the clear evidence of superior Soviet tank designs spurred them into rapid improvement of their own better types.

According to Professor Mary R. Habeck, from Johns Hopkins University in the United States, beyond unsatisfactory results, German officers drew two main conclusions on the use of tanks during the early part of the Spanish Civil War. The first was an affirmation of the initial lessons: Russian tanks performed better than Italian and German ones. Russian tanks were considered excellent for defensive action, but were also a good offensive weapon. The second lesson was that it was difficult to make conclusive decisions about tactics based on the Spanish experience, as conditions had been specific to the conflict alone; too few vehicles had taken part, and the terrain in Spain had been particularly difficult for the successful use of tanks, as opposed to the Northern European plains. The German General Staff concluded that the belligerents had not used the tanks "in accordance with their offensive purpose." Both German and Soviet tanks had been subordinated to infantry, and had been mostly treated as heavy infantry weapons. For all these reasons, the German High Command refused to draw any major conclusion on tank tactics or their operational use, reserving any judgment until witnessing the use of tanks in a larger conflict.[7]

Further details and lessons learned were recorded in the official report on the Spanish Civil War from the German Army General Staff (*Generalstab des Heeres*) dated March 30, 1939:

> *Panzer* tanks were never used in action in a battalion-size unit by the Nationalists. Usually in small packets, the *panzers* were attached directly to and escorted the infantry as armored heavy infantry weapons. Based on the judgment of the troops and their achievement the *Panzer I Ausf A "Krupp"* variant, covered 5,000 to 8,000 kilometers each and the *Ausf B "Maybach"* covered 2,000 to 4,000 kilometers each. Both tanks were considered a success from the viewpoint of mechanical reliability. Light tanks are useful only when armed with flamethrowers, as they can't hit anything by firing their machine guns while moving. However, they themselves are vulnerable to machine guns firing special ammunition. The nozzle for the small flamethrower can be readily secured in the right-hand machine-gun mount in the *Panzer I*. However, a longer range is desired because relatively high losses of crews tend to occur. In general, the *panzer* tanks employed in Spain in small numbers and without other supporting weapons have mainly proven to be inferior, very seldom superior to the antitank defense that was also only available in small numbers. The 45mm gun of the Russian tanks shoots high-explosive shells in an arcing flight path. The effectiveness of these shells is unsatisfactory. It also shoots armor-piercing shells at a flatter trajectory. Due to poor steel quality, the penetrating ability of the Russian armor-piercing shells is significantly lower than the corresponding German armor-piercing shells. The Russian AP shells can only penetrate 40mm armor plate at a range of 100 meters. In addition, up to 75 percent of the base fuses fail to detonate.

In a way, the Spanish Civil War established the axiom of the main battle tank as we understand it today. British General Fuller, a casual observer of the war, commented: "The three types of tanks that I have seen in Spain—Italian,

German and Russian—are not the result of tactical study but are merely cheap mass production, from the standpoint of a machine." He was clearly advocating for a gun-armed tank, with full protection and high reliability as a weapon system. Yet Fuller was not fair in his appreciation because by then, in 1936, not even the British Army was in much better shape than the three main nations involved in Spain.

British tanks, except for some heavily armored variants, were unsatisfactory. Most were weakly armored, still only carrying machine guns early in World War II. Emphasizing mobility, as Fuller did, the British had not paid enough attention to their tanks' ability to fight other tanks. More worryingly, the standard "cruiser" tanks were unreliable, often breaking down. Improved design was delayed by a lack of attention, and British tank design caught up with that of the Germans only near the end of World War II. By the mid-1930s, the British armored force was split between the relatively new Royal Tank Corps and a few reluctantly mechanized cavalry units that had only slowly adjusted to the change from horses to armored vehicles. The attitude of tank fanatics like Fuller and Liddell Hart actually hampered the armored units' development.[8] In the United States, even if the Tank Service was formed in 1918, it was disbanded following the war in 1920 and an armored force was not formed until 1940, only becoming a permanent branch of the U.S. Army in 1950.

Liddell Hart[9] made some interesting references on the employment of armor in the Spanish Civil War:

> It was a great mistake to consider the Spanish Civil War as proof of inefficiency of the mechanized forces. On the contrary the mechanized troops proved that they should move cross-country by preference and in a wide front and that when employed in such a way they contributed a great deal to the achievement of success. If mechanized troops were used extensively at their advantage, they contributed very efficiently to the defense. The most suitable procedure for the defense was the mobile defense rather than a strong-point based defense.

Against the 122 *Panzer Is* that Germany supplied to the Nationalists during the war, the Soviet Union provided the Republicans with some 281 heavier T-26 and 50 BT-5 tanks. The first notable impact of Soviet participation was felt on the Central front in combat around Madrid from mid-October to November 1936. The Soviet crewmen played a key part, entering battle on October 29 in a mobile counterattack against advancing Nationalist troops. However, Republican commanders were never able to develop effective combined-arms operations, so successful tank attacks were generally poorly supported and never sustained for long.

The mistakes made by the combined Soviet–Spanish leadership were not correctly understood, and the disbandment of the existing Soviet armored formations proved disastrous in 1941. The superiority of their equipment gave the Soviets some dangerous peace of mind, and by 1941, the T-34 had not yet been introduced in sufficient numbers. The Soviets also never understood the importance of close cooperation between air support and armor, or the key role of mechanized infantry working together with tanks. Nevertheless, their organization of armored units proved to be more efficient and has lasted even until today, with three tanks per platoon, 10 tanks and three platoons per company, 30 tanks and three companies in a regiment, and one independent tank regiment per division.

Mary R. Habeck,[10] one of the leading Western specialists in armored warfare, wrote on the Soviet experience in Spain: "Soviet officers unlike their German counterparts, believed that the conflict presented a valid picture of a future great war. The Soviet command staff became convinced that the Spanish war was a reliable model of modern war and treated each new experience of combat as a valuable lesson for how the Soviet Army should fight in the future." Soon after the Soviet military intervention began, Marshal Voroshilov issued orders detailing the specific tactics and technology that his men were to study and test.[11]

The Soviets formed a commission[12] reviewing the organization of the Red Army's tank forces. Soviet experiences during the Spanish Civil War led commanders who served there to recommend against the use of large, mechanized formations, chiefly due to technological limitations in communication and vehicle effectiveness. The 1935 Soviet tank corps (that had two tank brigades and one motorized rifle brigade on its force structure, with a total of 348 tanks) was disbanded in favor of a motorized division that had only 275 tanks but more infantry. The most important aspect of this change was that the new 1939 motorized division wholly emphasized the infantry-support role, with little focus on exploitation into the rear of an enemy force's disposition.

The Republicans were heavily influenced by the Soviet practice of massed armor attacks. It is interesting to note that the Soviets were notably reluctant to let Spanish crews operate their vehicles. Because they were unfamiliar with the peculiarities of the Spanish terrain, they were overly cautious with their tanks, and initially, operations orders reflected a high degree of indecisiveness. The Soviets finally agreed to mixed crews for political reasons, but this often caused more problems and resulted in considerable squabbling, which sometimes degraded mission accomplishment.

The Republicans often moved their tanks without any artillery preparation or the support of infantry. This made them vulnerable to enemy antitank weapons, and even to hand grenades or incendiary devices. Therefore, results on the battlefield were often disappointing, even when the Republicans held as much as a three-to-one advantage in the number of tanks. They were most successful in situations where their more powerful onboard weapons gave the Republican tanks no chance either to close or withdraw, such as when blocking known Nationalist avenues of approach or conducting armored ambushes. Little or no effort was made to combine armor and aerial assaults, an aspect of mobile warfare where the Germans undoubtedly succeeded. Conversely, Republican tanks were employed effectively in the defense and in counterattacks.

No other major European army apparently devoted as much attention to the presumed lessons of the Spanish war as did the Soviet Red Army. The study of operations in Spain, as well as of German and Italian equipment, was on a massive scale. But the issue is whether the Red Army commanders learned accurate lessons or merely managed to deceive themselves, as historian Stanley Payne concludes. Soviet commanders obviously made a fundamental mistake in taking the Spanish conflict as a valid scenario for a future European war. The armies in Spain for the most part lacked the weapons, firepower, leadership, and training to provide many lessons applicable to major mid-20th-century campaigns. This is especially true when Spain's topography is compared with that of Eastern Europe. Mountains played a major role in the Spanish struggle, but are almost absent in European Russia and most of Poland and eastern Germany. However, it must not be forgotten that German armor managed to advance through the hilly Ardennes on two occasions, as well as through the Balkans during the invasion of Greece in 1941.

The most serious error made by the Soviet commanders in trying to learn from Spain concerned armor doctrine and organization, but it is also a mistake to overlook improvements that the Red Army was able to make in many individual technical areas, ranging from administration and engineering to specific weapons systems. Though Soviet tanks were by far the best in Spain, they also revealed notable shortcomings, which prompted Soviet planners to accelerate the development of the T-34, which became one of the best tanks in World War II. The experience of the Spanish war was not decisive in any of these areas, but the intensive studies on the war did play a role in the development of better Soviet armaments and even in its technical execution.

The Soviet Army's lessons of the war in Spain were summarized in a 1939 study, which began by noting that such lessons were important as all modern combat arms had taken part in the fighting and the results were likely to be absorbed by the major European armies. Specific tactical lessons of the conflict were highlighted, including the need for infantry attacks to be supported by tanks, the need for coordination between the infantry, armor, and artillery, as well as the vulnerability of tanks to antitank defenses without such coordination. Regarding the use of tanks defensively, the report singled out their role as a key element in carrying out local counterattacks based on several examples of the 1st Armored Brigade in 1937. The study was extremely cautious in drawing any lessons on the use of armor en masse, as there was no experience on the use of large armor formations in Spain. The report was skeptical about the possibilities of using independent tank groups to achieve breakthroughs in the face of well-prepared defenses. The Soviet General Staff view was that the tanks' full potential had not been displayed in Spain and that the Soviet Army must continue to pursue plans to use tanks, but on a mass scale, with full artillery support. Marshal Georgiy Zhukov's later successful use of mechanized formations to defeat the Japanese Army at Khalkin Gol in 1939 further reinforced the advocates of armored warfare.

Armor–infantry cooperation was not the only area of concern in Soviet analyses of their experiences in Spain. Command, control, and communications were poor, with radio equipment, due to technological flaws and lack of experienced operators, never working well. Additional issues pointed out by Soviet observers included a lack of reconnaissance before tank attacks, which forced the Republicans to attack blind many times, and the inadequacy of depending on movement to save the tanks. Traveling at 35mph did not guarantee that vehicles would not be hit by artillery and increased the chances of falling into antitank traps. Visibility from inside the tanks was also poor, while the motion of the vehicles caused inaccurate fire. However, if the Soviet Army sometimes drew inaccurate lessons from the war, it was not alone. For most French military observers, the Spanish war tended to reconfirm the importance of defense and antitank warfare.

The outcome of these combined issues was inordinately high losses of tanks, which led to some interesting conclusions on the Soviet side about the future employment of armored units. Between October 1936 and February 1937, the Republican forces lost no less than 52 tanks—25–30 percent of their deployed tanks—destroyed each day of battle. By mid-September 1937, the Republicans only had 170 tanks serviceable out of a total of 256 T-26s delivered since mid-October 1936. It has been argued that if the Soviet Union sent 256 tanks to Spain, and during a half-year of combat, 63 had been lost; multiplying this by two would mean 126 lost in a year. Thus, the normal rate of attrition for tanks in a year would be around 50 percent of the total force employed. Unquestionably, this was a high figure.[13]

It must be taken into account that because tanks arrived in several shipments, and because the fronts where tanks became employed were widely separated from each other, the Republicans very rarely used more than 70–80 tanks at once, and the same was true for the Nationalists. With these parameters in mind, one can estimate that the rule for yearly permanent tank losses could be much higher, three to four times the initial strength of the combat force. The conclusion taken from this was that tanks would suffer massive destruction in a major war.

General Pavlov thought, nevertheless, that tanks had fought well in short, independent battles such as at Jarama, and even better when they had cooperated properly with infantry, artillery, and air support at Guadalajara. The infantry was helpless against tanks, while artillery and air forces did not pose a serious threat to an armored attack. Without question, tanks needed the infantry, but the infantry needed the tanks just as much.

Nationalist armor and antitank tactics were generally more sophisticated and effective. Their armored attacks were preceded by a thorough analysis of the enemy and the terrain. The Nationalists made up for the smaller caliber of their tank weapons by falling back at the appropriate time to bring enemy tanks within range of antitank guns and the 88mm guns of the Condor Legion, which proved to be excellent against armor.

The Republican People's Army never became a fully cohesive skilled army, though it sometimes fought well enough. Yet the Soviet advisers were not impressed by the Nationalist forces, even during the early stages of the war. Militarily speaking, the Spanish Civil War was a low-intensity conflict punctuated by occasional high-intensity battles. There is no question that Soviet assistance postponed the Republicans' defeat, though at no time was it of sufficient magnitude to give them a major chance of victory. German and Italian assistance was not much more decisive than that of the Soviets, but Mussolini made a major commitment to victory in Spain, while the technical quality of German assistance was markedly superior to that provided by the Soviets. Overall, the German and Italian escalation in military aid in November and December 1936 raised the stakes to a point where Stalin was no longer willing to make a direct bid for victory, in the hope of more favorable geostrategic conditions in Europe in the future.

The Spanish Civil War was the first conflict in Europe after World War I where an extensive use of tanks took place, following their debut on European battlefields in 1915. It happened at a key moment in armament history, when production was increasing in many European countries, but especially in Great Britain, France, Germany, Italy, the Soviet Union, and even Czechoslovakia. For many, the Spanish war was seen as a kind of laboratory to test out their equipment and doctrine.

Many authors insist that the Spanish Civil War provided few clear tactical lessons, whereas it actually provided many. It is another matter whether or not they were taken into account. Tank employment in Spain was certainly unique, but a bright observer could draw important conclusions about the nature of armored warfare there. The Spanish war demonstrated above all that tanks should not be split into small groups nor used by non-trained crews, and that senior commanders needed a better tactical understanding of the tank's capabilities. Using the Spanish experience to validate any preconception on armored warfare—as did the French and, to a point, the British—was a misuse of the lessons. A British military attaché in Spain during the war wisely observed that "the greatest caution must be used in concluding general lessons from this war as little adroitness and it will be possible to use it to prove any preconceived theory."[14]

While most military analysts in the mid-1930s had some firm ideas about tank warfare in Spain, a 1939 study at the U.S. Army Infantry School, Fort Benning, by Captain Thomas Stark mentioned that "the lack of detailed information precluded any comprehensive analysis."[15] Spain was indisputably not a proving ground for *Blitzkrieg*—after failing to take Madrid in the winter of 1936, it became obvious that Franco did not want a swift end to the war—but some significant technological lessons could be learnt.

To start with, the Spanish war showed that tank-versus-tank combat would be from then on the primary mission for main battle tanks. But it also proved that armored warfare would not be cheap, as better engines and armaments, combined with improved armor, would rapidly escalate both purchase prices and operating costs for a substantial tank fleet. It was clear that not all countries would be able to cope; indeed, the crippled economy of Spain never allowed the development of a reasonable armor force for the Spanish Army.

According to Spanish General Ignacio Despujol Sabater, who retired from the army in 1931, poor employment of tanks applied mainly to the Republicans. However, in November 1936, during the battle of Madrid, as can be seen in the documentary *Spain in Arms*,[16] Nationalist tanks advanced in a line, equi-spaced by about 60 meters, but with infantry strung out between the tanks rather than clustered behind them for cover. Similar tactics were also evident during the battle of Teruel. It was thus obvious that the Nationalists had much to learn abiout tank–infantry cooperation too.

Many former Spanish Nationalist combatants smiled when speaking of tanks. They recounted approaching tanks without risk from their blind side, then throwing a bottle of gasoline over it followed by a hand grenade. The tanks then often burst into flames. Moroccan soldiers were experts in capturing or destroying Russian tanks with just blankets, which they threw into the road wheels or tracks' cogs, often throwing the tracks out and stalling the tank. They then used another blanket soaked in gasoline, which they tossed over the turret and set on fire. Adequate infantry cooperation would have rendered such actions impossible. Yet it was not the tankers' fault, with the blame instead at the door of the commanders who employed the tanks under such conditions.

When tanks proved incapable of the tasks entrusted to them, such as clearing the way for the infantry, they were instead employed as assault artillery guns. However, accompanying the infantry and laying broadside to provide fire support made them more vulnerable to antitank guns. Nationalist troops at the battle of Brunete made a wiser use of their tanks, employing them in close liaison with the infantry.

Mechanized operations did not play a major role in the Spanish Civil War, as neither side had sufficient mechanized equipment. This reason may appear naïve, but one makes war with what one has. Before the war, the Spanish Army had neglected tanks and mechanized equipment as evidenced by its intervention against the leftist rebellion in Asturias in 1934 where it could field only infantry units with some artillery support and not a single armored vehicle. Public opinion and morals imposed a form of war applicable to the mass of mobilized population, not just to elite warriors. The consideration of making use of everything they possessed, men and arms, played a capital role in Spain in the composition of armies. Because of that, troops had certain traits and adopted specific methods of combat while equally lacking particular aspects of combat.

Both warring parties split their tank units and divided them piecemeal between their infantry, but especially the Nationalists. At the battle of Teruel, they even assigned tank platoons and sections to larger units such as brigades or divisions. The tank was employd as nothing more than a supplementary fire platform. The course of the Spanish war in 1938 was discouraging for anyone who thought that tanks were the decisive weapon of the future. Even though more tanks than ever took part in the conflict, they had not made a convincing impact in any battle, nor had they made an overwhelmingly positive impression on any of the observers of the war.

On the matter of the usefulness of armor and tanks, the Spanish Civil War provided no conclusions. When forced by circumstances, tanks were employed in close liaison with other arms. The war sought to use all available weapons in the best way. The main difference was that on the Nationalist side, these were combined for maneuver. Both sides did employ recently designed tanks, only to often find that they were not always ideally suited for the missions they were assigned.

It is difficult to find a balanced assessment of armored warfare in the civil war. Works that focus on World War II or deal with a comprehensive history of tanks, either avoid this issue altogether or treat it cursorily as a quick introduction to later more interesting events. Consequently, this review of tank employment in Spain aims to prove helpful in gaining a better understanding of Spanish armored combat. The technological superiority of Soviet armor came to matter only at the tactical level, and neither German nor Russian doctrine were fully put to the test. By default, what happened in Spain degenerated into a series of *ad hoc* tactical adjustments by commanders who were understandably more concerned with accomplishing missions than proving theories.

There is no doubt that the Spanish Civil War was not a successful testing ground for armored warfare. To be fair, much of the land where the main campaigns and battles were fought was unsuitable for a massive use of armor. Moreover, tanks were not developed enough, nor were the other arms trained to cooperate with them to conduct the sort of operations envisaged by the mechanization theorists of the 1920s and 1930s. Therefore, it must come as no surprise that the Spanish commanders did not think of any other use for tanks beyond the role of supporting the infantry. The only partial exceptions were Republican General Vicente Rojo's plan to seize Zaragoza in 1937 and the Nationalist breakthrough on the Aragon front in March 1938, but these were operations limited in time and space.

Nonetheless, there were differences between the Republicans and the Nationalists. Both based their use of armor on the Spanish pre-war doctrine, but the Nationalists remained attached to this concept and their German advisers—surely aware of their armor's limitations—seem to have been satisfied with only introducing minor tactical innovations, such as using larger tactical units or employing antitank guns as support. Indeed, evidence shows that the Germans were mainly worried about organizational matters and Spanish commanders' poor understanding of elementary tank tactics. However, above all, there was a single, coherent policy. By contrast, evidence does not show any such coherence on the Republican side. Officers were trained following the Spanish regulations in force before the conflict, whereas the Republican command issued instructions based on battlefield experience, which often differed significantly from pre-war doctrine. How did an officer reconcile the teachings of the staff college, where he learnt that tanks must not pursue the enemy, with General Rojo's new instructions on advancing deep into the enemy rear? This issue was made worse due to the nature of most of the Republican officer corps. If even the regular officer corps of foreign armies were hard put to assimilate the procedures of armored warfare, it is easy to understand why the improvised officers of the Republican Army so often failed to use and understand armor effectively. It was no different from present times, when tanks are still subordinated to the infantry.

The fighting in Spain ended on the last day of March 1939, and five months later much of Europe was at war. There was no time to ponder on data gathered and conclusions reached; war followed war much too quickly. Yet Spain held clues to the war that arrived in Europe. The weapons used in Spain by the Germans, Italians, and Soviets were not outdated relics surplus to their armies; they were largely their armies' standard equipment and were employed based on tactical doctrine learned during peacetime training in Germany, Italy, and the Soviet Union. Light, fast tanks sent to Spain by Germany and Italy proved vulnerable to antitank guns and to the heavier-armored and armed Soviet tanks. All tanks were in peril when employed individually or in small groups, without the protection of artillery or aviation. The attachés and their sources thus insisted that tanks had to be employed en masse and in combination with infantry, aviation, and artillery to be effective.

The use of tanks in Spain also proved that the advantages of heavy armor and armament outweighed the associated loss of speed. Effective antitank guns, especially when combined with obstacles, served to slow down or destroy enemy tanks. As the tanks of the future would surely become heavier, there were signs in Spain to suggest that antitank weapons would likewise become larger and more powerful. The Germans' successful use of the 88mm gun as both a direct-fire weapon and antiaircraft gun was an indicator of the direction in which defensive weapons could develop.

The stabilized conditions at the front when tanks arrived during the war, coupled with the relatively small numbers of vehicles deployed, created circumstances where the various theories of operations designed by other countries could not be executed. Instead, tanks became tactical weapons normally employed in support of operations, either offensive or defensive.

Tanks showed some value in pursuit, as demonstrated by the Italians at Malaga, and as a counterattack force, as shown by the Republicans at Madrid, but only if used prior to the enemy organizing their defenses and bringing forward antitank weapons. Tanks also took part in urban combat, in various villages and cities, where they were most vulnerable to antitank measures and improvised devices. One lesson was clear from all this: tanks, even during limited operations, required mobile infantry support to neutralize antitank defenses.[17] Regardless of the promise independent tank and mechanized action held, combined arms operations involving tank and dismounted infantry were to be expected.

German personnel avoided engagements with Russian tanks whenever possible and increasingly limited themselves to instructional duties only. Spaniards commanded the tanks in battle as they had before the Germans' arrival and it would not be until the war's closing months, during the offensive in Catalonia, that tanks would take part in a decisive operational offensive. Tank versus tank engagements, whenever they took place, continued to favor the Republican tanks but it was to no avail at all, as in a few weeks the Republic had lost the war. Despite the personnel turnover rate and the small number of tanks available, the tank's great potential as a close support weapon for non-mechanized infantry assaults became apparent and the still unfulfilled promise of independent operations did not make this occurrence any less true.

Soviet experience also showed that tanks, although they were real purpose-built offensive weapons, were often a front commander's most effective stop-gap, especially when neither artillery nor air support were available (and this is precisely what the Germans tried to do in Normandy, in 1944). The positive psychological impact of even just a single T-26 company on the defenders of Madrid was fully understood by both sides.

When considered in their true perspective, rather than in hindsight-aided assessments of later German successes against Poland, France and the Soviet Union, tank actions in the Spanish Civil War, especially the opening engagements, appear neither as flawless manifestations of later "*blitzkrieg*" doctrine nor as unqualified manifestations of the Soviets' intention in long range independent operations.

In the United States, attaché reports from Spain reinforced the somehow parochial attitude of most of the Army's leadership at the time and even the ground combatant arm branches. The Chief of the Army's General Staff, General Malin Craig, stated that a balanced army could never "dispense with a proper proportion of horse-mounted cavalry and horse-drawn artillery."[18] The field artillery also continued to view the tank as an infantry-accompanying weapon; an idea that had not changed much since 1918.

Most U.S. Army attachés stationed in Europe, beginning with Colonel Stephen Fuqua, the attaché in Madrid, who was the former Chief of Infantry, reported that lightly armored tanks armed only with machine guns were unable to overcome determined enemy fire. These lessons were misread in the United States, and in 1939, the M 2 medium tank, underpowered and underarmored, was introduced. Fuqua's opinion was that tanks did not prove themselves in separate offensive operations in Spain as they were effectively challenged by antitank guns. Therefore, the main conclusion was that tanks were only useful when in support of attacking infantry.

Regarding military operations in Spain, the view of the U.S. Army Chief of Staff was that tanks were not successful due to antitank weapons, insufficient armor protection, mechanical defects, tactical errors in their employment and inadequate support from artillery and aviation. In the meantime, General Adna Chaffee[19] was also paying close attention to events in Spain. A report he received from the General Staff stated that tanks used in Spain were unsuccessful in almost all operations. The issues identified were numerous, such as inadequate crew training and poor discipline, mechanical deficiencies, insufficient terrain reconnaissance, lack of infantry and artillery support, the questionable use of tanks against strong obstacles and villages, inadequate numbers, and the reported superiority of antitank guns. As far as the new mechanized cavalry was concerned, the Spanish Civil War provided ample evidence of what not to do.

American mechanized and armored cavalry pioneers at Fort Knox believed that the war's new weapons—armored cars, self-propelled artillery, tanks, and mechanized infantry vehicles—required new mission-oriented tactics rather than tank tactics inherited from World War I and demonstrated in Spain. The consensus among American armor specialists was that tank tactics used during the Spanish Civil War were unsound and tanks were improperly used.

Throughout the 1930s, the military debate had revolved around the issue of mechanization. After World War I, it was clear that airplanes and tanks had appeared on the battlefield and were there to stay, but there was not a clear view on how this should happen. The interwar era witnessed all the world's major armies looking for an improved solution, seeing the tank as a tool to overcome the trench–machine gun–artillery deadlock. Conservative thinkers, including most general staffs, were unimpressed by the new technologies. Spanish military minds were not particularly isolated on that issue, and like many others, considered that the new machines, especially tanks, were just role players, but that the battlefield still belonged to "the infantryman, and to the horse, to a certain extent."

In Spain, tanks restored mobility and maneuver to the battlefield, and in so doing, proved that war and tactics could consist of more than launching bloody frontal assaults with massed infantry. Even if the Spanish Civil War was quickly overshadowed by World War II, for a brief time in 1939 it was Europe's most modern war, fought with weapons newly developed since 1918, pitting industrialized European nations against each other. It was truly worthy of military interest.

CHAPTER 21

A Reappraisal of Equipment and Armament

The Spanish Civil War offered several lessons for the design of tanks and armored vehicles. The lightly armored tanks employed during the conflict were too vulnerable against almost any heavy weapon available on the battlefield, even to what we may call FEDs (Field Expedient Devices), such as "Molotov cocktails," the forerunner of today's IEDs. On the other hand, the conditions of Spain's battle-torn terrain and all kind of natural and artificial barriers made progress difficult for tanks and speed irrelevant. As the tanks could not travel at high speeds and had to slow down, they became easy prey: therefore they needed better protection.[1] On-board tank radios were necessary for command and control purposes.

Major General J. F. C. Fuller,[2] the great tank expert, wrote an interesting letter published in the London *Times* on April 6, 1937, after a visit to the Spanish front line. It included the following:

> The three types of light tanks I have seen, Italian, German and Russian, are mere runabouts, the offspring of cheapness and not of a tactical idea. Regarding tank tactics I could discover none. Tanks are used singly or scattered over wide fronts. Up to three weeks ago, the largest number used in an attack by either side, I was told, was 15; therefore, there have been no mechanized battles.
>
> So far, from the point of view of mechanization, this war has, I think, proved that the light tank is not really a combat machine at all. It is an indifferent armored scout but could be made a highly efficient one if its track base were lengthened.
>
> To sum up the experiences of tanks in Spain, it cannot be said that any final tactical lessons have been learnt and we are no nearer a conclusion as to whether a big breakthrough by mechanized forces is possible. But we have gained valuable experience regarding the performance of antitank guns and it seems certain that a tank attack will break down against them if they are present in sufficient quantity and if the element of surprise is lacking.
>
> Various means of defense against tanks have been improvised in Spain in addition to antitank guns. The Moors and Carlists have been adept at setting tanks on fire; gasoline is thrown on them and it is then ignited by a hand grenade. The inside of the tank becomes an inferno and the crew has the choice of remaining inside to meet a horrible death or of coming out and being shot down. A similar method is used against the tracks. The synthetic

> rubber in the track bearings is set alight; this brings the tank to a standstill and it is destroyed by gunfire. Yet another method is to dig a deep wide trench which the tank cannot straddle and from which, once it has entered, it cannot climb out on the farther side. The object of lengthening the track base would be to forestall this method of defense.

Fuller was being unfair, because in 1936, neither the Soviet Union, Germany, nor Italy had better tanks in service than those sent to Spain. Britain had no better armor either at the time. A major issue was that tank operations were poorly developed. The Soviets were rarely able to employ their superiority in tanks to good effect, which resulted in some Soviet Army commanders beginning to question their own doctrine. The small German and Italian tanks sent to Spain could only be used in limited ways. Indeed, by the end of the war, General Franco's best armor was made of by the Russian tanks captured from Republicans and organized into tank units of the Nationalist Army.

Fellow tank advocate Sir Basil Liddell Hart also commented[3] on the quality of tanks used in Spain, especially German and Italian ones:

> In weighing the difficulties met by tanks, account should be taken of the fact that the small German and Italian tanks that have been employed in Spain, were recognized as too small already, and otherwise unsuited for surmounting serious obstacles. This, of course, does not imply that larger and better machines would be unaffected by mud if sufficiently bad. Twenty years ago, Passchendaele taught a lesson in the folly of using tanks in swamp-like conditions, if pursuing an offensive by any means in such conditions.

Both Fuller and Liddell Hart saw the combination of tank and aircraft as the key to future success. Fuller went so far as to call for the abolition of infantry altogether and the conversion of the entire army to tanks. In a clash of armor, he wrote, a foot soldier was nothing more than "an interested bystander."

The Spanish Civil War proved not to have a major impact on the development of armored warfare, but neither did it have any significant influence on tank design. Everybody knew that the tanks used were far too light, too small, and underarmed, but even so, Germany went to war in 1939 with the bulk of its tank force comprising *Panzer I*s and *Panzer II*s, while Italy continued with its fleet of Fiat L3s. Britain and France were exceptions because in the end they built heavier and better tanks such as the Matilda, or the Somuas and Char B, while the Soviet Union was apparently happy with its T-26s and BTs, with only slight improvements.

Soviet equipment

The use of Soviet tanks during the Spanish Civil War provides a clear example of the potential of military technology, but also of the issues of its innovation. The war did have some important consequences in tank technology for the

Red Army, but on the tactical side, many lessons were ignored, distorted, or even worse, misunderstood.

In 1933, the Soviet Army had six types of tanks in service: the T-26 for tank battalions of infantry divisions, BT-5 for mechanized cavalry, T-35 for heavy tank brigades, and some amphibious T-37/T-38 and T-27 light tanks for reconnaissance and scout purposes, with the T-26 and BT models predominating. Of these, only T-26 and BT-5 tanks saw service in Spain. All these tanks varied in firepower and mobility, but none offered protection against anything more than small and medium-arms armor-piercing bullets all around and heavy machine-gun fire at the front.

The experience gained in Spain gave new impetus to Soviet tank design, sparking off some revolutionary thinking. The 1936–39 period saw the adoption of armor capable of keeping out shell splinters, the development of electric welding for armor plate, a special heavy duty engine for tanks—the Diesel C2, a forerunner for the T-34—and new types of running gear, including the excellent Christie suspension, invented in the United States but adopted by the Soviet Union after all other tank-producing countries had rejected it. The intense activity of the second half of the 1930s culminated in the introduction, in 1940, of the T-34/76. This was an outstanding tank that could be considered as the archetype for all successive successful tanks, from the *Wehrmacht*'s Panther to the British Centurion, the U.S. Patton and M60 series, without a doubt the Soviet T-54, and even, to a certain extent, the Federal German Leopard 1.

Soviet tanks mostly made a name for themselves due to their reliability in the field, low unit cost, and ease of manufacture. They proved to be simple, robust vehicles, requiring a minimum of daily maintenance, well suited to the average mechanically naïve tank crewman, as was the case with both Russian and Spanish tankers in 1936. Soviet tanks were generally designed with a ruthless no-frills philosophy that left them with a very rough-edged finish but without compromising any of their key performance requirements. Armor welding could have appeared appalling, but it never reduced the level of protection. Exterior machining also seemed crude, except in key joints and interfaces, where it was quite good. Nevertheless, the T-26 instantly played a dominant role wherever and whenever it appeared on the battlefield in Spain.

The T-26B used in Spain was indeed a light tank, with a combat weight of 10.6 tons and no more than 15mm of RHA (rolled homogenous armor). It was armed with the excellent 45mm Model 32 antitank gun plus two standard Russian 7.62mm DT machine guns. Power was derived from a single GAZ-type T-26 four-cylinder gasoline air-cooled engine[4] that delivered some 90 horsepower (67kw) and could reach a maximum road speed of 25mph, with a range of about 150 miles. The engine, which was a Soviet copy of the Armstrong-Siddeley engine used in the British Vickers 6-ton tank, was located in the rear part of the hull. With a crew of three made up of tank commander, gunner, and driver, it was the first all-Russian production tank armed with both cannon and machine guns.

Sufficiently armored against its machine-gun equipped German and Italian counterparts and well armed with the 45mm gun, the T-26 was only susceptible to antitank guns, artillery, and land mines. However, its potential in Spain was not exploited in full because coordination of infantry and armor formations was virtually non-existent, resulting in tank attacks lacking infantry support and vice-versa. Not surprisingly, there were bounties offered by the Nationalists for every tank captured; when this occurred, all were instantly integrated into Nationalist tank units. Thus the T-26 remained in action until the end of the war, taking part in almost all major battles and with both sides.

The first Soviet T-26 tanks delivered to Spain through Cartagena's harbor were intended for Republican tankers training at the Tank School recently established in Archena, southeastern Spain, about 75 miles away. However, with the situation around Madrid becoming complicated, 15 tanks quickly formed a tank company under Soviet Captain Paul Arman and were sent to the capital. By mid-November 1936, poor handling in combat and Nationalist antitank weaponry had already taken their toll, the Republicans losing no less than 13 tanks, four of them captured.

The way combat was developing during the civil war in Spain allowed Russian tanks to spot the smaller Nationalist tanks, stop, fire from almost a mile away, and penetrate their thin armor. Consequently, the main battle tank of the Spanish Civil War was clearly the T-26, the most widely used and most successful tank on both sides. As was the case with many other Soviet tanks of the early 1930s, the T-26 tank was developed from a British model purchased from the Vickers-Armstrong company; it was commonly known as the "Vickers tank" by Spanish soldiers. More than 12,000 of the T-26 series were built between 1931 and 1940 in the Soviet Union, and at the time of the German invasion in 1941, it still formed the backbone of Soviet armored troops. The T-26 saw action not only in Spain and Russia, but also in Manchuria against the Japanese in 1939 and in the Russo-Finnish War in 1940. It was against the Japanese when its weaknesses in armor were clearly revealed, and subsequently a newer version with improved armor was introduced.

By the time of the battle of Madrid in mid-December 1936, Krivoshein's initial small armored force of T-26 tanks was largely spent, not only due to battlefield casualties, but to mechanical fatigue. There were no established maintenance facilities in the Madrid area, and spare parts were at the time almost non-existent. While Krivoshein's tank force had succeeded in its immediate mission of bolstering the Republican troops defending Madrid, it could not continue to do so forever.[5]

The immediate lessons from the early fighting in the autumn of 1936 mainly concerned technical issues, to keep the force in a fighting state. The Soviet Army had never conducted prolonged tank operations away from their peacetime training bases, so combat experiences in Spain were an eye-opening introduction to the day-to-day technical realities that had plagued tankers ever since World War I. It was clear from the initial fighting that tank units could not be employed non-stop, day and night like infantry, but had to be carefully preserved for the most important missions.

The new Republican Spanish tank crews provided a discouraging experience, and the Soviet practice of assigning a junior crewman to driving duties usually left the tanks in the hands of inexperienced Spanish tankers. This led to abnormally high breakdown rates, forcing the Russians to reorganize crew tasks, with tank commanders sometimes shifted to the driver's position in the hope of keeping the tanks in operating condition. However, this adversely affected the tanks' combat capabilities because the more experienced Soviet commanders were then unable to command the tank and direct gunfire from the driver's position. The loader in a Russian tank was the lowest man in the crew hierarchy, and his inability to reload main gun rounds quickly in combat led many times to losing a gunnery duel against the less capable but quicker German or even Italian tanks.

The T-26 lacked any heating system, as was usual then. So in cold winter weather, such as during the fighting for the town of Teruel, the combat compartment of T-26 tanks was ice cold; a constant draught caused by the engine drawing in air made it even colder for the crew. Turret ventilation was also poor, and when the guns were firing, the crew was almost asphyxiated during prolonged combat.

T-26 tanks were poorly equipped when it came to radio sets for communicating between tanks and with other units, as well as interphone used for communication between individual members of the tank crew. The first production models had no radios, and as a replacement of a proper interphone system they had a speaking tube. Later T-26 tank models were sometimes equipped with radio, but these remained a minority. The rail antenna was vulnerable and usually became inoperative after a few days of fighting. The single most troublesome technical feature on the T-26 was the standard Russian 71-TK-12 radio set.[6] This required very precise and constant tuning, which was soon lost during combat movement. Due to poor radio performance, T-26 tank commanders used flags for signaling, but enemy gunners soon fired on tanks that were seen doing so.

Vision from inside the tank was poor, and it was difficult to identify targets during battle. By Western standards, the T-26 tank was considered to have rather poor optics, which limited visibility outside the tank. Many tanks were limited to the telescopic sight and lacked the optional periscopic sights. Early T-26B tanks only had a periscope for the loader, with late models usually having two, one for the tank loader/commander and another for the gunner. The tank loader's periscope was poorly suited for spotting targets and estimating their range. Likewise, the driver's episcope offered poor vision when the tank was buttoned-up for combat. The gunner's periscope had an aiming reticle for the 45mm gun, but was quite poorly suited for shooting targets. The main gun sight was much better suited for this task and was used for aiming both the 45mm gun and the coaxial DT machine gun. The tank turret and combat compartment had several observation slots, but the turrets were only manually rotated.

As was typical with other tanks of the time, they lacked a built-in fire extinguisher system. There was a manual fire extinguisher, but to use it a crew member had to get outside the tank. The basic design of the engine and its cooling system made T-26 tanks especially vulnerable to attacks with "Molotov cocktails." The main weak point was the radiator, located just above the engine, through which the engine dragged in air. Due to the rear deck location, on top of the armor compartment was an armored grill, which provided a highly vulnerable target for "Molotov cocktails." Since the engine also took air from the fighting compartment, where the tank crew was located, the two were partially connected and any fire in the engine compartment was likely to spread very quickly.

To further extend the life of tanks, the Russians began to use trains or heavy trucks to transport them to their combat positions whenever the units had to move more than a few miles. This was a practice also adopted by the Spanish Army after the war.[7]

The BT-5 fast tank was the other main battle tank employed by the Soviets in Spain. The BT (*Bistrokhodny Tank* = Fast Tank) derived from the American Christie design and was intended for large, independent long-range armored and mechanized units. One of its basic attributes was the tank's ability to run either on tracks or just on the road wheels, but this advantage was never exploited in Spain. The tank running system proved to be unreliable, and due to mechanical failure and bad employment, all tanks of this type were lost by mid-1937 and were never replaced. BT series tanks also saw service during battles against the Japanese in Manchuria and during the Russo-Finnish War, like the T-26. All BT tanks were also employed during early operations following the German invasion in 1941, resulting in their destruction by the then technically superior German forces. Nevertheless, the experience gained with the BT tank was of great use later for the designers of the T-34.

Unquestionably, the designs of American engineer Walter Christie laid the foundations of modern Soviet tanks. During their modification and production, both the Soviet designers and the workers along the entire production line gained immense experience. The first opportunity to deploy and test the new fast tanks in combat was during the Spanish Civil War. This somewhat confusing conflict ultimately became the main weapon proving ground for the future enemies of the Axis powers and the Soviet Union.

On July 24, 1937, the Spanish cargo ship *Cabo San Agustin* sailed from Sevastopol, loaded with 50 BT-5 tanks. These were not new tanks, all having undergone a general retrofit in the Soviet Plant No.48 factory before being shipped to Spain. The tanks were accompanied by a group of Soviet "instructors": mostly members of the V Mechanized Corps of Konstantin Kalinovskiy. The ship broke through the embargo blockade, arriving in Cartagena's harbor on August 18. Spare parts arrived later on board the Soviet ship the *Kursk*. The 50 BT-5 tanks delivered to Spain were mainly deployed during the battles of Zaragoza and Ebro. Unlike what happened with the T-26, captured BTs were never used by the Nationalists.

The BT-5 Model 34 tank was what was called a cruiser tank by the British, with a combat weight of 12 tons and armor of no more than 13mm. Its main armament was the same antitank gun as in the T-26, the ubiquitous 45mm Model 1932, plus a DT machine gun. Equipped with a more powerful Mikulin M-5 gasoline engine, a copy of the American Liberty engine—delivering 400 horsepower—it could reach speeds over 50mph (which offered active protection) and had a range of over 150 miles.

The BT tanks were a type of "convertible tank," a feature designed by Walter Christie to reduce wear of the unreliable tank tracks of the 1930s. In about 30 minutes, the crew could remove the tracks and engage a chain drive to the rearmost road wheel on each side, allowing the tank to travel at high speed on roads. In wheeled mode, the tank was steered by pivoting the front road wheels. However, Soviet tankers soon found the convertible option of little practical use in a country with few paved roads, and as it consumed space and added needless complexity and weight, the feature was dropped from later Soviet designs.

The BT tanks represented significant progress in Soviet armor development. To many observers, BT tanks were the best tanks sent to Spain. They were so significant that they allowed the Soviets to completely change the way tanks were used. BT tanks also played an important role in training new crews and command staff. Unfortunately, the experience gathered in various conflicts was completely wasted during the defense of the Soviet Union in 1941. By mid-August 1939, it was decided to proceed with the development of a new integrally tracked medium tank that began with a modified version, renamed as the BT-7, with a redesigned and distinctive hull, well-shaped sloping frontal armor, but still armed with a 45mm gun. This model ended up becoming the famous T-34, up-gunned and up-armored.

The main armament of both the T-26 and BT-5 tanks was the standard Soviet 45mm M-1932/35 L46 antitank gun, firing an armor-piercing round with a muzzle velocity of 820 m/sec. It also fired HE shells with lower muzzle velocity in an arcing flight path. As secondary armament, both types were armed with one DT 7.62x54mm coaxial machine gun. Sometimes an additional externally mounted machine gun was provided to be used by the tank commander. The T-26 carried a total of 122 rounds[8] for the main gun, while the BT-5 had 115 rounds (about three times the normal loading of modern tanks).

Armor was without doubt a weakness in both types, as maximum thickness was only between 15 and 16mm of RHA. This was later improved, and by 1940, the latest T-26C version had an equivalent of 25mm of RHA, but was still no match for almost all antitank guns then in service with the German *Wehrmacht*. Nevertheless, at the time of the German invasion of the Soviet Union in 1941, the bulk of Soviet armored forces were still equipped with T-26 and BT tanks, and it took some time for better-protected tanks like the T-34 and KV-1 to appear in force with front-line units. Combat weight was slightly over 10 tons for the T-26B, while the BT-5 was slightly heavier, about 12 tons.

Italian Colonel Valentino Babini, head of the armored component of the Italian Volunteer Corps (CTV), made some interesting comments about Soviet equipment after carefully inspecting all vehicles captured during the Spanish Civil War. He referred to the T-26B as "Vickers-Armstrong A" and the BT-5 as "Vickers-Armstrong B," and considered that notwithstanding both being cannon-armed tanks with the excellent Soviet 45mm gun, they had many mechanical failures that ultimately made them unreliable. However, Colonel Babini claimed that a detailed check-up before operations and efficient maintenance would have solved the problem.

Babini was very critical of Soviet logistics: "A Russian tank commander knows how many tanks he has, but doesn't know with how many tanks he will be able to start his mission and what is even worse is that he knows even less with how many tanks he would be able to implement his concept of maneuver or whether he will be able to do so at all." However, the Italians viewed Russian tanks as excellent for carrying out ambushes.

The Italians were more impressed by the Soviet BA-10 armored cars, armed with the same 45mm gun as the tanks, which were much sought after, especially when compared to the obsolete Lancia 1 ZM in service with the Italian CTV. The Soviet 45mm Model 1932 antitank gun was also rated much better than the Italian 47mm gun. The Italians were concerned about the powerful armament of the T-26, often used at very long ranges up to 2,000 yards, and rated the small and older 65mm Model 13 65/17 assault gun better than any other high-velocity guns they had, even if it was not used primarily as an antitank gun.

The T-26 was the most widely used tank of the Spanish Civil War by both armies. Out-gunned, out-maneuvered, and hard-pressed, the Nationalists initially had no effective response to the Russian tank, sparking several interesting developments in tank design and antitank tactics. Despite the T-26's superiority over the German *Panzer I* and Italian L3 CV-33/35 light tanks armed only with machine guns, the Spanish Civil War uncovered a vulnerability of the T-26: its weak armor. Even the frontal armor of the T-26 was easily penetrated by German and Italian machine guns at close range. Italian reports claimed that 20mm Italian and German antiaircraft guns were effective against the T-26 at distances up to 400 meters, while antitank guns such as the German 37mm *Pak 36* were effective up to 500 meters and the Italian 47mm 47/32 M5 up to 600 meters.

Much greater danger was posed by the German 88mm *Flak 18* antiaircraft gun, which was capable of destroying any tank at long range. The 15mm bullet-proof armor of the T-26 provided no protection against it, even when *Flak 18*s were firing HE rounds.

The Soviet Union provided a total of 281 T-26 Model 1933 tanks that were used by the Republicans in almost all battles of the Spanish Civil War. Turrets from T-26 and BT-5 tanks and from BA armored cars that were beyond repair were mounted on Chevrolet 1937s and other armored trucks designed and produced by the Republicans. T-26 tanks often attacked enemy trenches or defensive positions in the narrow streets of Spanish towns without support, where they met strong resistance. Nationalist infantry, especially the Moroccan regulars, attacked them courageously despite heavy casualties, throwing hand grenades and gasoline bombs that were effective against the tanks' engines.

However, not all Soviet commanders recognized the T-26 light tank's obsolescence in the mid-1930s, and projects designing tanks with stronger armor were slow in the USSR. The effect of such decisions was fatal for the Soviet Army in 1941. They also failed to take into account the results of the confrontation between Japanese and Soviet forces in Mongolia in 1939.

The BT-5 tank had few opponents which could match it, so the conclusions from antitank combat in Spain were not deemed relevant. Experience from street fighting and the tank's vulnerability to short-range infantry assaults should have acted as warnings, but little heed was paid to them. Despite all its failures, the BT tank laid down the foundation for modern Soviet tanks. Developing the concept gradually through various prototypes, Soviet engineers reached the balanced T-34 tank concept that later became the symbol of the Red Army's victory in World War II. But the price paid by Soviet tank crewmen was enormous.

Due to the incompetence of their military commanders in Spain, the Republicans were not able to exploit their superiority in armor. Russian tanks took part in several engagements during the first months of the war but did not make a significant contribution to any of them. In the early defense of Madrid in 1936, the Republicans even deployed some tanks on the barricaded streets of the University campus, with little or no impact upon the struggle.

Italian equipment

The Italian tank design used in Spain, called a "tankette" by some authors, was the brainchild of British Lieutenant Colonel Martel,[9] a skilled engineer and veteran of the British Tank Corps in World War I. The idea was to provide advancing infantry with their own automatic weapons, but under protection; unlike heavier tanks, tankettes would be part of an infantry unit's normal compliment of equipment, which is how both Italian and German tanks were used in Spain.

Of all the countries that produced their own tankettes, Italy proved to be the most enthusiastic convert to the concept: by 1939, when the Spanish Civil War ended, the Italian Army had more than 1,300 Fiat CV-33/35 L3 tankettes in active service. The primary attraction of these light tanks was their low cost, proving popular among foreign customers and leading Italy to export around 290 L3 tanks to 11 countries, excluding Spain, before the outbreak of World War II.

In general, Italian combat vehicles used in the Spanish Civil War were handicapped due to the inferiority of their armament, being no match for the heavier enemy Soviet tanks armed with rapid-fire 45mm weapons on rotating turrets. There were other equipment issues; for example, the air intake systems on the tanks and armored cars were not equipped with appropriate filters to protect crewmen from the fine dust that is so prevalent in the Spanish countryside. To protect their faces and mouths from dust, the Italians adapted their gas masks, but to little avail.

The *Carro Veloce* Fiat CV-33 or L3 CV-33 was a light tank of just 3 tons, originally built in 1933. Many CV-33s were retrofitted to meet the specifications of the CV-35 in 1935. In 1938, the CV-33 was renamed the L3/33, while retrofitted CV-35s became known as Light Tank L3/35s. The original CV-33 carried a two-man crew protected by 13mm of welded front armor and 8mm of side armor. Initially, it was armed with a single 6.5mm machine gun, but this was replaced by a twin mount with 8mm machine guns. It was the most numerous of Italian armored fighting vehicles and saw service almost everywhere the Italians fought in World War II, but proved inadequate for modern warfare; its armor was too thin and its armament of only machine guns too weak.

Differences between the L3/CV-35 and L3/CV-33 were few. Both featured riveted and welded construction. The vehicle's commander/gunner sat on the left, while the driver sat on the right. The engine—a FIAT-SPA CV3 water-cooled unit delivering 43 horsepower (32kW)—which allowed a top speed of 26 mph on roads and a range of just 78 miles, was mounted transversely in the rear. A circular radiator was mounted behind the engine. The transmission went from the front to the final drive. The Vickers-Carden-Lloyd type suspension had two three-wheel bogies on leaf springs and a single unsprung wheel on each side.

The usual outcome of meeting Soviet tanks on the battlefield should have forced the Italian command to face the fact that their tanks were hopelessly obsolete. But even though the process of designing and building heavier and better-armed tanks was already under way in Italy, it took a long time for the Italian Army to replace its entire fleet of light tanks. In Spain, Italian as well as German tanks were always outgunned by the Soviet-supplied Republican tanks. The only ways for the Italians to overcome such a weakness were to either rely on their flamethrower tanks carrying out an ambush or to count on the support of attached antitank guns, either the German 37mm *Pak 36* or the Italian 47mm M35. Italian tanks started to tow antitank guns after the battle of Guadalajara, but it was a dangerous and difficult task to dismount and set up the antitank gun, especially when performed in the vicinity of the enemy. Both these Nationalist antitank tactics were close combat procedures that were mostly avoided by the Republicans, who preferred to engage at long ranges.

The Italian antiaircraft Breda 35 cannon, firing its 20mm armor-piercing round, also proved to be an effective weapon when dealing with enemy tanks armored with only 13–15mm of protection. This gun, only recently fielded by the Italians, quickly acquired an excellent reputation due to its success against both ground and aerial targets. Its popularity was such that the Germans refitted several of their own *Pzkw I*s with the Breda 35 and the Nationalist Army asked the Italians to manufacture a modified CV3/35, equipped with the Breda gun for the Spanish Army after the war. Although Spain ordered 40 Italian L3/35 tanks replacing the original armament with the 20mm Breda model 35 gun, this order was subsequently canceled after it was thought that the adaptation of the same gun to the German *Panzer I* would yield better results.[10]

The Nationalist idea of using a 20mm Breda gun instead of the twin 8mm machine-gun mount was not the right answer, as what was really needed was a cannon-armed tank able to confront Soviet tanks rather than a hastily devised interim solution. Italy even considered sending to Spain 40 Fiat 3000 tanks, an Italian version of the French Renault FT-17, but this idea was soon dismissed as unpractical and unreliable. The Italian Fiat L3 required high-intensity maintenance, with sometimes up to 15 hours in a single day for field repairs, resupplying, and tuning up. Such demands put heavy stress on crewmen, some consequently requiring medical attention or transfer to rest areas.

Colonel Babini made an astonishing reference in view of the results of employing Fiat L3 CV-33/35 tanks in Spain, saying that "the assault tank has earned its place in the battlefield." In reality, far from confirming the L3 as a useful breakthrough tank, he wanted to establish once and for all what its tactical role was. He didn't refrain from saying that there were still many aspects which needed improvement on the Fiat L3: starting procedures, avoiding the danger of turning over, its short operational range (just scarcely 78 miles), difficulties in handling and opening of hatches, the lack of radio communications, poor visibility from the inside, and the need for better armament and armor protection. The Fiat L3 relied more on mobility than armor for protection. Thicker armor would have signified more weight and then a more powerful engine, but the L3's size made it virtually impossible to achieve this. A different tank was the only possible answer.

It is easy, in hindsight, to dismiss the Italian concept of a light tank. However, such a judgment is not fair. Martel's notion of small armored vehicles armed only with machine guns as an integral part of an infantry unit, providing them with fire support as they advanced, was never actually put to the test in Britain. Ironically, both Italians and the Nationalists in Spain came closer to fulfilling Martel's original intentions.

In general, the weakest aspect of Italian tank design was their technology. The small size of Italian tanks placed on them unavoidable restrictions that fatally compromised their effectiveness. Mobility required adequate power, but restrictive space limited the types of engines that could fit within a small tank. The small size also interfered with their ability to clear even modest obstacles. Despite being tracked vehicles, Italian light tanks had poor off-road capabilities.

Restrictions on the strength of the power plant of the Italian tanks in turn led to restrictions on the armor thickness they were able to carry; a typical Fiat L3 barely offered protection from small-arms fire. Armor thick enough to resist antitank weapons was out of the question. A crew of two proved to be inadequate, with the commander having to divide his attention between firing the vehicle's weapons and performing the functions of command, yet this was a weakness that also plagued the German *Panzer I*. Once again, it was size that had dictated a crew of no more than two. Size also severely restricted firepower. Even when a few Italian L3 tanks were upgraded with 20mm cannons, that was the limit of what they could accommodate. Consequently, regarding the main characteristics by which the effectiveness of an armored fighting vehicle is judged—mobility, armor protection, and firepower—the Italian light tank, much like the German one, failed on all three counts.

The solution to the dilemma was obvious: what was needed, and not just for Spain, was a larger vehicle than the Italian tank, free of unreasonable restrictions. But it was already too late for Italy. It had neither the financial nor the industrial capacity to manufacture heavier vehicles. Mussolini was only deluding himself by believing that his fleet of "tankettes" represented a force of some armored might.

German equipment

The *Panzer Kpfw* light tank had been designed and was originally intended only as a training tank, but saw front-line service up until 1942. The limitations imposed on Germany following World War I made it necessary to hide the vehicle's real purpose, so it was called the *Landwirtschaftlicher Schlepper* (*La S*), or agricultural tractor, until 1938, when the name *Panzer I* (*PzKpfw I*) began to be used. The first variant (*Ausf A*) weighed only 6 tons, had a two-man crew and was armed with two 7.92mm machine guns on a small turret. The main production version (*Ausf B*) had a more powerful engine and was slightly longer.

The name "*Panzer I*" is short for *Panzerkampfwagen I* (armored fighting vehicle Mark I), and is abbreviated as *PzKpfw I*. However, the tank's official German ordnance inventory designation was *SdKfz 101* (special purpose vehicle 101). In July 1932, the Krupp corporation revealed a prototype with a sloped front glacis plate and a large central casemate, a design heavily influenced by the British Carden Lloyd tankette like in the case of the Italian L3. As the tank's twin 7.92mm MG-13 Dreyse machine guns had already been seen to be largely useless against even the lightest tank armor of the time, the *Panzer I* was restricted by its design to a training and anti-infantry role. Power was provided by a Krupp M305 four-cylinder air-cooled gasoline engine delivering 59 horsepower (44kW), with a quarter-elliptical leaf spring suspension. Its performance was not impressive: it had a range of just 120 miles on roads and a top speed of 31mph.

A mass-produced version was designed by a collaborative team from Daimler-Benz, Henschel, Krupp, MAN, and Rheinmetall, exchanging the casemate for a rotating turret, and was accepted into service, after testing, in 1934. Its official name was *Panzerkampfwagen I Ausführung A* (model A, or more accurately, batch A). The *Ausf A* was under-armored, with steel plates of only 13mm RHA at its thickest. The tank had several design flaws, including suspension problems that made the vehicle pitch at high speed, as well as engine overheating. The driver was positioned inside the chassis and used conventional steering levers to control the tank, while the commander was positioned in the turret where he also acted as gunner. The two crewmen could communicate by means of a voice tube. Machine-gun ammunition was stowed in five bins, containing 25-round magazines.

Many of the issues in the *Ausf A* were corrected with the introduction of the *Ausf B*. The engine was replaced by the water-cooled, six-cylinder Maybach NL 38 TR, developing 98 horsepower (73kW), and the gearbox was changed to a more reliable model. The larger engine required the extension of the vehicle's chassis by 16 inches, which allowed the improvement of the tank's suspension by adding another bogie wheel and raising the tensioner; however, the tank's weight increased by 0.4 tons. The *Ausf A* proved to be underpowered and its very loud 59hp Krupp engine overheated. Both models had an identical turret and superstructure, but the *Ausf B* was longer (it had an additional roadwheel) and had a modified engine deck due to its new engine. In 1935–36, the *Panzer I Ausf A* was experimentally mounted with a Krupp M601 diesel engine, but it could only produce 45hp, so the idea of a diesel-powered vehicle was rejected.

The *Panzer I* first saw combat during the Spanish Civil War. It also saw extensive service during the invasion of Poland in 1939 and France in 1940, but by 1941 it began to be withdrawn from the front line; something that should have happened much earlier. Subsequently, there were numerous variants based on the *Panzer I* chassis: command vehicles which had a large fixed superstructure in place of the turret; self-propelled artillery vehicles fitted with a 150mm assault howitzer; a few chassis were converted to flamethrowers; and the *Panzerjäger I* was armed with a 47mm antitank gun.

The Spanish Nationalist forces dubbed the *Panzer I*s the "*negrillos*" (blacks) due to their dark grey paint. Most were quickly painted in a new lighter scheme. In a report on October 23, 1936, Lieutenant Colonel Warlimont of the German General Staff wrote that "the machine made a somewhat worn-out and by no means modern impression. Its effect is very slight, and it can hardly be considered a decisive weapon in local combat formations."[11]

While *Panzer I* tanks were outclassed by the Soviet T-26s and BT-5s provided to the Republicans, they were also a propaganda tool to showcase the Third Reich and its military might in the years leading up to World War II. The only option for the *Panzer I* when facing Soviet tanks was to get into close combat and use the special armor-piercing 7.92mm ammunition of its twin machine guns, which was not easy to achieve as the Republicans wisely tried to avoid such situations. Although the *Panzer I* was initially able to knock out T-26s at ranges of about 165 yards, the Republican tanks soon began to engage only at longer ranges where they were immune to the *panzer*'s machine guns.

*Panzer I*s were used by the Nationalists on October 30, 1936, near Madrid, and immediately experienced issues. As the Nationalist tanks advanced, they were engaged by the International Brigade's *Commune de Paris* battalion, equipped with Soviet BA-10 armored cars. The 45mm gun in the BA-10, the same as in the T-26, was more than sufficient to knock out the *Panzer I* at ranges below 550 yards. Colonel von Thoma, analyzing several early engagements between German and Russian tanks, remarked that the superiority of tanks with guns versus those armed only with machine guns was well known. As the situation then stood, the conclusion was that the Nationalists must not use German tanks when Russian tanks were expected to enter into battle.[12]

Von Thoma sent repeated dispatches to Berlin noting the weaknesses of the *Panzer I* armor against Russian tanks and antitank guns. The tank crews also noticed the better power and quality of the Soviet tanks' armaments in the field. They soon realized that their *Panzer I*s had an inferior defense and the two machine guns that served as its main armaments were practically useless against Soviet armor. Even the early model of the BA-10 armored cars fitted with a 37mm gun proved lethal for the lightly armored *Panzer I*, and von Thoma soon offered substantial rewards for all captured Republican T-26s and BA-10s that could bolster the Nationalist's capabilities.

In the struggle around Madrid at the end of 1936, the Nationalists handled their German-supplied tanks no better than the Republicans, and von Thoma complained bitterly about the pointless use of armor in close urban combat, which resulted in "bloodying the best troops to no avail." Von Thoma soon found that it was easier to improve tactics than to wait for a better tank to be produced to effectively fight the Russian T-26.

The *Panzer I* was upgraded to increase its lethality. The gun chosen for this was the Italian Breda Model 35, due to the simplicity of its design. The 20mm Breda was capable of piercing 40mm of armor at 275 yards, which was more than enough to penetrate the frontal armor of the T-26. The mounting of the Breda into the *Panzer I* required the original turret to be modified at the top and then extended with a vertical supplement. Four of these tanks were finished at the armaments factory in Seville, but further production was canceled as a number of Republican T-26 tanks had already been captured and could fulfill the Nationalists' request for more lethal tanks. The Breda modification was not particularly liked by German crews, as an unprotected gap in the turret—designed to allow the tank commander to aim—was found to be a dangerous weak point.[13]

The light command vehicle named the *Kleiner Panzer Befehlswagen I* (*SdKfz.265*) was conceived in 1935 by Krupp and was based on the *Panzer I Ausf B* chassis and components. From 1935–37, Daimler-Benz produced a total of 190 of these. Two slightly different versions based on the *Ausf B* were produced—2 Kl B and 3 Kl B—both mounted with two radio sets, the Fu2 and Fu6. They were operated by a three-man crew. These vehicles were also first tested in Spain, but Germany only ever supplied four of them.

Lessons learned from the *Panzer I* provided German designers and manufacturers with valuable experience in designing and producing the next generation of *panzers* that would soon come. Although the *Panzer I* was not a valuable combat tank, it proved to be an excellent training tank; most of the *panzer* crews were trained on the *Panzer I*, almost until the end of World War II, or operated it in combat as their first armored vehicle. So the *Panzer I* did eventually prove to be far more robust and durable in automotive terms than the T-26.

The war in Spain made clear to the German High Command that they could not rely on the *Panzer I*, even as a stopgap. The *Wehrmacht* had to have a better-armed and protected generation of tanks to engage in a war against a major power in Europe. Issues with tank production and design explain why Germany shipped only the *Panzer I* to Spain. After Germany, Spain fielded the largest number of *Panzer I* tanks, and as late as 1945, the Spanish Army's Armored Division still fielded 93 *Panzer I*s. They remained in active service in Spain until 1954, when they were replaced by modern U.S.-made tanks.

A special case: Captured Russian tanks in service with the Spanish Nationalist Army

Although it has been shown that captured Russian tanks became in time the core of the Nationalist armored force, the particularities of how this happened deserve special attention. Never in military history had a major weapon of a warring party become the main weapon of choice for the opposing warring party. Although *Luftwaffe* Major Adolf Galland (a leading German ace and a veteran from the Spanish Civil War) told *Reichsmarschall* Goering at the peak of the battle of Britain in 1940 that to succeed in the air war against the RAF all they needed were Spitfires,[14] this never actually happened and was merely a pipe dream. In Spain, from October 1936, enemy tanks were much sought-after by the Nationalist troops to make up for their inferiority in armor on the battlefield.

No matter how much aid Germany and Italy sent to Nationalist Spain, the Soviet Union ultimately became the main purveyor of tanks for Franco's army. About half of the Soviet tank force sent to Spain was captured by the Nationalists, most of them re-entering the conflict against their previous owners.

On October 29, 1936, during the Spanish war's first tank combat—and the real first tank vs tank clash in history—the Nationalist troops captured three Republican T-26 tanks that had been partially damaged but not destroyed. On November 3, another four T-26 tanks were captured on the Madridfront, and during the following days, more Soviet tanks were taken. All these supplied the Nationalists with enough parts and spares to attempt to repair and put back into service some of the tanks captured. On March 10, 1937, Nationalists troops also recovered from the battlefield at Guadalajara five T-26 tanks that were immediately taken to Zaragoza, where they underwent urgent repairs and maintenance. By March 13 that year, the Nationalists were able to effectively deploy in combat a full platoon of five Soviet T-26 tanks, under the command of a Spanish officer, Lieutenant Ramon Fernandez, which was assigned to a company of German *Panzer Is* operating in the Jarama valley, south of Madrid. They suffered several losses there, and only three tanks remained in service in June.

In mid-June 1937, General Joaquin Garcia Pallasar[15] of the Nationalist Army had established just how many Russian tanks had so far been captured by Nationalist troops. He found that there were 12 T-26 tanks at a main logistical base in Seville being serviced and repaired, plus five more in Zaragoza, along with the first platoon of five still around Madrid. Consequently, he ordered all T-26 tanks to be sent to Seville to be put into operational readiness. Afterwards, it was decided to transport all tanks capable of being taken into combat to the main base of the German Condor Legion at Cubas de la Sagra on the Madrid front. Once there, it was up to the German Colonel von Thoma to organize them, train the appropriate crews, and deploy them.[16]

For the Germans to be able to train the Spaniards on captured Soviet tanks, they first had to learn how to operate these unknown tanks themselves. While this was certainly a major intelligence boost for the Germans, it may have led them to underestimate the Soviet Army's capabilities, as the new Soviet T-34 and KV tanks took the *Wehrmacht* completely by surprise when Operation *Barbarossa* was launched in 1941.

Initially, the idea was to organize for combat two tank companies equipped with 12 ex-Soviet tanks each within the Nationalist tank battalion—which fielded *Panzer Is*—and to employ them as a reserve force. In the end, only 18 T-26 tanks were service-ready and with full combat capabilities. However, the central issue was the main gun ammunition, as only 1,300 captured 45mm rounds were available. Ammunition proved to be a key issue when employing Soviet tanks, despite orders given at the time to start studying, copying, and producing Soviet rounds. Nevertheless, General Garcia Pallasar issued orders to speed up the production of 3,000 rounds at the artillery workshops at Seville.

Special orders were issued to all fronts in Spain to collect parts and spares, ammunition, and armament from captured or destroyed Soviet tanks and armored cars and to ship them to Seville. On July 20, 1937, another operational Russian T-26 tank was captured on the Andalusia front and was immediately shipped to Cubas de la Sagra. A key part much sought-after was the aiming sight and fire control system of the T-26, as this was a relatively vulnerable item that was difficult for Nationalist industry to copy and produce. Between July 18 and 23, 1937, at the battle of Brunete, the first Nationalist tank company equipped with T-26 tanks and trained by German personnel entered combat, integrated into the German-equipped tank battalion. During the battle, until July 23, 10 more T-26s were captured, all of them being sent to Seville. Nationalist T-26s subsequently took part in the battle of Belchite on the Aragon front in September 1937. A platoon with three T-26s was assigned to the Italian tank battalion. The Italians captured another four T-26 tanks following the campaign in Santander, and these were also sent to Seville for repairs.

By October 1937, two tank companies equipped with captured T-26s were in service within the Nationalist tank force. Both *Panzer Is* and T-26s were employed at the battle of Teruel between December 1937 and February 1938. To facilitate the capture and recovery of more Russian tanks, the Nationalist Army's combat service support managed to "produce" some crude armored recovery vehicles based on the chassis of the T-26. When such a recovery tank became severely damaged at the battle of Teruel in January 1938, it was replaced by one of the BT-5s captured at Fuentes de Ebro the previous October, equally crudely transformed.

When the Nationalist Army reached the Mediterranean in April 1938 at the town of Benicarlo, six more T-26 tanks were captured in almost perfect condition. By the following month, the Nationalist Army was deploying 39 T-26B Russian tanks plus four BT-5 fast tanks, all captured from Republican troops; however, the BT-5 tanks were never employed in combat. The number of *Panzer I A/B* tanks in active service was 67, all within the same original unit under the supervision of Colonel von Thoma. Three T-26 tanks were assigned for training duty only.

By October 1, 1938, Nationalist tables of organization and equipment displayed a total of 66 German *Panzer Is* and 41 Russian T-26s available. In other words, the number of captured Russian tanks in service was more than half of the total German fleet available. By November 1938, the newly created "Tank Task Force of the South" (*Agrupacion de Carros del Sur*), within the Army of the South in Andalusia, also had 12 more T-26 tanks.

Captured T-26 tanks were employed during the final offensive in Catalonia, and also during the last combats in the provinces of Andalusia and Toledo, together with Italian troops. They were mostly reinforcing the *Panzer Is* or Fiat L3s, and never fighting alone or without other tanks as support. Despite the T-26's superiority over the *Panzer I* and L3, the Spanish Civil War uncovered a vulnerability of the T-26: its frontal armor was easily penetrated by German and Italian antitank guns at close range.

It is interesting to note that while for the Nationalists it was customary to capture Russian tanks and put them back into operational status, returning them to battle, the Republicans did not bother capturing either German or

Italian armor, obviously considering them inferior and of no real military value. Capturing Russian equipment was not limited to tanks: the Soviet 45mm Model 1937 antitank gun was also highly prized as it offered better performance that the original German 37mm *Pak 36*.

Summary of tanks supplied by foreign powers

Tank	Nation of origin	Number supplied	Side supplied to
BT-5	Soviet Union	50	Popular Army
Renault FT-17	France & Poland	64	Popular Army
Fiat L3 CV-33/35	Italy	155	Nationalist Army
Panzer I A/B	Germany	122	Nationalist Army
T-26B	Soviet Union	281	Popular Army
Vickers	Paraguay	1	Popular Army
Total tanks received by the Republic		396	
Total tanks received by the Nationalists		277	

Comparison of main battle tanks employed in the Spanish Civil War

	T-26	*Panzer I*	L3 CV-33	L3 CV-35
Weight	10 tons	6 tons	3.5 tons	4 tons
Gun	45mm cannon	2×7.92mm MG-13 machine gun	2×8mm Breda machine gun	2×8mm Breda machine gun
Ammunition	122 rounds/ 45mm	2,250 rounds/7.92mm	3,200 rounds/8mm	3,200 rounds/8mm
Range	150 miles	120 miles	78 miles	78 miles
Armor (RHA)	7–16mm	7–13mm	5–15mm	5–15.5mm

Spanish Army experiences of captured T-26 tanks were varied. Generally, the steering of the tank was considered nimble, while the road speed was reasonable and so was terrain mobility. But the suspension made aiming difficult while the tank was moving, and the spotting of the enemy also somewhat complicated. However, compared to the BT-series, captured T-26 tanks proved much more practical and reliable in Spain. The main technical issues with captured T-26 tanks were related to their engines. Due to a cooling problem, their practical sustainable maximum road speed was less than 30mph. Due to poorer manufacturing quality, oil leaks and starting problems were common too. Also likely due to poor manufacturing, the Spaniards noted that the service life of the GAZ T-26 engine was remarkably short, requiring extensive overhaul after every 250 hours of use.

By the end of the war, the Nationalist Army had captured a total of 178 Republican Russian tanks, while 98 T-26s were used effectively in combat by Nationalist troops. Thirty were captured but almost destroyed, while another 50 needed major repairs. Between May and July 1939, the French government returned to Spain 14 more T-26 tanks that the fleeing Republican soldiers had taken into French territory following the final Nationalist offensive in Catalonia.

By 1942, the total number of Soviet T-26 tanks in service with the new Spanish Army was 139. They were integrated and mixed with German and Italian tanks, within five tank regiments, which must have become a real logistical nightmare and impossible to sustain. By late 1940, there were merely 60 or 70 T-26s in operational status, the rest being "cannibalized" for spare parts and repairs. It was of little use as an armored force. The arrival of newly supplied U.S. tanks in 1954 finally sent them to the scrapyard; only a handful survived, that can still be found today in Spanish military museums or memorials.

The Spanish Civil War offered several lessons for the design of tanks. It became obvious that tanks needed turrets that could traverse 360 degrees, as well as guns and accurate fire-control systems capable of dealing with other tanks. They also required heavier armor to increase survivability and vehicle speed was to be sacrificed to this end, but mechanical reliability and off-road capability needed improvement too; the relatively crude vehicles used by both sides were often subject to breakdowns and consequently "ditched" and thus frequently roadbound. Better radio communications were also required to coordinate movement and integrate support of other arms.

Epilogue

"The Spaniards were quick to learn but were also quick to forget."

The tank was undisputedly the most sensational weapon of 20th-century land warfare, combining mobility, armor, and firepower. Tanks have been able to maneuver where other weapons systems could not, survived in environments where no others could (including under NBC—nuclear, biological, chemical—attacks), and led mobile operations which contributed to a rapid end to wars and glamorous victories. Combined with technology and tactics, the tank first dominated the imagination of great military thinkers such as Fuller, Guderian, and Liddell Hart; and subsequently, the doctrine of the present era's war theorists, including generals like Creighton Abrams, Donn Starry, Frederick Franks, Tommy Franks, or Stanley McChrystal. Yet in terms of Spain's military, the tank failed to make any difference, as the outcome of the civil war would probably not have changed even without the existence of tanks. According to most of the Spanish military, even today, the civil war was won by the infantry, the "queen of battles."

Political and general historians are not usually too concerned with technical details or ancillary and circumstantial events, the result of events being what matters most. For military historians, it is different: details, weaponry, equipment, and procedures count a great deal, as does decision-making; aspects that together may help to clarify situations and events, perhaps rewrite history another way, even if the overall result or general picture remains the same. This is what this book is about.

It is difficult to assess just what contribution tanks made to the outcome of the Spanish Civil War. Events such as Nationalist operations on the Aragon front early in 1938, which led to them reaching the Mediterranean and splitting Republican-held territory in two, or the final offensive in Catalonia a year later, would not have been possible without tanks, or not at the speed with which they were carried out. Even if the tanks did play a crucial role at some critical events, the final result would have been the same, with or without the tanks.

The tank made little difference to the Republicans, as they would have lost all the same even if armored forces had not been present on either side. The Republicans' defeat was rooted in issues other than the weaponry or equipment supplied to them. The Republicans were a hotchpotch of anarchists, communists, socialists, and other groups that were ill-suited to fighting a war in a cohesive manner. The Soviet contribution had the additional negative effect of creating political instability within Republican Spain, as Stalin eventually wanted full control of the whole country.[1] The communists eventually gained control on the Republican side, but created such divisions among the various factions that they merely precipitated the final defeat. As British military historian Antony Beevor says, "It was the Republic's own high command and its Soviet advisers' disastrous conduct of the war in engaging in conventional offensives, normally implemented for propaganda purposes against a better-armed and trained army, which gradually destroyed the Republic's army and resistance."

Indeed, tank employment in Spain offered many lessons, but these were not always related to what had been done or accomplished, but on what had not been done or accomplished. Following events at the beginning of the Spanish Civil War and the surprise that came with the first Russian tanks, it is difficult to understand how the German *panzer* divisions were still so inefficiently equipped, not just when World War II began in Poland, but even in 1941, when Operation *Barbarossa* was launched against Russia. It is equally difficult to understand the shape of Italian armor in 1940, and why Fiat L3 light tanks had not been withdrawn from service or at least improved with a rotating turret and better armament.

Those were lessons that both Italy and Germany should have learnt, but did not. Victory is not the best recipe for learning in war, and it has been said that only defeat offers good teaching. But the Soviet Union, despite being on the side that lost the war in Spain, did not learn much either, as the enormous defeats suffered throughout 1941 and into 1942 proved.

The Spaniards also failed to learn anything, nor did they wish to. The outcome of the civil war precluded any learning. Ultimately, the victorious Nationalists were convinced that everything they did was right, and that was why they won. As armor had been mainly used or supervised by the Germans and Italians, they did not pay much attention to that either. Tanks had been just one more tool, useful but certainly not decisive. The end of the war meant ultimately that the new Spanish Army was left with a bunch of various tanks and armored vehicles from three different origins, already quite obsolete, even if the Spanish military was as yet unaware of this or simply chose to ignore it. These tanks remained in service until the mid-1950s and early 1960s, continuing to be distributed proportionally between the infantry and cavalry. For the Spanish Army, the tank was another weapon in its inventory and nothing else. The Spanish Army was, and still is, one of the few military land forces in the Western world within NATO that has never organized an armored branch, still maintaining an organization that has changed little from the times of World War II or even World War I; keeping tanks and armored fighting vehicles distributed among the traditional infantry and cavalry branches.

Perhaps one of the most noteworthy lessons and experiences obtained from the civil war was the employment of combined arms, even though for practical reasons the Nationalists had been using the concept from the very outset. Both the Germans and Italians learnt how to proceed along such operational lines. The Italians had already tried the concept in Abyssinia, while the Nationalists performed their great advance from Seville to Madrid by organizing their "columns" with combined arms, even understanding the great value of airpower, despite having almost none in the earlier days of the conflict.

The Germans understood the role of close air support and developed its use, even integrating communications with the advancing ground elements that kept them in touch with supporting attack aircraft. Tanks were without a doubt an essential element in these tactical procedures. In Spain, close air support was often just to help the attacking infantry. Meanwhile, the Republicans and their Soviet advisers failed miserably in this field, which made it easier for the Nationalist forces to succeed.

From the beginning of the civil war, tanks were embedded into whatever military organization both sides had, the Spaniards rarely having any views on it. The Italians did as they pleased, organizing their own armored force within the Italian Volunteers Corps, while the Germans had the Condor Legion, even if the crewmen and commanders ultimately going into combat were Spanish. The Soviets did exactly the same, but went even further, to the point of requiring the use of tanks to have Soviet approval.

The conclusion that may be drawn from a rapid survey of the opposing forces, and what is convenient to bear in mind in order to appreciate accurately the conception and execution of operations, is that these forces were deter-mined—both in terms of quality and quantity—by political considerations, circumstances, and the resources available, rather than doctrines or even the will of the various commanders.

Tanks were not initially even requested by Spaniards of either side. The Italians decided to send them on their own initiative and because it was the logical thing to do. Meanwhile, the Germans acted on the advice provided to Berlin by Colonel Warlimont after he noticed the scarcity of modern equipment available to the Nationalist Army. Tanks were already in use with the Russian armed forces, and it was logical to have them if they intended to win the war. Nevertheless, the Spaniards did not at first know what to do with them, which is why the first Italian tanks were put under the administrative control of an artillery regiment. When German equipment arrived later, it was under the control of an infantry regiment, then later under the administrative leadership of a practically disbanded tank regiment, ending up within the Foreign Legion, a military organization that was basically made of shock troops and infantry, with no understanding whatsoever of tanks. On the Republican side, the Soviets took effective control of everything from the start; it was much simpler that way.

Even if the war in Spain showcased the tank's potential, it also revealed its serious weaknesses. Tanks were better at attacking than defending; they could not hold ground on their own; and if they came across unsuppressed enemy artillery or antitank guns, they became easy targets. The Germans saw clearly that tanks could succeed, but only if they worked with other weapons systems in a close, cooperative, combined-arms arrangement: the tanks to take the ground, the infantry to hold it, and the artillery to suppress enemy weapons that might harm the tank.

In Germany, it was General Guderian who, overseeing a key series of exercises in 1931–32, uncovered what might be called tank warfare's "first principle": "In order to support the tank, the other arms had to be mobile enough to keep up. Infantry and artillery had to move as rapidly, reliably and relentlessly as the tank, and chaining the tank to the pace of infantry on foot was a fundamental mistake."[2] However, the Spanish conflict did not provide an adequate environment to prove such an idea.

Ideally, tank warfare should rarely take place without mechanized infantry, yet this element was completely absent from Spain's battlefields, as it was to a great extent during the early years of World War II. Perhaps we should consider the Republicans as the first to try out the idea when infantry at times climbed on top of the Russian tanks, using them purely as transport when approaching the enemy, but this was not a standard procedure. The Italians tried the concept in a much more orderly manner within their Volunteer Troops Corps, but only by transporting infantry aboard conventional cargo trucks which had almost no off-road mobility whatsoever. The Germans did not even bring up the issue for discussion until later in World War II, when they came to master the technique with their *Panzergrenadieren*.

It is a curious reflection that these lessons appear to have been ignored by the Spanish Army, as the natural outcome should have been to regard them as a useful revelation on mechanization. All those who have thoroughly studied the subject of mechanized warfare have long insisted on the importance of distinguishing between fully mechanized and just merely motorized troops. It should be pointed out that the scale of manpower and consequently of superfluous vehicles must be greatly reduced, that the force must be composed of cross-country armored vehicles, and these must be trained to keep off the roads and to be able to move on wide fronts, maintaining a good state of controlled dispersion. Only when these conditions are fulfilled can a force be said to be wholly mechanized.[3]

The fighting in Spain did not offer any easy solutions on the issue of infantry–armor cooperation, primarily because the tanks supplied did not perform well and were supplied in small quantities, regardless of the fact that the Republicans organized an "armored division." The situation with tanks on the Nationalist side was so bad in practical terms that they had to reuse captured Russian armor in their units, a decision successfully implemented in 1937. All these factors did not allow for a serious test of how armored units would fare in modern warfare, and even prevented an examination of the various ideas on coordinating infantry and tank operations.

Also absent from the Spanish Civil War was the concept of armored reconnaissance, as tanks or even armored wheeled vehicles were rarely used for such a purpose. Reconnaissance was a mounted cavalry mission, and both Nationalist and Republican cavalry were horse-mounted for the duration of the war.

The opposing armies in Spain were a heterogeneous lot, with all nationalities mixed up against each other. Idealism was rife and discipline inconstant: sometimes a decision to attack was made by a show of hands. Organizations such as these did not equate with the sort of small, highly professional tank force envisaged in Britain and Germany, in which mutually disciplined cooperation by all arms was mandatory.

Nationalist commanders stuck to preconceived ideas. Von Thoma complained of General Franco, who "wished to parcel out tanks among the infantry. I had to fight this tendency constantly in the endeavor to use the tanks in a concentrated way. Nationalist successes were largely due to this." Up to the spring of 1937, never had more than 50 tanks been used at once on the battlefield.

No plan or operation order for either side has been found giving tasks or missions to tank units; tanks were simply viewed as supplementary or additional assets. At the most, an army corps or division would be signaled as having tanks assigned, but that was all. Only during the campaign in Catalonia, late in 1938, are Nationalist tanks mentioned as having been given missions and specific orders regarding their employment,[4] as advised by Colonel von Thoma, and regarding only German *Panzer* tanks, but only with the aim of providing support to infantry. Italian tanks were always directly dependent on the Italian Volunteer Troops, receiving direct orders from their command.

As pointed out[5] by Dr John L. S. Daley, a scholar and a former armor officer, more than 80 years since the start of the Spanish Civil War, the conflict continues to pose a problem for all those interested in armored warfare. Most opinions, even those diametrically opposed on the issue of Spain's viability as a testing ground, share the assumption that only grand tactics deserve the military intellectual's attention. As it happened in Spain, small-unit tactics, meaning cooperation of tanks with non-mechanized infantry, scarcely mattered as tank formations were too small to achieve significant success. Neither side possessed enough tanks to execute the tactically independent offensives and uses envisioned by interwar theorists such as Fuller, Martel, or Liddell Hart. Tanks were mainly used in support of dismounted infantry, and most of the time without the element of surprise. Nevertheless, tanks proved useful once effective procedures had been developed.

Unlike early machine guns, the tank had a faster acceptance as a weapon within the Spanish Army because it had proven its value on the battlefields of World War I. Nevertheless, as with the machine gun, the infantry and artillery contended for having the early tanks, even though both corps displayed limited enthusiasm towards the new weapon. There is evidence that the Spanish military did consider the compromise of creating a functional service which grouped all tanks under a single corporate command, but creating a fully fledged armored corps was without doubt too daring an idea at the time. Finally, corporate factionalism prevailed and the Spanish armor was divided into two separate forces of infantry and artillery tanks. The actual consequences were not serious due to the Spanish tank arm's small size during the 1920s and early 1930s. Indeed, the artillery corps seemed to have lost interest in having its own armor when the civil war broke out in 1936. Therefore, the infantry was the sole corporate operator of tanks during the conflict, as neither the Republicans nor the Nationalists sought to set up a separate tank branch. It should thus come as no surprise that tanks were usually employed as a support weapon for the infantry, and that the overall performance of armor, despite the presence of foreign advisers on both sides, was in the end unremarkable.

On the other hand, keeping in mind the contemporary thinking on armored warfare and the conditions of the Spanish Civil War, it would not be unfair to blame the Spanish officer corps for failing to implement a new doctrine on armor, especially its leadership and above all those who, influenced by the Moroccan campaigns, were blind to material factors. However, they only considered those that displayed a morally motivated offensive spirit as ultimately decisive. An outcome of the psychological image of colonial warfare was the trend to underrate technology. Such a tendency was clearly seen in the cases of the machine gun and the tank. Even the events of World War I did not change such thinking by much.

Technology-based solutions to the tactical stagnation of trench warfare were reckoned, at best, as temporary remedies for quite exceptional circumstances, or, at worst, as aberrations. Although the Spanish Army was undoubtedly interested in the tank before the Great War was over, this did not turn into the pursuit of a policy of mechanization. Indeed, financial constraints ruled out the creation of a large armored force, while the Spanish military did not show any remarkable enthusiasm for one.

Official doctrine, embodied in the Spanish Army's 1928 tactical regulations, recognized the tank only as a support weapon for the infantry. This was not because the pioneers of mechanization and their ideas were unknown, but they were judged as too radical. Nonetheless, there were signs during the early 1930s, such as a slight increase of interest by the cavalry in the use of armored vehicles, which showed that the Spanish Army did gradually develop a more positive attitude towards mechanization. During the civil war, the Spanish field commanders continued to be attached to pre-war doctrine on armor and did not introduce any significant change. In fairness, this is not surprising. Armored warfare could not really be tested out in the Spanish Civil War, as the armor used by both sides was not adequate in terms of quality or quantity for operations by mechanized armies. Furthermore, the terrain where many of the major battles and campaigns were fought was mostly unsuitable for armored forces. The Republicans, unlike the Nationalists, seem not to have maintained a fully coherent policy on the use of tanks. On the one hand, pre-war regulations were the official doctrine, but the Republican command issued instructions based on operational experience that sometimes were in open conflict with these. This would have been just a minor issue for an army where its field commanders were versed in the essentials of tank warfare. But this was not the case in the Republican Army, where many of the commanders were not even professional officers. Therefore, the underperformance of Republican armor should hardly come as a surprise.

Republican military planners soon learned that the high speed of tanks on the battlefield only made things worse, as the infantry quickly became separated from the tanks. With motorized infantry on trucks careering around the battlefield at speed, and aircraft also inserted into the mix, command and control was lurching toward chaos. The solution was radio communications, but they were scarce in Spain, especially within the Republican Army. While tanks and aircraft were the obsession in most contemporary military discourse, radio communication was the real military breakthrough of the period. Unfortunately, that went almost unnoticed for both sides in the Spanish Civil War. The Germans, however, understood this from the beginning, which is why they sent command vehicles (*befehlspanzerwagen*) to Spain designed to carry both radio-senders and receivers.

In conclusion, the Spanish Army at the outbreak of the Civil War was short of material resources. This was a situation for which the army itself was to a large extent responsible, due to its reluctance to undertake reformist policies, but it was not out of date in terms of doctrine and knowledge of military developments. Indeed, from the later point of view, it could bear comparison with other similar European armies. Its overall professional preparation would have been better if the narrow-minded spirit of the corps of each service had not been an obstacle to implement reforms in the way officers were trained and promoted, and if the distrust of technological innovation had not been such an impediment to the modernizing of its weaponry.

What the course of the Spanish Civil War could have been if the army had been better prepared and equipped is a matter of guesswork. But one may also wonder whether the events which led to up to the civil conflict of 1936 would have taken place at all if the exclusive interest of the Spanish military during the early 20th century, untroubled by non-professional issues, had been to prepare for war and not meddle in politics.

The conflict was limited to a country that had for many years been on the periphery of the great affairs of Europe, and yet within a couple of months, three out of the four major European powers—Italy, Germany, and the Soviet Union—decided to intervene. Spain was thought to be the perfect proving ground to carry out controlled, realistic experiments with live weapons and troops. Whether or not the lessons learnt by all armies involved in Spain could ultimately help them to organize and fight the next war was another matter.

The use of tanks during the Spanish Civil War wedded traditional war to modern technology. However, it would take years for the Spanish Army to catch up. Spain was lucky not to have a need for such technology while its defense planners were planning to accept the tank and to establish the necessary allocations in the military budget to have an armored component at last.

Bibliography and Further Recommended Reading

Albert, F. C. *Carros de combate y vehículos blindados de la guerra 1936–1939* (Barcelona: Borras, 1984)

Alvarez, José E. "Tank Warfare during the Rif Rebellion, 1921–1927" in *Armor Magazine* (Fort Knox, KY: U.S. Army Armor Center, January 1997)

Alvarez, José E. "Between Gallipoli and D-Day: Alhucemas, 1925" in *Journal of Military History*, Society for Military History (January 1999)

Baryatinskiy, Mikhail. *Light Tanks T-27, T-38, BT, T-26, T-40, T-50, T-60, T-70* (Surrey: Ian Allen, 2006)

Beevor, Antony. *The Spanish Civil War* (New York: Penguin Books, 1982)

Bishop, Chris. *The Encyclopedia of Tanks and Armored Fighting Vehicles: From World War I to the Present Day* (San Diego: Thunder Bay, 2006)

Bowers, Claude. *My Mission to Spain: Watching the Rehearsal for World War II* (New York: Simon and Schuster, 1954)

Candil, Antonio J. *Carros de Combate: Evolución, Presente y Futuro* (Madrid: ISDEFE, 1999)

Candil, Antonio J. "Soviet Armor in Spain: Aid Mission to Republicans Tested Doctrine and Equipment" in *Armor Magazine* (Fort Knox, KY: U.S. Army Armor Center, March 1999)

Cattell, David *Soviet Diplomacy and the Spanish Civil War* (Berkeley, CA: University of California Press, 1957)

Ceva, L. and Curami, A. *La Meccanizzazione dell'Esercito fino al 1943,* Vol. 1 and 2 (Roma: Ufficio Storico dello Stato Maggiore dell'Esercito, 1994)

Cockburn, Andrew. *The Threat: Inside the Soviet Military Machine* (New York: Random House, 1983)

Colonna, Ugo and Benvenuti, Bruno. *Fronte Terra—Carri Armati*, Vol. 2/II (Roma: Edizioni Ateneo Bizzarri, 1974)

Coverdale, John F. "The Battle of Guadalajara, March 8–22, 1937" in *Journal of Contemporary History* (January 1974)

Daley, John. "Soviet and German Advisors Put Doctrine to the Test: Tanks in the Siege of Madrid" in *Armor Magazine* (Fort Knox, KY: U.S. Army Armor Center, May 1997)

Daley, John. "An Experiment Reconsidered: The Theory and Practice of Armored Warfare in Spain" in *Armor Magazine* (Fort Knox, KY: U.S. Army Armor Center, March 1999)

van Dyke, Carl. *The Soviet Invasion of Finland 1939–40* (London: Frank Cass, 1997)

Erickson, John. *The Soviet High Command: A Military Political History 1918–1941* (Boulder, CO: Westview Press, 1984)

Fernández Mateos, Francisco. *Carros de Combate y Vehículos Acorazados en la Historia de España*, *Revista Ejercito* (1984)

Fuqua, Colonel Stephen O. National Archives U.S. Army Military Intelligence Division, 2724-S-16/8, Military Intelligence Division, Record Group 165, Washington, D. C., 1937

García, Dionisío. *Renault FT 17 en España: la Guerra Civil* (Madrid: Ed. Almena, 2004)

García, Dionisío, *Trubia: el primer Carro de Combate español* (Madrid: Ed. Almena, 2008)

Habeck, Mary R. *Storm of Steel (The Development of Armor Doctrine in Germany and the Soviet Union 1919–1939)* (Ithaca, NY: Cornell University Press, 2003)

Habeck, Mary R. *Spain Betrayed: The Soviet Union in the Spanish Civil War* (New Haven: Yale University Press, 2011)

Hill, George. *The Battle for Madrid* (London: Vantage Books, 1976)

Gladnick, Robert. *Between the Bullet and the Lie: American Volunteers in the Spanish Civil War* (New York: Holt, Rinehart & Winston, 1969)

Gladnick, Robert. *Report on the Combat Use on the 13th of October (1937) of the Regiment of BT-5 Tanks,* Commander of Tank #7, 1st Section, 1st Company, Yale RSMAC, Box 14

Harvey, A. D. "The Spanish Civil War as Seen by British officers" in *RUSI Journal* (August 1996)

Herrero Perez, José Vicente. *The Spanish Military, and the Evolution of Warfare, 1899–1939* (London: King's College, 2017)

Hofmann, George F. "The Tactical and Strategic Use of Attaché Intelligence: The Spanish Civil War and the U.S. Army's Misguided Quest for a Modern Tank Doctrine" in *Journal of Military History*, Society for Military History (January 1998)

Infiesta Perez, José Luis. *El empleo de los carros de combate en la Guerra de España* (Madrid: Servicio Historico del Ejercito, 1995)

Jackson, Gabriel. *The Spanish Republic, and the Civil War, 1931–1939* (Princeton, NJ: Princeton University Press, 1967)

Jentz, Tom. *Tank Combat in North Africa: The Opening Rounds* (Atglen, PA: Schiffer, 1997)

Johnson, Captain Wendell G. "The Employment of Supporting Arms in the Spanish Civil War" in *The Command and General Staff School, Quarterly, Review of Military Literature*, no. 72 (1939)

Juntunen, Captain Kim M. *U.S. Army attaches and the Spanish Civil War, 1936–1939: the gathering of technical and tactical intelligence* (West Point, NY: May 1990)

Kiesling, Eugenia *Arming Against Hitler: France & the Limits of Military Planning* (Lawrence, KS: University of Kansas Press, 1996)

Liddell Hart, Sir Basil. *Storia di una Sconfitta* (Rome: Biblioteca Universale Rizzoli, 2002)

Luraghi, Raimondo. "Carri Armati" *in Storia Militare* (November 2002)

Luraghi, Raimondo and Pedriali, Francesco. "Dialogo—Guadalajara: due tesi contrapposte" in *Storia Militare* (January 2000)

MacDougall, Ian, *Voices from the Spanish Civil War: Personal recollections of Scottish Volunteers in Republican Spain 1936–39* (Edinburgh: Polygon, 1986)

de Mazarrasa, Javier. *Los Carros de Combate en España* (Madrid: San Martin, 1977)

de Mazarrasa, Javier. *Blindados en España 2ª Parte: La Dificil Postguerra 1939–1960* (Valladolid: Quiron Ediciones, 1994)

de Mazarrasa, Javier. *Carro de Combate Verdeja* (Barcelona: MC Ediciones, 1994)

de Mazarrasa, Javier. *Los Carros de Combate en la Guerra de España 1936–1939* (Vol. 1) (Valladolid: Quiron Ediciones, June 1998)

Manrique, José María and Molina Franco, Lucas. *Las Armas de la Guerra Civil Española* (Madrid: La Esfera de los Libros, 2006)

Manrique, José María and Molina, Lucas. *Blindados Soviéticos en el Ejército de Franco* (Valladolid, Spain: Galland Books, 2007)

Medina Tornero, Manuel Enrique. *Instalaciones Militares en Archena durante la Guerra Civil: Escuela de Tanques y Aeródromo* (Madrid: Siglo Cero, 2007)

Molina, Lucas. *Panzer I: El inicio de una saga* (Valladolid: Quiron Ediciones, 2005)

Montanari, Mario. "Santander" *in Storia Militare* (June 2002)

Muñoz, Carlos. *La Batalla de Brunete: El fallido contraataque republicano* (Madrid: Serga, November 2007)

Payne, Stanley G. *The Spanish Civil War, the Soviet Union, and Communism* (New Haven: Yale University Press, 2004)

Payne, Stanley G. *¿Por qué la Republica perdió la guerra?* (MadridL Espasa Libros, 2011)

Pedraza, Jorge. *Unidades Blindadas Republicanas durante la Guerra Civil Española* (Madrid: Serga, 2003)

Pedriali, Francesco. "Guadalajara: Le due Verità" in *Storia Militare*, no. 73 (October 1999)

Perrett, Bryan, *German Light Panzers 1932–42* (Oxford: Osprey, 1998)

Pirella, A., Caiti, P. and De Lia, E. "The Role of Italian Armor in the Spanish Civil War" in *Armor Magazine* (May–June 1986)

Preston, Paul. *The Spanish Civil War. Reaction, revolution & revenge* (London: Harper Perennial, 2006)

Reese, Roger R. *Stalin's Reluctant Soldiers: A Social history of the Red Army 1925–41* (Lawrence, KS: University of Kansas Press, 1996)

Rosselli, Alberto. *Breve Storia della Guerra Civile Spagnola 1936–39* (2019)

Rovighi, Alberto and Stefani, Filippo. *La Partecipazione italiana alla Guerra Civile Spagnola*, Vol. 1 and 2 (Roma: Ufficio Storico dello SME, 1993)

Russian State Military Archives Collection, Record Group 1670, Yale University Sterling Memorial Library, Box 13

Salas Larrazabal, Ramón. *Historia Ejército Popular de la Republica*, Vol. 2 (Madrid: La Esfera de los Libros, 1973)

von Senger und Etterlin, General F. M. "Sevilla 6 November 1936: Die Panzergruppe Thoma der 'Legion Condor', der spanishche Burgerkrieg und die Folgen" in *Soldat und Technik*, no. 10 (1986)

Sgarlato, Nico. "La Battaglia di Madrid" in *Esercito nella Storia*, no. 13 (September–October 2002)

Surlemont, Raymond. "German Tanks in Spain 1936–39" in *AFV News* (January–April 1992)

Surlemont, Raymond. "Blindati Italiani in Spagna (1936–1939)" in *Storia Militare*, no. 35 (August 1996)

Thomas, Hugh. *The Spanish Civil War* (London: Penguin Books, 2001)

Tocci, Patrizio. "Le Autoblindo Lancia 1ZM—Parte 3ª" in *Storia Militare*, no. 69 (June 1999)

Weeks, John, *Men Against Tanks: A History of Anti-Tank Warfare* (New York: Mason/Charter, 1975)

Zaloga, Steven. *The Renault FT Light Tank* (London: Osprey, 1988)

Zaloga, Steven and Grandsen, James. *Soviet Tanks and Combat Vehicles of World War Two* (London: Arms and Armour Press, 1984)

Endnotes

Preface

1　For a thorough explanation of how the Spanish war differed from World War II, as well as other revolutions throughout modern European history, see Stanley Payne, *The Spanish Civil War, the Soviet Union, and Communism* (New Haven: Yale University Press, 2004), pp. 313–315.

2　The American ambassador and the American military attaché to Spain also recognized the war as a testing ground. The Ambassador, Claude G. Bowers, used that very phrase after the war: "Spain then was to be the testing ground. Here would be staged the dress rehearsal for the totalitarian war on liberty and democracy in Europe." Colonel Stephen O. Fuqua, the U.S. attaché, wrote in the spring of 1937: "It is generally accepted that the civil war in Spain had not only been a laboratory for testing equipment, particularly of German and Russian designs, but a dress rehearsal for the next war."

Chapter 1

1　These columns were no more than reinforced battalion-size units with scarce fire support and almost no logistics whatsoever.

2　In spite of the Republic having most of the Spanish Navy's assets, its value was limited due to the fact that Republican militias had assassinated most of the naval officers, thus making the Navy leaderless.

3　Apparently, Hitler said that: "Franco ought to erect a monument to the glory of the Junkers-52"; Hugh Thomas, *The Spanish Civil War* (London: Penguin Books, 2001), p. 357.

4　Stanley G. Payne, *Por qué la República perdió la Guerra?* (Madrid: Espasa Libros, 2010), "*Dos modelos de Guerra*," p. 207.

5　*Ibid.*, p. 198.

6　General Emilio Mola died on June 3, 1937, when the aircraft in which he was travelling crashed due to bad weather while returning to Pamplona. The deaths of generals Sanjurjo and Mola left Franco as the preeminent leader of the Nationalist side. This has led to the suspicion that Franco contributed in some way to the deaths of his two rivals, but no evidence has ever been produced.

7　Submarine warfare on the Nationalist side—conducted mainly by the Italians—was so effective that supplies from the Soviet Union through the Mediterranean stopped and had to be deviated through the Baltic to France, and then by road to Catalonia; a much more expensive and more time-consuming way which eventually crippled the Republic's logistics.

8　Stanley G. Payne, "*Dos modelos de Guerra*," in *¿Por qué la República perdió la Guerra?*

9   The Nationalist Army was reorganized into six army corps, including the Italian Corps (CTV), which constituted the so-called *Ejército de Maniobra* (Army of Manoeuver) (Madrid: Spanish Army Historical Service, SHM, *Síntesis Historica de la Guerra de Liberación*, 1968).

10   It was in the Castle of Figueras—the Castle of Saint Ferdinand—where, on February 1, 1939, the last meeting of the Republican government's cabinet took place, and where Prime Minister Negrín even dared to make a proposal of unconditional surrender to Franco when the war was already lost.

Chapter 2

1   On July 29, 1936, the *Manchester Guardian* argued against sending arms to Spain as "there exist on both sides of the barricade considerable forces which submit to no control. We are therefore free to wonder whether arms dispatched to the Spanish government would fall into the hands of extremists who, though fighting the insurgents show no obedience to the central authority." Quoted by David Pike in his book *Conjecture, propaganda and Deceit and the Spanish Civil War*, this was indeed what happened.

2   Pierpaolo Barbieri, *Hitler's Shadow Empire, Nazi economics in the Spanish Civil War* (Cambridge, MA: Harvard University Press, 2015). Many years later, in 1954, Torkild Rieber, no longer at Texaco, was awarded the Order of Queen Isabella by General Franco's government for his services to Spain.

3   Jose M. Doussinague, *España tenia razon, 1939–1945* (Madrid: Espasa Calpe, 1949).

4   Paul Preston, "Mussolini's Spanish adventure: from limited risk to war" in Helen Graham and Paul Preston (eds), *The Republic Besieged: Civil War in Spain, 1936–1939* (Edinburgh: Edinburgh University Press, 1996), pp. 21–51. Paul Preston, "Italy and Spain in civil war and world war, 1936–1943" in Sebastian Balfour and Paul Preston (eds), *Spain and the Great Powers in the Twentieth Century* (London: Routledge, 1999), pp. 152–55. John Coverdale, *Italian Intervention in the Spanish Civil War* (Princeton: Princeton University Press, 1975), pp. 69–74.

5   John Coverdale, *Italian Intervention in the Spanish Civil War.*

6   Hugh Thomas, *The Spanish Civil War*, 3rd edition (London: Penguin, 1977), p. 353.

7   M. Muggeridge (ed.), *Ciano's Hidden Diary, 1937–1938* (New York: Dutton, 1953), diary entry October 29, 1937, p. 26.

8   Stanley G. Payne, "Fascist Italy and Spain, 1922–1945," *Mediterranean Historical Review, Vol. 3, Spain and the Mediterranean since 1898*, 1998, pp. 98–115.

9   Glyn Stone, *Spain, Portugal, and the Great Powers, 1931–1941* (London: Palgrave Macmillan, 2005), p. 29.

10   Stone, *Spain, Portugal, and the Great Powers*, pp. 34–35.

11   As Paul Preston has shown, Franco's slow and deliberate attritional strategy was based on his determination to conduct a war of annihilation to ruthlessly crush for the foreseeable and even distant future all and any remnants of Republican Spain. "General Franco as military leader," *The Royal Historical Society*, 6th series, vol. 4 (1994), pp. 21–41.

12   Hassell to the German Foreign Ministry, October 19, 1937. Hassell to the German Foreign Ministry, December 20, 1937, *Documents on German Foreign Policy, 1918–1945* (hereafter DGFP), series D, vol. III, pp. 444, 468, 489, 533.

13   Juan Beigbeder y Atienza was a Spanish military and political leader who served as Minister of Foreign Affairs during the early days of the rule of General Franco between 1939 and 1940, just after the Civil War. In the Protectorate of Morocco, he held the positions of Chief of

Local Affairs and High Commissioner. Before the military uprising and after his promotion to lieutenant colonel, he had been appointed military attaché to the Spanish embassy in Berlin. After the end of the civil war, he was appointed Minister of Foreign Affairs of Franco's government between August 12, 1939, and October 16, 1940.

14 Burns, "Nazi Conspiracy in Spain," Christian Leitz, "Nazi Germany's Intervention in the Spanish Civil War and the Foundation of HISMA/ROWAK" in Paul Preston and Ann L. Mackenzie (eds), *The Republic Besieged: Civil War in Spain 1936–1939* (Edinburgh: Edinburgh University Press, 1996).

15 Heinz Hohne, *Canaris, Hitler's master spy* (New York: Doubleday, 1979).

16 For details see Angel Viñas, *Hitler, Franco y el Estallido de la Guerra Civil: Antecedentes y Consecuenias* (Madrid: Alianza Editorial, 2001), pp. 368–84; Angel Viñas and Carlos Seidel, "Franco's request to the Third Reich for military assistance" in *Contemporary European History*, Vol. 11 (2002), pp. 200–05; and Christian Leitz, "Nazi Germany's intervention in the Spanish Civil War and the foundation of HISMA/ROWAK" in Graham and Preston (eds), *The Republic Besieged*, pp. 53–57.

17 For details see Raymond Proctor, *Hitler's Luftwaffe and the Spanish Civil War* (Westport, CT: Greenwood Press, 1983), pp. 10–19.

18 Ewald Banse, *Raum und Volk im Weltkriege* (Stalling, Germany: Oldenburg, 1933).

19 Michael Muller, *Canaris, the life and death of Hitler's spymaster* (Annapolis: Naval Institute Press, 2007).

20 Viñas and Seidel, "Franco's request," pp. 208–09.

21 Ulrich von Hassell, German ambassador at Rome, to the German Foreign Ministry, DGFP, 18 December 1936, series D, vol. III, no. 157, 170.

22 See, for example, Weinberg, *Foreign Policy of Hitler's Germany, 1937–1939*, pp. 143–44, 163.

23 The Hossbach conference was a meeting on November 5, 1937, between Adolf Hitler and his military and foreign policy leadership where Hitler's future expansionist policies were outlined. The meeting marked a turning point in Hitler's foreign policies, which then began to radicalize. It outlined Hitler's plans for expansion in Europe. Apparently, at the conference, Hitler did not want war in 1939 with Britain and France. What he wanted was small wars of plunder to help support Germany's struggling economy, such as the Spanish Civil War.

24 Minutes of the Conference in the Reich Chancellery, Berlin, November 5, 1937. DGFP, series D, vol. I, 19, p. 37.

25 State Secretary Mackensen to the German embassy in Spain, February 28, 1938. DGFP, series D, vol. III, 539, p. 611.

26 Muggeridge (ed.), *Ciano's Hidden Diary* (diary entries: 24, 26 and 29 August 1938), pp. 146–48.

27 *Ibid.*, diary entries 3, 7, 9 and 11 September 1938, pp. 150–54.

28 For Italian reinforcements see Coverdale, *Italian Intervention*, pp. 374, 381.

29 Both Italy and Germany acted mainly on General Franco's request; however, General Mola and the exiled Spanish Monarchists had also been asking for help.

30 Stalin did indeed receive an early direct request for military aid from the Republican government, in a letter signed by Prime Minister Jose Giral and delivered by the Spanish ambassador to the Soviet ambassador in Paris on July 25, 1936. The request came this way because Spain and the Soviet Union hadn't yet established diplomatic relations, which was not uncommon as at its founding, the Soviet Union was considered a pariah by most Western governments because of the communist revolution, consequently being denied diplomatic recognition by most states. In the case of the United States, President Roosevelt ended the almost 16 years of American non-recognition of the Soviet Union only in November 1933.

31 Paul Preston endorses the historical consensus that "Stalin helped the Spanish Republic not to hasten its victory but rather to prolong its existence sufficiently to keep Hitler bogged down in an expensive venture."

32 Stanley Payne, *The Spanish Civil War, the Soviet Union and Communism*, p. 127, quoting NKVD agent Walter Krivitsky.

33 Walter Krivitsky, *In Stalin's Secret Service* (New York: Enigma Books, 2000), p. 76.

34 Stanley Payne, *The Spanish Civil War, the Soviet Union and Communism*, p. 142.

Chapter 3

1 Spain's ignominious rout at the hands of Riffian tribesmen was the greatest defeat suffered by a European power in an African colonial conflict in the 20th century. Following the Annual disaster, the Spanish military realized the importance of utilizing the best weapons available to crush the rebellion. A commission led by the then Director of Studies of the Infantry's Central Gunnery School (*Escuela Central de Tiro*) visited several European countries in the hope of acquiring tanks. They considered the British Whippet tank, but financial and political reasons led them to pass on it in favor of French equipment. Jose E. Alvarez, "Tank warfare during the Rif rebellion. 1921–1927" in *Armor Magazine* (January/February 1997).

2 The battle of Ambar, or Anvar, in northern Morocco, fought on March 18, 1922. Ambar saw the first use of tanks by the Spanish Army, and their earliest deployment on the African continent. Jose E. Alvarez, "Tank warfare during the Rif rebellion. 1921–1927" in *Armor Magazine* (January/February 1997).

3 The Alhucemas landing was an amphibious operation which took place on September 8, 1925, in northern Morocco. It involved the Spanish Army and Navy and, in lesser numbers, an allied French contingent, and was intended to put an end to the Rif War. It is considered the first amphibious landing in history involving the use of tanks and massive seaborne air support.

4 The initial evaluation was that the Trubia tank satisfied the requirements for a modern light tank and could even outmatch other contemporary models. However not everybody shared this assessment, and an engineering report stated that the Trubia had "poor armor, weak tracks and was too bulky for its performance."

Chapter 4

1 Some cavalrymen didn't care much about mechanization. General Monasterio, a key cavalry officer in the Nationalist Army, refused to accept that his branch was in decline and considered it wrong to think that mechanization would substitute the horse.

2 In 1922, Vicente Rojo was at the Infantry School at Toledo as an instructor, where he held diverse educational and administrative positions. He was one of the editors of the curricula on the subjects of tactics, weaponry, and firepower for the new section of the General Military Academy at Zaragoza headed by General Franco. During this period at the Infantry School, he collaborated on the establishment and management of the Military Bibliographical Collection, along with Captain Emilio Alamán, who would later become a general in the Nationalist Army.

Chapter 5

1   As a matter of fact, the T-26 tank was always known and referred to as the "Vickers Tank" in Spain.

2   It was stated as such in Soviet Army regulations from 1931.

3   Rodion Malinovsky volunteered to fight for the Republicans, and upon his arrival in Spain participated in planning and managing several main operations. In 1938, he returned to the Soviet Union, being awarded the top Soviet decorations in recognition of his service in Spain and was appointed a senior lecturer at the Frunze Military Academy. In February 1943, Malinovsky took command of the Soviet Southern Front and ended his campaign in Europe with the liberation of Czechoslovakia, observing the meeting of his troops with American advance forces. In August 1945, he led the last Soviet offensive of World War II when he invaded Manchuria and crushed the Japanese in 10 days, in what has since been considered a model of mechanized *blitzkrieg* warfare. In 1956, Khrushchev promoted Malinovsky to Commander-in-Chief of the Soviet Ground Forces, and made him Minister of Defense from October 1957 until March 1967. Malinovsky built the Soviet Army into the most accomplished and powerful force in the world by achieving nuclear parity with the United States and modernizing its huge conventional force, and is regarded as one of the most important military leaders in the history of Russia.

4   Ivan Stepanovich Konev led the Red Army forces that retook much of Eastern Europe in World War II and helped in the conquest of Berlin. In 1956, as the Commander of Warsaw Pact forces, Konev led the suppression of the Hungarian Revolution with Soviet armored divisions.

5   In 1936–37, Nikolai Voronov was a military adviser. From 1937–41, he was in the artillery command in the Red Army, as deputy commander of the Main Artillery Directorate and commander of the National Air Defense Forces. From 1950–53, he was president of the Academy of Artillery Sciences; from 1953–58, he was head of the Military Artillery Command Academy; and from 1958, he held a senior post in the USSR's Ministry of Defense.

6   Pavel Batov was selected to "volunteer" for service during the Spanish Civil War, under the name "Fritz Pablo." He first served as military adviser to the 12th International Brigade defending Madrid. He fought on the Teruel front and was wounded twice, and won his first Orders of Lenin and of the Red Banner as a result. After recovering, he fought at the battle of Guadalajara and on the Aragon front, where he was wounded again. Batov became the commander of a military district from 1955–58. During this period, he also took part in the suppression of the 1956 Hungarian Revolt. Although mostly unknown to the general public, Batov had a well-deserved reputation of competence and took hisplace among the myriad of talented generals who, after surviving the first part of the Soviet–German war, contributed greatly to the final victory over the Nazis.

7   Kirill Meretskov fought for the Republicans under the pseudonym of "General Pavlovich." In 1939, he was appointed commander of the Leningrad Military District. After the war, Meretskov commanded several military districts until 1955, when he was made Assistant Minister of Defense; a post he held until 1964.

8   Vladimir Gorev had combat experience in the Russian Civil War and had been a military advisor in China during the Chinese Civil War. Gorev went to Spain in late August 1936 as military attaché. Upon his return to the Soviet Union, he was arrested by the NKVD in January 1938, sentenced to death, and shot the same day on orders from Stalin. He was posthumously rehabilitated in October 1956.

9   By the end of the war, in 1939, all BT-5s had been destroyed in combat, and the only surviving sample was apparently presented as a trophy by General Franco to Mussolini after the war, still being preserved to this day in Italy in a military museum.

10 There were 281 T-26B tanks and 50 BT-5s, both being superior to the ones delivered by Germany and Italy.

11 There is a document in the Spanish Military Archives which states that between January 1937 and May 1939, the total number of Vickers tanks captured by the Republicans was 178, in different levels of operational status. It also records that the number of Vickers tanks in active duty by April 1, 1939, was 80. Later, in 1942, the official total number of Vickers tanks in service with the Spanish Army was 139. The T-26B tank was renamed as Tank Type 2 after the war by the Spanish General Staff.

12 Modern armor equipment only started to arrive in Spain after 1954, a consequence of bilateral agreements between Spain and the United States.

13 There are some discrepancies about the total number of tanks delivered to Spain. Most Russian sources quote a figure of 347 tanks (297 T-26s and 50 BT-5s), while others quote figures as high as 362. However, recent archival evidence would suggest that the figure is lower: only 331 tanks (281 T-26s and 50 BT-5s). The various discrepancies were probably caused by one of several events. On its second voyage to Spain, the transport ship *Komsomol* was sunk by the Spanish Nationalist cruiser *Canarias* on December 14, 1936, probably while carrying tanks that may have been counted in some records. An attempted shipment of 25 T-26 tanks on the transport ship *Iciar* in the summer of 1937 was blocked when the crew refused to sail. Finally, there was at least one shipment of 40 T-26 tanks that was returned to the USSR late in the war. The figures of 347 and 362 tanks probably refer to the number of tanks shipped, while the figure of 331 is the number of tanks actually delivered to Spain. Gerald Howson, *Arms for Spain: The Untold Story of the Spanish Civil War* (London: John Murray, 1998).

Chapter 6

1   It was Major W. E. Donohue, of the British Army's Mechanical Transport Committee, who earlier suggested fixing a gun and armored shield on a British type of track-driven vehicle, and in July 1907 an improved chain-track was demonstrated at the British Army's HQ at Aldershot. It was explained that there were plans for a trailer, also fitted with a chain-track, on which a gun could be mounted; John Glanfield, *The Devil's Chariots: the Birth and Secret Battles of the First Tanks* (Stroud: Sutton Publishing, 2001). In 1911, a lieutenant engineer in the Austrian Army, Gunther Burstyn, presented to the Austrian and Prussian War Ministries plans for a light, three-man tank with a gun in a revolving turret; D. Angwetter, *Gunther Burstyn* (Austria: Verlag der Österreichischen Akademie der Wissenschaften, 2008).

2   CV is the abbreviation for *Carro Veloce* (Italian for "fast tank") and "33" is the year of adoption.

3   Together with the tanks came 38 light infantry 65mm assault guns, under the command of Italian Captain Terlizzi, which were soon found good use for as antitank guns.

4   Colonel Faldella's initial role was to be liaison officer and military observer at Franco's HQ. He nevertheless assumed a much more important role, taking command of all Italian forces in Spain between October and November 1936, becoming chief of staff of the Italian Volunteer Corps in December 1936, and therefore contributing to the plans for the attack on Malaga in February 1937. After Guadalajara, he took over the command of an Italian infantry regiment and as such took part in the fighting on the Northern front, especially the conquest of Bilbao

and later at Santander. Following World War II, he became military commandant of the city of Milan and was promoted to major general in 1951. He died in 1975.

5   The new office's functions were very broadly defined: "centralization of all requests from the Military Mission in Spain; coordination of the activities of the three military ministries to expedite reply to the requests; and handling of all the affairs related to collaboration with the Spanish Nationalist forces"; final report of the Ufficio Spagna, Ministero degli Affari Esteri/MAE, Ufficio Spagna, p. 1; John Coverdale, *Italian Intervention in the Spanish Civil War*, p. 165.

6   See Stone, *Spain, Portugal and the Great Powers*, pp. 33–35.

Chapter 7

1   Walter Warlimont became deputy chief in Germany's Supreme Armed Forces Command (OKW) during World War II. Following the German defeat in May 1945, Warlimont was held as a prisoner-of-war. In October 1948, Warlimont was tried as a war criminal before a U.S. military court, and was convicted and sentenced to life imprisonment. However, in 1951, his sentence was reduced to 18 years. In 1957, there was an amnesty for certain prisoners, and he was finally released. After the war, he engaged in writing various war-historical studies.

2   Apparently, Von Blomberg told Warlimont that Hitler had decided to send limited ground aid to Spain. Although German air support would be provided, the decision was that "any ground support would consist only of armaments and sufficient personnel to train Spanish troops on its use."

3   On August 26, Warlimont, accompanied by Admiral Canaris, Chief of German Intelligence, flew to Rome, where they met with Benito Mussolini and General Mario Roatta. Mussolini agreed to Hitler's program in Spain and promised to provide help too. Warlimont then boarded an Italian cruiser and sailed to Tetouan in Morocco. At Tetouan, Warlimont adopted an alias and called himself "Guido Walteradorff." A German plane flew him to Seville, where he and Roatta conferred with Spanish General Gonzalo Quiepo De Llano, Nationalist commander of Southern Spain. The latter accompanied them to a first meeting with Franco at Caceres. Warlimont and Roatta each promised to send three companies of light tanks to fill a deficiency in Franco's forces. In October, the three promised German companies arrived, but General Franco was upset when he examined the German light tanks that were equipped only with machine guns.

4   Michael Alpert, *A new International History of the Spanish Civil War* (London: Palgrave McMillan, 1998).

5   General Wilberg was a department leader in the Reichs Air Ministry. Curiously, Wilberg was, in the meaning of Nazi ideology, a half-Jew, but was declared an Aryan by Hitler himself in 1935. He was appointed as the Commander of the War Air School in 1935 and later of the Higher Luftwaffe School in Berlin. Wilberg was one of the strategists of the *Blitzkrieg* and had a lot of influence in the German Air War Doctrine. He died after an air crash in 1941.

6   According to Warlimont, the whole conception of the Condor Legion was Goering's. He wanted to give to the *Luftwaffe*'s recruits some battle training. "Still Franco was fearful of eventual defeat and he demanded greater help."

7   Hugo Sperrle became a field marshal of the *Luftwaffe* during World War II. By 1944 he had become Supreme Commander of the *Luftwaffe* in the West but was subsequently dismissed when his heavily outnumbered forces were unable to hamper the Allied landings in Normandy.

He was captured by the Allies and charged with war crimes at the Nuremberg Trials, but was acquitted. He died in 1953.

8 As a major in the German General Staff, in 1936 von Funck served in the Spanish Civil War as military attaché to the headquarters of the Nationalist government in Burgos in northern Spain. At the beginning of 1939 he was appointed military attaché to the German embassy in Lisbon, Portugal. He was promoted to full colonel the same year, and in 1940 was appointed commander of the 3rd *Panzer* Brigade. In 1941, he was promoted to major general and given the command of the 7th *Panzer* Division as successor to General Rommel on the Russian Front. After the war, von Funck was held as a prisoner-of-war by the Soviets from August 1945 until his release 10 years later in 1955.

Chapter 8

1 Gosbank—the State Bank of the USSR—was the central bank of the USSR, and the only bank whatsoever in the entire Soviet Union from the 1930s to 1987.

2 The pronouncement in the communist newspaper *Mundo Obrero* on October 16, 1936, has an almost Orwellian sense of irony: "*La solidaridad de la URSS con nuestro pueblo en armas no puede pagarse con oro*" (The solidarity of the USSR with our people in arms cannot be compensated with gold). In fact, it could, and it was.

3 A copy of the receipt for the gold, signed by Soviet and Republican officials, is available in the papers of Marcelino Pascua, Spanish ambassador to Moscow, in the National Historical Archives, AHN-Madrid.

4 The U.S. Senate, meanwhile, concluded in 1973 that the shipment of gold to Moscow was illegal—in effect, a theft. See the published testimony entitled *The Legacy of Alexander Orlov*, issued by the Committee on the Judiciary, U.S. Senate (Washington, DC: United States Government Printing Office, 1973).

5 Gerald Howson, *Arms for Spain: The Untold Story of the Spanish Civil War* (New York: Murray, 1998).

6 After the outbreak of war in September 1939, the Allies put HISMA on the blacklist of enemy companies. The Spanish government therefore came to regard HISMA's existence as a burden to Spain's neutrality and repeated the request for its closure.

Chapter 9

1 Located in the premises of the recently abandoned Military General Academy, the regiment was commanded by Colonel of Infantry Manuel Rodriguez Arnau.

2 Written by Lieutenant Colonel Yague after the Battle at Badajoz, on August 14, 1936.

3 The Spanish Army has always been obsessed with administration and bureaucracy; therefore, an isolated platoon was not acceptable, and it had to be under the umbrella of a superior unit. The first thing coming to someone's mind when the Italian platoon arrived was to put it under the organization of an artillery unit. There was no other reason.

4 The Tank Company *Navalcarnero* was named after the successful combat actions on the Madrid front on October 21, 1936, in the vicinity of the small town of Navalcarnero.

5 *Corpo Truppe Volontarie*, or Italian Volunteer Corps.

6 As written by Sir Basil Liddell Hart in *The Other Side of the Hill: The German Generals talk* (London: Pan Books, 1959).

7   Eberhard Von Ostman was later the commander of the *Panzerlehr* Regiment until May 1942, and then took over *Panzer* Regiment 25 of the 7th *Panzer* Division. Von Ostman led the German liaison staff to the Hungarian 2nd Army from June 1942 to February 1943, and spent the rest of the war with the *Heerespersonalamt* (Army Personnel Office) in Berlin.

8   Heinrich Becker became a highly decorated *Wehrmacht* officer in *Panzer* Regiment 31 during World War II. He was a recipient of the Knight's Cross, which was awarded to recognize extreme battlefield bravery or successful military leadership. He was also a recipient also of the Spanish Cross in Silver with Swords. Becker was captured by British troops in May 1945 and released in 1947.

9   Rudolf August Demme was a German general during World War II. He was also a recipient of the Knight's Cross with Oak Leaves. He was Head Trainer for the Condor Legion. He was given command of the 17th *Panzer* Division in 1944, was captured by the Soviets on May 8, 1945, spent the next 10 years in Soviet captivity, and was released on October 6, 1955.

10   Ziegler was awarded the Spanish Cross for his participation with the Condor Legion. In 1939 he served in the 3rd *Panzer* Brigade and was awarded the Iron Cross. In 1943 he was promoted to full colonel and later received a command position in the *Waffen-SS*. From June 1943, Ziegler was the Chief of General Staff of the *III SS Panzerkorps*, until July 1944, when he was asked to take over command of the 11th *SS Panzergrenadier* Division *Nordland*. In September 1944, he was awarded the Knight's Cross in action, followed by the Oak Leaves in April 1945. Ziegler was gravely wounded in Berlin and died from his wounds in May 1945.

11   Gerhard Willing became a battalion commander, and in July 1943 took over the 506th Heavy Tank Battalion equipped with Tiger I tanks. The unit was engaged in the Dnieper battles on the Eastern Front, and *Oberstleutnant* Willing was killed in action in October 1943.

12   From September 19, 1939, to March 5, 1940, he acted as commander of *Panzer* Regiment 3 in the 2nd *Panzer* Division with the rank of colonel. In 1941 he was assigned the leadership of the 20th Panzer Division on the Russian Front with the rank of brigadier. At the end of December 1941, von Thoma received the Knight's Cross after organizing and holding a defensive position despite being closely pursued by strong Soviet forces. After continuing to serve on the Moscow Front, von Thoma relinquished command and having been promoted to lieutenant general, in September 1942, was transferred to North Africa and appointed as commander of the German *Afrika Korps* in the absence of General Walter Nehring. On November 4, 1942, von Thoma was captured by the British at the hill of Tel el Mampsra, west of El Alamein. With his tank hit several times and on fire, von Thoma dismounted and stood quietly amongst a sea of burning tanks and dead German soldiers scattered around the small hill, where he was taken prisoner by Captain Allen Singer of the 10th Royal Hussars.

13   Steven F. Hayward, *Churchill on leadership: executive success in the face of adversity* (New York, N.Y.: Three Rivers Press, 1998), p. 105.

14   By the spring of 1937, the intensive use of tanks on the battlefield, and the losses suffered, meant the German tanks supplied to the Condor Legion were insufficient and the Spanish Nationalist HQ asked Germany for more tanks, even if that meant purchasing them. Two orders were made, one in July 1937 and a final one in November 1938.

15   These tanks came in two batches, with 18 tanks arriving at Vigo's harbor and then 12 more at Seville.

16   The battalion was named Tank Battalion 1/Infantry Regiment *Argel* 27 and was structured into three tank companies, each with 16 *Panzer I A* "Krupp" tanks, three platoons per company with five tanks each. In addition, the battalion had an antitank platoon with *Pak* 37mm guns, plus a headquarters company, and support and logistic elements.

17 The Spanish word "*Bandera*" (flag) has no equivalent in American or British military terms, but it is basically equivalent to a battalion-size unit. This expression is used only by *La Legion* within the Spanish Army, even up to the present day.

18 Apparently, it was General Franco's personal decision to place the tank forces under the control of the Foreign Legion. There is still speculation whether it was done just to raise their prestige or to give them a salary increase, or both. In any case, it was a bureaucratic step of no relevance whatsoever. The official name was *Bandera de Carros de Combate del Tercio de Marruecos*, a very complicated name.

19 This meant that each tank company of the Nationalist Army was composed of nine German tanks and seven Russian tanks. On October 1, 1938, the Nationalist Army fielded 64 German tanks and 42 Soviet tanks.

20 Captain Felix Verdeja Bardales was a Spanish artillery officer and armaments engineer who later designed the Spanish *Carro Verdeja* medium tank, a kind of *Panzer I* cannon-armed tank with a 45mm gun, which never went beyond the prototype stage.

21 According to Spanish Army TOEs (Tables of Organization and Equipment) of 1942, there were a total of 139 Russian T-26B tanks still in active duty and fully operational that year. Italian, German, and Soviet armor formed the basis for creating five tank regiments of the new Spanish Army in 1940. Ironically, it can be said that Stalin had become the main tank purveyor for the Nationalist Army. With the war already over, nobody stopped to think what a logistical nightmare such an organization brought about. Russian T-26 tanks even formed the basis of the Spanish Army's Armored Division *Brunete 1*, serving until 1953. The Spanish Army tried to develop its own light tank prototype after the war, with the wide use of elements from the *Panzer I* and especially from the T-26, but the *Carro Verdeja* program was doomed by lack of finance and technology.

Chapter 10

1 Its commanding officer, Colonel Angel Cuadrado Garces, was executed in July 1936 by the Republicans after being suspected of sympathizing with the military uprising. His deputy commander, Lieutenant Colonel Rafael Sanchez Paredes, remained loyal to the Republic and became the commanding officer of the Tank School established by the Soviets at Archena, Murcia, in late October 1936.

2 Cavalry Colonel Segismundo Casado, *The Last Days of Madrid* (London: Peter Davies, 1939). Colonel Casado was in command of what was left of the Republican Spanish Army in Madrid in March 1939. He conducted a *coup d'etat* against the government of Prime Minister Negrin, claiming Negrín wanted a Communist takeover. However, Casado's efforts to negotiate a peace with General Franco failed. He insisted on unconditional surrender, and Casado went into exile to Venezuela, not returning to Spain until 1961.

3 George Kennan wrote: "Soviet tanks and aircraft had been sent, and were in operation; Soviet officers were in effective charge of military operations on the Madrid front ... Moscow simply took control over whole great areas ... The Soviets had their own tank and air units, which they operated entirely independently ... with no other purpose, at the time, than to save Madrid and to assure the victory of the Republic"; *Russia and the West under Lenin and Stalin* (Boston: Little Brown, 1961), p. 309. George Frost Kennan was an American adviser, diplomat, and historian, best known as "the father of containment." He later wrote great accounts of the relations between the Soviet Union and the Western powers.

4 Ulyanovsk, curiously, is Lenin's birthplace.

5   It is unclear whether Captain Arman, who was made a Hero of the Soviet Union, was later shot, apparently under suspicion of conspiracy in one of the purges conducted by orders of Stalin. Some unconfirmed sources claim that he died in the Volkhov sector of the front at Leningrad, early in 1943, fighting against the Germans, in the sector assigned to the Spanish volunteers of the German Blue Division.

6   Krivoshein's nickname in Spain was "*Mele*." In January 1937, Krivoshein was recalled to the Soviet Union to rest after his combat experience. He was promoted to brigade commander and appointed commander of a mechanized brigade. In the summer of 1938, he led his brigade against the Japanese in Mongolia, at the battle of Lake Khasan. Krivoshein's next tour of duty was against Finland during the winter of 1939–40. Krivoshein fought with distinction and was quickly promoted. In less than two years, he rose from commander of a motorized rifle division and then a tank division to commander of tank forces for a key Baltic Special Military District. Krivoshein received command of the 25th Mechanized Corps in April 1941. From 1941–43, Krivoshein was a head of the Department of Training in the Army Tank Forces. By the end of 1939, when a reorganization of the Soviet armored forces had taken place, Krivoshein had been appointed commanding officer of the 2nd Tank Division under the III Mechanized Corps, commanded by Lieutenant General Yeremenko. Later, already promoted to lieutenant general, Krivoshein commanded the III Mechanized Corps, one of the main Soviet armored formations that suffered heavily the beginning of the battle of Kursk in July 1943. Krivoshein was severely wounded in the battle. In 1945, for his outstanding combat leadership and personal courage in the capture of Berlin, Krivoshein received the highest Soviet war honor, the order of Hero of the Soviet Union. The death of Stalin in 1953, brought an end to Krivoshein's military career as the new leadership began to reduce the huge Soviet army and, on May 4, 1953, the Soviet Ministry of Defense retired him after 35 years of the service. He spent the last quarter century of his life writing books of his war memoirs.

7   A Red Army light tank brigade at the time had around 256–267 tanks, organized into four tank battalions, and supported by a motor transport battalion and maintenance battalion. Pavlov's brigade was organized around three instead of four tank battalions, a planned but never completed machine-gun battalion, an enlarged transport battalion, and special factory technical support, repairs, medical, and food supplies departments.

8   Colonel Enrique Navarro Abujas was later the chief of staff of the Republican Armored Division. He had been, in 1931, the commanding officer of Tank Regiment 2 at Zaragoza.

9   General Pavel Rotmistrov fought at the battle of Kursk in the summer of 1943, commanding the Soviet Fifth Guards Army with the rank of lieutenant general, opposing the powerful *panzer* forces of Colonel General Hoth. His account of the massive tank battles around Prokhorovka hills remains among the best in modern Soviet military history. He ended the war as a marshal after his Guards Army had been one of the crack units under leading Soviet generals like Konev and Zhukov, advancing into Germany and reaching Berlin by April 1945. Following the war, Rotmistrov commanded the mechanized forces of the Group of Soviet Forces in Germany and became a Deputy to the Supreme Soviet and an assistant Minister of Defense. He became the first Chief Marshal of Armored Troops in 1962.

10   Colonel Rafael Sanchez Paredes was a professional infantry officer loyal to the Republic, who had been the deputy commanding officer of Tank Regiment 1 at the beginning of the war, and remained leader of the Armor School at Archena from October 1936 until the end of the war.

11   General Dimitry Grigorevich Pavlov commanded the key Soviet Western Front during the initial stage of the German invasion of the Soviet Union in June 1941. After his forces were heavily defeated within the first few days of the campaign, he was relieved of his command, arrested, charged with military incompetence, and executed. He was exonerated in 1956.

12 He was made a Hero of the Soviet Union after his experience in Spain. Nevertheless, in contrast to many other officers who took part in that war, Pavlov was not purged after his return to the Soviet Union, and was made the Head of the Directorate of Tank and Armored Car Troops of the Red Army, which gave him considerable influence in their development. In particular, he insisted that tanks be shifted to infantry support roles, which in hindsight turned out to be incorrect. He participated in the war against Finland, as well as in the border clashes with Japan in 1938–39.

13 The division was organized into two armored brigades, an infantry brigade, and a company of antitank guns. In fact, the infantry were seldom available, and the tank strength steadily declined.

14 This tank regiment was initially called the *Regimiento de Carros Rapidos* (Fast Tanks Regiment). Pablo Otez was the commander of the unit, but his real name and rank was Major Pavel Kondratyev. These tanks underwent their baptism of fire at the battle of Fuentes de Ebro, close to Zaragoza, where the tanks supported the assault of the 15th International Brigade. One of the most prolific Russian writers on tank operations in Spain was Aleksandr Vetrov, Kondratyev's assistant commander in charge of technical matters. He published numerous articles and at least two books, among which are his memoirs of the regiment's fighting in Spain.

15 In theory, the armored units within Army Group Center were organized into three brigades, under the command of Colonel Rafael Sanchez Paredes.

16 Army Group East had two brigades under the command of Major Juan Ibanez Lugea.

17 Professor Michael Alpert, from the University of Westminster, concludes: "Russian control of Soviet tanks was, of course, another matter and there is abundant proof that they were not controlled by the Republicans and that they were often unavailable when needed."

18 Stanley Payne, according to Mikhail Novikov, quoting Marshal Voroshilov, in the USSR, Comintern, 1995.

Chapter 11

1 The unit comprised 12 regular battle tanks and three flamethrower tanks.

2 Frank L. Kluckhorn was the *New York Times* journalist who filed the report. The action actually took place at Navalcarnero, where the Fiat Tank Company earned its nickname of Tank Company *Navalcarnero*, a name officially given to honor the Italian unit by the Spanish General Enrique Varela, one of the key Nationalist commanders.

3 The Medium Mark A Whippet tank was a British tank of World War I. It aimed to complement slower heavy tanks by using its relative mobility and speed in exploiting any break in the enemy lines. There were none of these tanks in Spain.

4 Apparently, there were only 15 tanks available as less than 40 Spanish crewmen were ready. The other 35 T-26s so far delivered remained at Archena, waiting to have all their crew trained and ready for action. Dr John Daley, "Soviet and German advisors put doctrine to the test: Tanks in the siege of Madrid" in *Armor Magazine* (May–June 1999).

5 According to Nationalist Captain Anselmo Sánchez Perez, later a colonel in the Spanish Army, who was then in command of the town of Seseña; Lucas Molina, "*Seseña, Llegan los rusos!*" (Valladolid: Quiron Ediciones, 2006), p. 97,

6 General Batov was commander of the Soviet 65th Army in 1941, subordinated to Marshal Budenny, and his forces were destroyed by the Germans in the first battle of Kiev. After that, nothing more was ever heard of General Batov.

7   The arrival of Captain Arman's tank company in the Madrid sector provided a much-needed boost to Republican morale. Prime Minister Largo Caballero's text was also printed in the propaganda newspaper *Solidaridad Obrera* on October 30, 1936, according to Dr John Daley's article "Soviet and German advisors put doctrine to the test: Tanks in the siege of Madrid" in *Armor Magazine* (May–June 1999).

8   It is not clear whether the gasoline bottles were a spur-of-the-moment improvisation, or if the newspaper accounts of the arrival of Soviet tanks had prompted the Nationalists to prepare for possible fighting against tanks. The use of these "*Molotov* cocktails," named after the Soviet Foreign Minister of the time, was a surprise to the Soviet tankers, and details of how they were put together were duly forwarded to Moscow.

9   Semyon Krivoshein, *Tanquistas voluntarios soviéticos en la defensa de Madrid* (Moscow: Editorial Progreso, 1971), p. 325.

10 On October 28, 1936, a weapons shipment arrived from the USSR with 30 armored cars: 16 BA-6s, four BA-3s, and 10 FA-1s. With all this equipment, plus the 35 T-26 tanks received initially, Colonel Krivoshein organized three tank companies and one mixed armored car company. Most crewmen were Spaniards. They went to the Madrid front on November 2.

11 Dr John Daley, "Soviet and German advisors put doctrine to the test: Tanks in the siege of Madrid" in *Armor Magazine* (May–June 1999).

12 The *Fuerzas Regulares Indígenas* (Indigenous Regular Forces), known simply as the *Regulares* (Regulars), were volunteer infantry units largely recruited in the Spanish enclaves in Morocco, the cities of Ceuta and Melilla. Consisting of indigenous infantry and mounted cavalry, under the command of Spanish officers, and forming part of the Army of Africa, these troops played a significant role in the war. They still exist still as garrisons for these cities.

13 It is likely that Captain Vidal-Quadras, not being an expert in armored operations, endangered himself and ventured with his tank into unsuitable ground, getting into a small ravine where the tank couldn't maneuver and was easily destroyed with hand grenades.

14 Lieutenant Daniel Gómez Perez, nicknamed "Bakali," was an infantryman, not an expert on tanks; however, he had volunteered to transfer into the new armored units that were being organized. This action was probably the result of a lack of expertise. He was severely wounded, eventually losing his sight, and I remember meeting him at a military celebration in Madrid during the mid-1980s. Lieutenant Daniel Gómez became a veteran wounded in combat and took no further part in the fighting. Highly decorated nevertheless—he was promoted to honorary brigadier general after the war—his alias "Bakali" became the nickname of the AMX-30 tank company of the Spanish Foreign Legion in the Western Sahara in the mid-1970s.

15 Manfred Stern was a member of the GRU, or Soviet military intelligence. He gained fame in Spain under his nickname "General Kleber" as leader of an International Brigade during the Civil War. *The New York Times* correspondent Herbert Matthews interviewed Stern after the fighting around Madrid. After that he was quietly removed to the rear, briefly returned to command the Republican 45th Division for several battles, and was then recalled to Moscow. In May 1939, he was condemned to 15 years' hard labor and died of exhaustion at a labor camp in Sosnovka in 1954.

16 Colonel von Thoma sent an urgent message to OKH, in Berlin, asking for cannon-armed tanks to be sent to Spain as soon as possible, but his request was never answered. Obviously, such an action was not considered appropriate then, perhaps for fear of escalating the war, besides the fact that in 1936, Germany did not have many cannon-armed tanks in service. The *Panzer II* light tank had originally been designed as a stopgap, after the *Panzer I*, while larger and more advanced tanks were developed. Nonetheless, it went on to play an important role during the early years of World War II. The *Panzer II* became

the standard light tank in the German *panzer* divisions and was used to great effect as a reconnaissance and scout tank, beginning with the invasion of France. The *Panzer II*, though, could be penetrated by towed antitank weapons such as the Soviet 45mm Mod 1932 and even the German *Pak 36*.

Chapter 12

1   General Mario Roatta initially helped direct Italian assistance to the Nationalists, until Mussolini appointed him as commander-in-chief of Italian troops in Spain from September 1936 to December 1938. Roatta was then replaced by General Ettore Bastico. Late in 1943, when the Italians had abandoned their Axis partners following the invasion of Sicily and southern Italy, the Allies requested that Roatta be removed from his post as Chief of Staff of the Italian Army. On March 5, 1945, Roatta escaped from arrest and was never brought to justice. He later lived in Rome until his death in 1968.

2   These two tank companies were under the command of Italian captains Oreste Fortuna and Paolo Paladini. The third unit was the already famous *Navalcarnero* Tank Company, under Spanish Captain Vicente Gomez Salcedo.

3   Emilio Faldella, *Venti mesi di guerra in Spagna* (Firenze: Editions Le Monnier, 1939), p. 248.

4   Antony Beevor, *The Battle for Spain. The Spanish Civil War 1936–1939* (London: Penguin Books, 2006), pp. 216–220.

5   Non-intervention had been proposed in a joint diplomatic initiative by the governments of France and the United Kingdom. It was part of a policy of appeasement, aimed at preventing a proxy war—with Italy and Germany supporting the Nationalists on one side and the Soviet Union supporting the Republicans on the other—from escalating into a major pan-European conflict.

6   According to Paul Preston, *Concise History of the Spanish Civil War* (New York: Harper & Collins, 2014), p. 117, the Republican Government had "divisively and controversially" moved itself to Valencia on November 6, 1936, when it was considered likely that the capital city might fall to the rebels.

7   Antony Beevor, *The Battle for Spain; the Spanish Civil War, 1936–1939* (London: Penguin Books, 2006), p. 153.

8   Peter Kemp was a British soldier and writer. He was given journalistic cover for entry into Spain by Collin Brooks, then editor of the *Sunday Dispatch*, "to collect news and transmit articles for the *Sunday Dispatch* from the Spanish Fronts of War." He later transferred to the Spanish Foreign Legion with whom, in a rare distinction for a non-Spaniard, he commanded an infantry platoon. His memoirs on the Spanish Civil War are in his book *Mine were of trouble* (London: Cassell & Company, 1957).

9   The *Littorio* Division acquitted itself very well later in North Africa under Field Marshal Rommel, even if eventually defeated and annihilated by the British Eighth Army.

10   General Annibale Bergonzoli, nicknamed "Electric Whiskers" (*Barba elettrica*), commanded the defense of Bardia in Libya in 1940 after the short-lived Italian offensive into Egypt. By the end of 1940, the British Operation *Compass*, led by General Richard O'Connor, took Bardia and forced the Italians to retreat into Cyrenaica. Bergonzoli continued to command the Italian troops during the retreat and, in February 1941, following the disastrous Italian defeat at Beda Fomm, surrendered to Australian forces. He was held as a prisoner in India and the USA before being repatriated after the war to Italy, where he died in 1973.

11 Italian Colonel Carlo Rivolta—commander of the Special Units Task Force of the Italian Volunteer Corps (*Raggruppamento Reparti Specializzati/RRS*)—in his report written on March 31, 1937.

12 It is common knowledge that the Italians started calling their L3 tanks "sardine cans" (*Scatolette di sardine*) after the battle of Guadalajara.

13 *Carristi italiani in Spagna: l'occasione mancata*, report written on March 31, 1937, by Emanuele Cattarossi.

14 The Republican government was so confident that they invited many press correspondents to see the anticipated great victory. Unfortunately, their planned operation had not been kept secret. Combat developed around Cerro Garabitas (Garabitas Hill), located on the edge of the city, above the wooded hills of the Casa de Campo, from where Nationalist field artillery trained their sights on Madrid's landmarks.

15 James W. Cortada, *Modern Warfare in Spain, American military observations on the Spanish Civil War, 1936–1939* (Williamsport, MD: Potomac Books, 2011).

Chapter 13

1 General Roatta was replaced by General Ettore Bastico, who had commanded an Army Corps in Ethiopia, and Colonel Faldella was replaced as chief of staff by Colonel Gastone Gambara. Some 3,700 men were pulled out of the CTV and sent back to Italy.

2 The "Iron Belt" or "Iron Ring" was a vast, labyrinthine fortification around Bilbao, consisting of bunkers, tunnels, and fortified trenches in several rings, protected by artillery. Hurriedly built by the Basques, it was an antiquated defense concept, vulnerable to modern weapons such as aircraft and artillery, and was easily overcome by the Nationalist troops.

3 *Ejército del Centro, Estado Mayor, Sección de Operaciones, General Ejército Centro to jefe Brigada de Carros*, June 28, 1937, AMA-ZR 59/664/9; *Ejército del Centro, Estado Mayor, Sección de Operaciones, General Ejército Centro* to *Jefe Brigada de Carros*, June 30, 1937, AMA-ZR 59/66419.

4 The brigade had suffered eight tanks burned out and 51 others knocked out, including 25 hit by antitank guns or other artillery and 26 by other means. Many of these were recoverable, but not in time to continue with the fighting at Brunete. Casualties had been the equivalent to 44 tank crews. The force on July 11–12 consisted of only 13 tanks attached to Lister's 11th Division, 12 to the 15th Division, and the remainder in reserve. Ramon Salas Larrazabal, *Historia del Ejercito Popular de la Republica*, Vol. 2 (Madrid: Editora Nacional, 1973), p. 1255.

5 *Ejército de Maniobra, Estado Mayor, 3ª Sección, Instrucción reservada número 28*, July 19, 1937, AMA-ZR 64/778/22.

6 The Italian force, led by General Ettore Bastico, comprised the *Littorio* Infantry Division, a fully motorized infantry division of the Italian Army that had been at Guadalajara.

7 Hugh Thomas, *The Spanish Civil War* (London: Penguin Books, 2001), p. 705.

8 The Republican Staff College included references to Nationalist instructions on armored forces in its teaching, according to evidence which can probably be dated from late 1937 onwards. "*Escuela Popular de Estado Mayor, Táctica de Infanteria, Resumen de las instrucciones del enemigo a las Unidades de Tanques,*" n. d., AMA-ZR 55/520/1.

9 "*Escuela Popular de Estado Mayor, Carros de combate,*" n. d., AMA-ZR 55/520/1, "*Escuela Popular de Estado Mayor, Carros blindados, Segunda promoción, Conferencias 3 y 4,*" n. d., AMA-ZR 55/520/1.

10 The tanks also lost the advantage of their speed when they got bogged down in an area of marshes and muddy soil near the town of Fuentes de Ebro. The result was the loss of 19 BT-5 tanks out of the 50 committed.

11 The details of the attack were approved by the Soviet advisers to Army of the East, as the instructions for it were handed over to Colonel Kondryatev by advisers Grigoriev and Leonidov, as well as to the front's chief of staff, Spanish Lieutenant Colonel Antonio Cordon.

12 Report on the "Combat Use on the 13th of October (1937) of the Regiment of BT-5 Tanks" by Robert Gladnick, Commander of Tank #7, 1st Section, 1st Company (Yale RSMAC, Box 14).

13 Robert Gladnick, *Between the Bullet and the Lie: American Volunteers in the Spanish Civil War* (New York: Holt, Rinehart & Winston, 1969), pp. 129–130, quoting Cecil Eby.

14 There are numerous accounts of the battle from many other perspectives in English, since the accompanying infantry units were from the British International Brigade. See Ian MacDougall, *Voices from the Spanish Civil War: Personal recollections of Scottish Volunteers in Republican Spain 1936–39* (Edinburgh: Polygon, 1986), pp. 214–218.

15 Antonio J. Candil, "Soviet Armor in Spain" in *Armor Magazine* (March–April 1999).

16 James W. Cortada, *Modern Warfare in Spain* (Williamsport, MD: Potomac Books, 2011), p. 219.

17 Peter Wyden, *The Passionate War* (New York: Simon & Schuster, 1983), p. 421.

18 Hugh Thomas, *The Spanish Civil War* (London: Eyre and Spottiswoode, 1961), p. 504.

19 Stoyan Minev "Stepanov," *Las causas de la derrota de la República Española* (Madrid: Encinas Moral A.L., Miraguano Ediciones, 2003).

20 Paul Preston, *The Spanish Civil War, an Illustrated Chronicle 1936–39* (New York: Grove Press, 1986), p. 149.

21 Carl Geiser, *Prisoners of the Good Fight, the Spanish Civil War, 1936–39* (New York: Lawrence Hill Books, 1986), p. 42.

22 Laurie Lee, *Moment of War, a Memoir of the Spanish Civil War* (New York: Penguin Books, 1991), p. 158.

23 With one of his hands blown off, Corporal Zanardo nevertheless drove his tank to the aid of another tank under attack, and then drove it for almost four miles back to his lines. He was awarded the Italian Gold Medal for Bravery and the Spanish *Laureada de San Fernando*, the highest combat award of the Spanish Army, which was finally awarded to him much later, in May 1967, at the Spanish General Military Academy, at Zaragoza, when he was already retired in Italy after having survived World War II, I he had the privilege of attending the ceremony as a junior cadet officer.

Chapter 14

1 John Coverdale, *Italian Intervention in the Spanish Civil War*, p. 357.

2 Jesús Salas Larrazabal, *La Guerra desde el aire* (Barcelona: Editorial Ariel, 1969), p. 365. The Republican Air Force only appeared over the Ebro on July 31, 1938, when the largest air battles of the war took place. In the end, the battle of the Ebro provided a good opportunity for the Nationalists to destroy the Republican Air Force once and for all.

3 Most of the Italian Fiat tanks were overhauled at a main logistics base in Pamplona before the Catalonia offensive.

4 Antony Beevor, *The Battle for Spain, the Spanish Civil War, 1936–1939* (London: Penguin Books, 2006), p. 354.

5   Deep battle was a theory developed during the 1920s and 1930s by a number of influential Russian military writers and thinkers, such as Mikhail Tukhachevsky, who envisaged the breaking of the enemy's forward defenses, or tactical zones, for fresh, uncommitted mobile operational reserves to exploit by breaking into the strategic depth of an enemy front.

6   Helen Graham, *The Spanish Civil War, A Very Short Introduction* (Oxford: Oxford University Press, 2005), p. 111.

7   Maurice Duval, *Les Leçons de la Guerre d'Espagne* (Paris: Librairie Plon, 1938).

Chapter 15

1   Hermann Lichtenberger was later a highly decorated major general in the *Luftwaffe* during World War II, commanding a Flak-Brigade. He was also a recipient of the Knight's Cross. Lichtenberger retired from active duty on October 31, 1943.

2   Georg Neuffer was also a highly decorated general in the *Luftwaffe*. He was captured by British troops in Tunisia in May 1943 following the surrender of German troops in North Africa. He was held prisoner until 1947.

3   Out of all the Soviet antitank guns produced, the "*sorokopyatka*" (forty-fiver) was neither the biggest nor the most powerful, but it retains a special place in history. The Soviet Union produced numerous guns that were 45mm in caliber, and each different gun was improved and had a different name, but they were all known colloquially as "*sorokopyatka*."

4   Steven Zaloga, *Spanish Civil War Tanks, the Proving Ground for Blitzkrieg* (Oxford: Osprey Publishing, 2010), p. 8.

5   *The Times*, London, April 6, 1937.

Chapter 16

1   In January 1937, the U.S. Congress passed a joint resolution outlawing the arms trade with Spain. The Neutrality Act of 1937, finally passed in May that year, included the provisions of earlier acts, this time without expiration date, and extended them to cover civil wars. Furthermore, U.S. ships were prohibited from transporting any passengers or articles to belligerents, and U.S. citizens were forbidden from traveling on ships of belligerent nations. In a concession to Roosevelt, a "cash-and-carry" provision was added so that the president could permit the sale of materials and supplies to belligerents in Europe as long as the recipients arranged for the transport and paid immediately in cash, with the argument that this would not draw the U.S. into the conflict.

2   James M. Anderson, *The Spanish Civil War: A History and Reference Guide* (Westport, CT: Greenwood Press, 2003).

3   Antony Beevor, *The Battle for Spain: The Spanish Civil War 1936–1939* (London: Penguin Books, 2006), p. 139.

4   The Germans supplied at least eight special trucks for transporting tanks with the initial shipment of tanks in October 1936, and another 18 or so trucks were especially prepared for transporting tanks. This practice had begun in World War I for the same reason, namely the low endurance of early tanks and the need to carefully reserve their running time for actual combat missions. The French Army began by using semi-trailers for the tanks, later switching to heavy trucks as they became available. The same practice is widely used in many armies today, since the operating costs for a tank transporter are far lower than those for a tank.

Chapter 17

1 *"Cuartel General del Generalisimo, Estado Mayor, Sección Tercera to General Jefe del Ejercito del Norte,"* January 7, 1938, *Archivo Militar Avila*, AMA-ZN 15/23/49.

2 Captain Enrique Crespo, "The maintenance section of the tank companies" in Spanish Army magazine *Ejército*, April 1945.

3 Colonel von Thoma, *"Informe del Arma de Carros de Combate,"* April 29, 1938, AMA-CGG 8/3 88/ 10.

4 *"La Legion, Bandera de Carros de Combate, Mando to General Jefe del Ejercito del Norte,"* October 10, 1938, AMA-ZN 15/27/32.

5 *"Von Thoma to General Jefe de Movilización, Instrucción y Recuperación,"* October 3, 1938, AMA-ZN 15/27/24.

6 It goes without saying that Lieutenant Colonel Pujales was never promoted to the rank of general, regardless of his professionalism and military achievements.

Chapter 18

1 Nikolai G. Kuznetsov, *Memoirs of Wartime Minister of the Navy* (Moscow: Progreso, 1990).

2 "Document 60," in Ronald Radosh, Mary R. Habeck and Grigory Sevostianov (eds), *Spain Betrayed, the Soviet Union in the Spanish Civil War* (New Haven: Yale University Press, 2001).

3 Report from General Dimitry Pavlov, chief of the Armor Directorate, to Voroshilov, "Armor forces in the Spanish Civil War," Russian Military Archives; Mary R. Habeck, *Storm of Steel*, p. 259.

4 To make up for the lack of Soviet spare parts, Spanish industry produced almost 20 tons of tank parts, including tracks, wheels, and other components (Yale RSMAC, Box 17).

5 In general, Spanish tankers were used as tank turret crews, both commanders and gunners. In following the practice of earlier units in Spain, most of the regiment's drivers were Soviet tankers, as were all company commanders and higher staff. International Brigade tankers were usually tank commanders. *Report on the Combat Use on the 13th of October (1937) of the Regiment of BT-5 Tanks* by Robert Gladnick, Commander of Tank #7, 1st Section, 1st Company (Yale RSMAC, Box 14).

6 Steven Zaloga, *Spanish Civil War Tanks*, p. 38.

7 Wendell G. Johnson, "The employment of supporting arms in the Spanish Civil War" in *Command and General Staff School Quarterly* (March 1939), p. 5.

Chapter 19

1 Colonel Sanchez Paredes' promotion was published in *La Gaceta de Madrid* on August 6, 1936.

2 These four officers were captains Alfonso Arana, Vicente Paredes, Carlos Faurie, and Manuel Cristobal.

Chapter 20

1 During the Spanish Civil War, foreign military officers wrote highly elaborate reports of their experiences at the front. One was attaché Colonel Stephen O. Fuqua of the U.S. Army, who

later became a major general. His presence was highly unusual, for most military observers were less-experienced captains, majors and lieutenant colonels. Fuqua's reports contained important observations about Spanish armament and troop movements, and he managed to acquire Nationalist propaganda and information despite being situated entirely within the Republican military lines. His reporting was considered so valuable that during World War II, Fuqua was tapped to be TIME's military commentator. James W. Cortada (ed.), *Modern Warfare in Spain: American Military Observations on the Spanish Civil War, 1936–1939* (Washington D.C.: Potomac Books, 2011).

2   *"Esperienze dalla Offensiva Santander,"* RRS/CTV, September 15, 1937.

3   *"Note sull'impiego delle minori unità di fanteria e artiglieria nella guerra di Spagna,"* Italian War Department, May 1938, Rome, Italy.

4   Colonel Babini wrote: *"Bisogna finalmente avere il coraggio di confessare questo bisogno generale di carri nel senso dinamico della parola. Succede questo: alla vigilia della battaglia tutti pretendono i carri ed nessuno ne può fare a meno; il giorno dopo la battaglia non si riconosce più il grande compagno d'armi. Perché non c'è posto per tutti anche nei consuntivi tattici?"* This can be translated as: "We must finally have the courage to confess this general need for tanks in the dynamic sense of the word. This is what happens: on the eve of the battle, everyone wants tanks and no one can do without them; however, the day after the battle the great comrade in arms is no longer recognized. Why cannot we include everyone in tactical statements?"

5   Translating Babini's words into today's terminology, he was already then asking for more battle tanks and fighting vehicles for mechanized infantry.

6   Colonel Babini at times comes across as a little confusing when talking of "tank units" (*unità carriste*) or "high mobility units" (*unità celeri*), concepts he often mixed.

7   Guderian, *Achtung – Panzer!* (London: Cassel Military Books, Orion Publishing, 2007), p. 210.

8   Corelli Barnett, *The Collapse of British Power* (Guilford, CT: Prometheus Books, 1986).

9   Basil Liddell Hart in his book *The Memoirs of a Captain*, but first presented in his *Europe in Arms*.

10 Mary R. Habeck is an associated professor of Strategic Studies at the Johns Hopkins University. Her book *Storm of Steel: The Development of Armor Doctrine in Germany and the Soviet Union, 1919–1939* is a masterpiece on armored warfare and development.

11 Copious and detailed reports were sent to Russia by the Soviet military advisers, ultimately composing an entire section in the Red Army archives, and specialists returning to the USSR after combat in Spain were interrogated exhaustively on the effectiveness of the equipment supplied; R. Higham and F. W. Kagan, *The Military History of the Soviet Union* (London: Palgrave McMillan, 2003), pp. 93–108.

12 Jonathan House, *Toward Combined-Arms Warfare: A Survey of 20th Century Tactics, Doctrine, and Organization* (Fort Leavenworth: U.S. Army Command and General Staff College, 1984), pp. 67–68.

13 A report by Soviet General Kirill Meretskov to Marshal Boris Shaposnikov, Chief of the General Staff, on August 5, 1937. Mary R. Habeck, *Storm of Steel*, p. 260.

14 Steven Zaloga, *Spanish Civil War Tanks*, p. 40.

15 Reports of U.S. Army Military Intelligence Division at the U.S. National Archives and Records Administration (NARA), also cited by Steven Zaloga in *Spanish Civil War Tanks*.

16 A short, black and white documentary based on the book *Spain in Arms*, 1937, by Anne Louise Strong, a partisan reporter and journalist from Seattle, who covered the SCW. It was shown in Spanish Republican territory only.

17 See the author's article "Soviet Armor in Spain: Aid mission to Republicans" in *Armor Magazine* (March–April 1999), p. 38.

18 George F. Hofmann, *Camp Colt to Desert Storm, the History of U.S. Armored Forces* (Kentucky: The University Press of Kentucky, 1999), p. 124.

19 U.S. Army Major General Adna R. Chaffee Jr was called the "Father of the Armored Force" for his role in developing the U.S. Army's tank forces. He was commissioned in the cavalry in 1906 after graduating from West Point and won recognition as the "Army's finest horseman." He predicted in 1927 that mechanized armies would dominate the next war and assisted in the first program for the development of a U.S. Army armored force. In 1938, he assumed command of the reorganized 7th Cavalry Brigade; the Army's only armored force. Chaffee battled continuously during the prewar years for suitable equipment and the creation of armored divisions. With the collapse of France in June 1940, Chaffee's 1927 predictions of the importance of armored forces in modern warfare were confirmed. The M24 Chaffee light tank was later named after him. Fort Chaffee, Arkansas, was also named in his honor.

Chapter 21

1 David E. Johnson, Adam Grissom, and Olga Oliker, in *In the Middle of the Fight* (California: RAND Corporation, 2008), p. 176.

2 Major General John Frederick Charles Fuller was a British Army officer, military historian, and strategist, notable as an early theorist of modern armored warfare, including categorizing principles of warfare. His ideas on mechanized warfare continued to be influential in the lead-up to World War II, ironically more with the Germans, notably General Guderian, than with his countrymen.

3 Sir Basil Liddell Hart, *Europe in Arms, Lessons from Spain* (New York: Random House, 1937), p. 7.

4 The T-26 (Armstrong-Siddeley) engine did not have a speed limiter, which often resulted in overheating and engine valve breakage, especially in summer. A 48 U.S. gallons fuel tank and 7.1 U.S. gallons oil box were placed alongside the engine, which caused some unwanted vulnerability. The engine required top-grade gasoline, as the use of second-rate fuel could cause damage to the valve units due to engine detonation.

5 Steven Zaloga, *Spanish Civil War Tanks*, p. 18.

6 The early 71-TK tank radio set could only use voice communication at short range, over a few miles. Therefore, the only reliable means of communication was by code; before each major engagement, a list of coded numerical abbreviations was provided to the tank units, but these were inflexible and became difficult to employ.

7 The Spanish Army used White 920 6x4 18-ton American trucks as tank transporters. The White company was acquired by Volvo in 1981.

8 The T-26 Model 1933 carried 122 rounds of 45mm ammunition, firing armor-piercing rounds with a muzzle velocity of 2,700 ft/s, or lower-velocity high-explosive (HE) munitions.

9 Sir Giffard Le Quesne Martel was a British Army Royal Engineers officer who served in World War I, familiarly known as "Q Martel" or just "Q." He was a pioneering British military engineer and tank strategist, developing a keen interest in tank theory and believing them to be the future of warfare. In November 1916, he wrote a paper, "A Tank Army," suggesting an army composed entirely of armored vehicles. From 1936 until 1939, Martel served at the War Office, first as Assistant Director of Mechanization, then from 1938 as

Deputy Director. In 1936, he attended a large-scale tank exercise in the Belorussian military district of the Soviet Union in which large numbers of the Soviet variant of the Carden Loyd tankette, the T-27, took part. During his retirement, as a lieutenant general, Martel wrote on military matters.

10 Apparently, General Franco expressed the need in 1937 for a *Panzer I* armed with a 20mm gun. Obviously, he was asking for the new *Panzer II* that was entering service with the German Army, but none were ever sent to Spain. The *Panzer II* was around 50 percent heavier than the *Panzer I* and added a 20mm Solothurn cannon as main gun as well as an increase in armor up to 30mm RHA. Production began in 1935, but it took another 18 months for the first combat-ready tank to be delivered. Other developments were delayed even longer. All came too late to be fielded in Spain.

11 Mary R. Habeck, *Storm of Steel,* pp. 248–249; Report no. 6, "Guido," October 23, 1936, BA-MA, RM 20/1241, p. 108.

12 Report from Colonel von Thoma on December 6, 1936, "*Erfahrungen im Kampf zwischen dem Deutschen MG-Panzer und Russischen Kanonen-Panzern,*" BA-MA, RH 2/288, pp. 34, 36; Mary R. Habeck, *Storm of Steel,* pp. 248–249.

13 As a personal analysis, after having worked alongside the German military and technicians, I believe that as the improvement was not of German design, it was flatly rejected. German pride would not have accepted the Spaniards telling them how to improve their own weapons systems.

14 Sometime in early September 1940, *Reichsmarschall* Goering asked *Luftwaffe* ace Major Adolf Galland if there was anything he wanted so he could beat the RAF, to which Galland replied: "Give me a squadron of Spitfires." Obviously, Goering was not amused.

15 General Joaquin Garcia Pallasar, an artillery officer, was a close friend and subordinate of General Franco from his time at the Canary Islands. He was in charge of equipment, weaponry, and manufacturing ammunition for the Nationalist Army.

16 Note of the Nationalist General Staff, G-4, Logistics, June 25, 1937, AGMA, CGG/6/314/47/1 and 2.

Epilogue

1 The *New York Times*, in an article on August 6, 1936, predicted that "a government victory would involve Spain's going quickly Communist"; John F. Coverdale, *Italian Intervention in the Spanish Civil War*, p. 81.

2 Heinz Guderian, *Panzer Leader* (New York: Da Capo Press, 1952).

3 Curiously, the modern Spanish Army still keeps a high proportion of commercial wheeled vehicles integrated into their mechanized forces, unable to move off-road. Even until the mid-1980s, the Spanish Army continued having "motorized infantry battalions," simply truck-borne on unprotected commercial trucks unable to follow tanks, or even APCs, on cross-country movements and off-road. It seems that they did not learn anything at all from the civil war.

4 *Instruccion General n. 50*, Nationalist Army, December 11, 1938, VII *Modalidades de Ejecucion*: 2 "*Carros: Para los afectos al Cuerpo de Ejercito de Aragon, la zona precisa, el momento y la forma de intervencion seran determinados de acuerdo con el coronel inspector de la Unidad, estableciendo despues el necesario enlace entre el Mando de esta, y la infanteria asaltante.*"

5 John L. S. Daley, "The theory and practice of armored warfare in Spain" in *Armor Magazine* (March–April 1999), p. 30.

Index